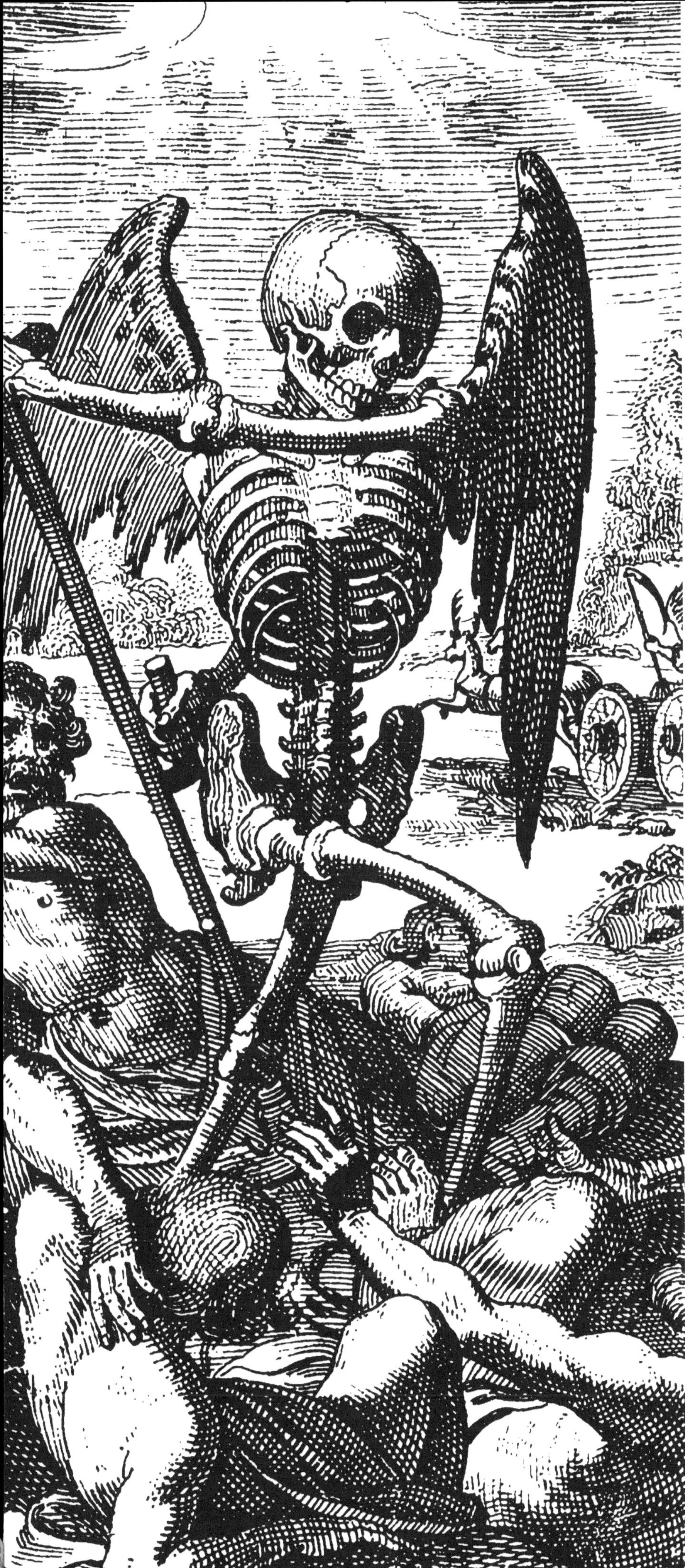

THE DANCE OF DEATH

AN IMAGE ARCHIVE FOR
ARTISTS *And* DESIGNERS

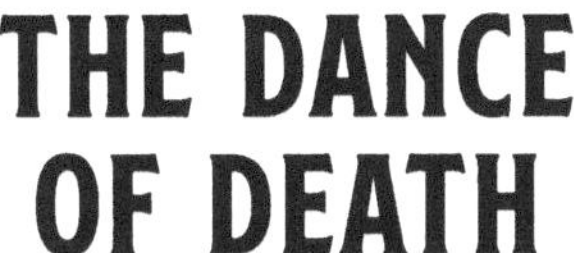

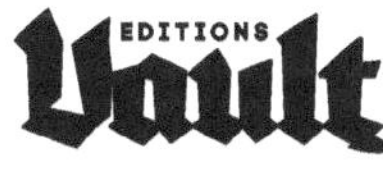

BIBLIOGRAPHICAL NOTE

This publication is a new work by Vault Editions Ltd.

AUTHOR

This publication was curated and authored by Kale James.

INTRODUC

PREFACE

By Kale James

Welcome to *Dance of Death: An Image Archive for Artists and Designers*, a meticulously curated collection designed to ignite your creativity and imagination. Within these pages lie centuries of artistic interpretations, each offering a unique perspective on the timeless theme of mortality.

The Dance of Death is a visual allegory that serves as a poignant reminder of life's transient nature. Originating as a medieval motif, it depicts death as an equaliser, ushering souls from all walks of life to the same inevitable fate. From kings to peasants, none are spared the grasp of the skeletal figure that personifies mortality.

In this archive, we present to you a diverse array of images

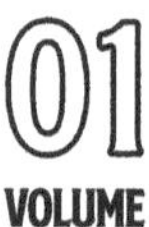

meticulously restored and selected to inspire and captivate. Whether you're a seasoned artist seeking historical accuracy or a budding designer in search of unconventional motifs, these illustrations offer a wealth of creative inspiration.

As you delve into these haunting yet captivating images, reflect on their profound message. Though the Dance of Death may evoke thoughts of morbidity, its true purpose is to encourage introspection and appreciation for the fleeting nature of existence. Through the contemplation of mortality, we are reminded to live fully and embrace the present moment.

We hope these images stir your imagination, provoke thought, and inspire a creative fervour that drives you to produce works of art that reflect the human condition in its rawest form and strive to break free from the constraints of time. May this exploration encourage you to blend tradition with innovation, merging historical themes with contemporary insights to create art that resonates with today's audiences while paying homage to the past.

In this dialogue between the ages, let the Dance of Death remind you that while life may be fleeting, art endures, transcending generations and speaking to the universal experience of existence. May your creations contribute to this ongoing conversation, adding your unique voice to a chorus that spans the ages, and in doing so, may you find a timeless quality in your work that echoes beyond the present, reaching into the future and touching the souls of those yet to come.

Through this journey, we hope that you not only discover the beauty and complexity of this age-old motif but also recognise the power of art to navigate the intricacies of life and death, casting a light on the fragility and the strength of the human spirit.

Disclaimer:

PUBLISHER	ISBN	W
Vault Editions Ltd vaulteditions.com	978-1-922966-32-2	vault…

TABLE OF CONTENTS

ACKNOWLEDGMENTS

Vault Editions extends its deepest gratitude to the extraordinary artists whose timeless talents have paved the way for this publication: Hans Holbein the Younger, Rudolf Meyer, Conrad Meyer, Matthieu Merian, Wenceslaus Hollar, Abraham Van Dipenbeek, Alfred Rethel, and Daniel Chodowiecki. Their profound artistry and remarkable works, which serve as the foundation of The Dance of Death: An Image Archive for Artists and Designers, continue to inspire awe and admiration.

This book is a tribute to their legacy, and through the meticulous process of restoring and curating their historical images, we aim to bridge the past with the present. We sincerely hope that contemporary audiences will find as much inspiration and fascination in these captivating images and their enduring messages as we have.

The journey of assembling this archive has been a profound reminder of the power of art to transcend time, communicating universal truths through the ages. We are honoured to play a role in ensuring that the talent of these artists remains accessible and influential in today's world.

To our readers, we extend our heartfelt thanks for joining us in appreciating the remarkable contributions of these masters. May their visions continue to enrich our lives and kindle creativity in artists and designers for generations to come.

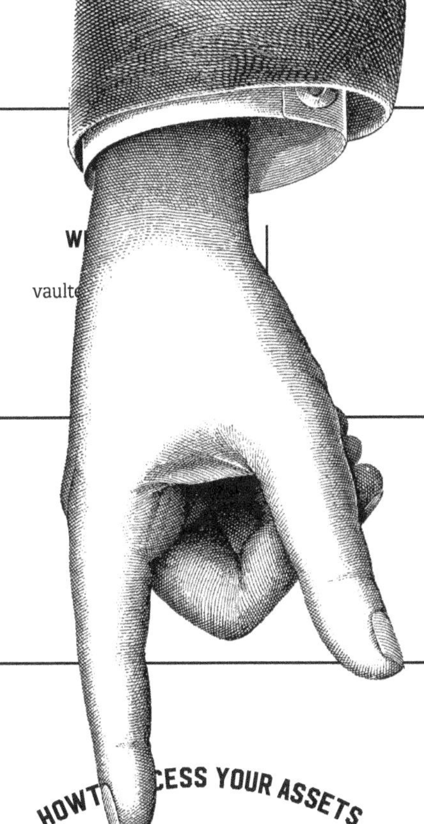

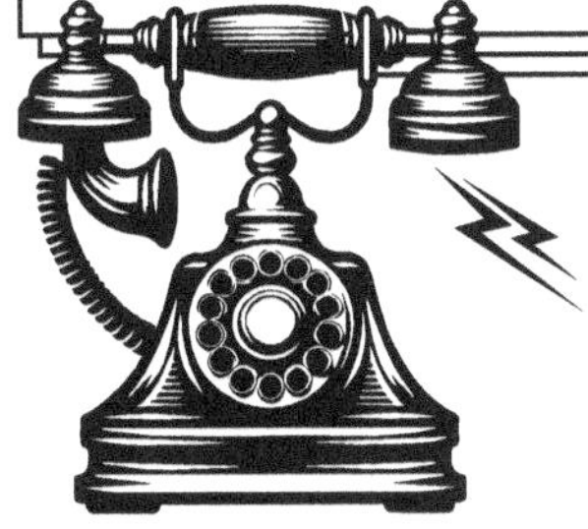

CONTACT

Do you need assistance accessing your files? Or do you have a questions about our products and services? If so, our team will be more than happy to help you. Please contact Vault Editions via: info@vaulteditions.com

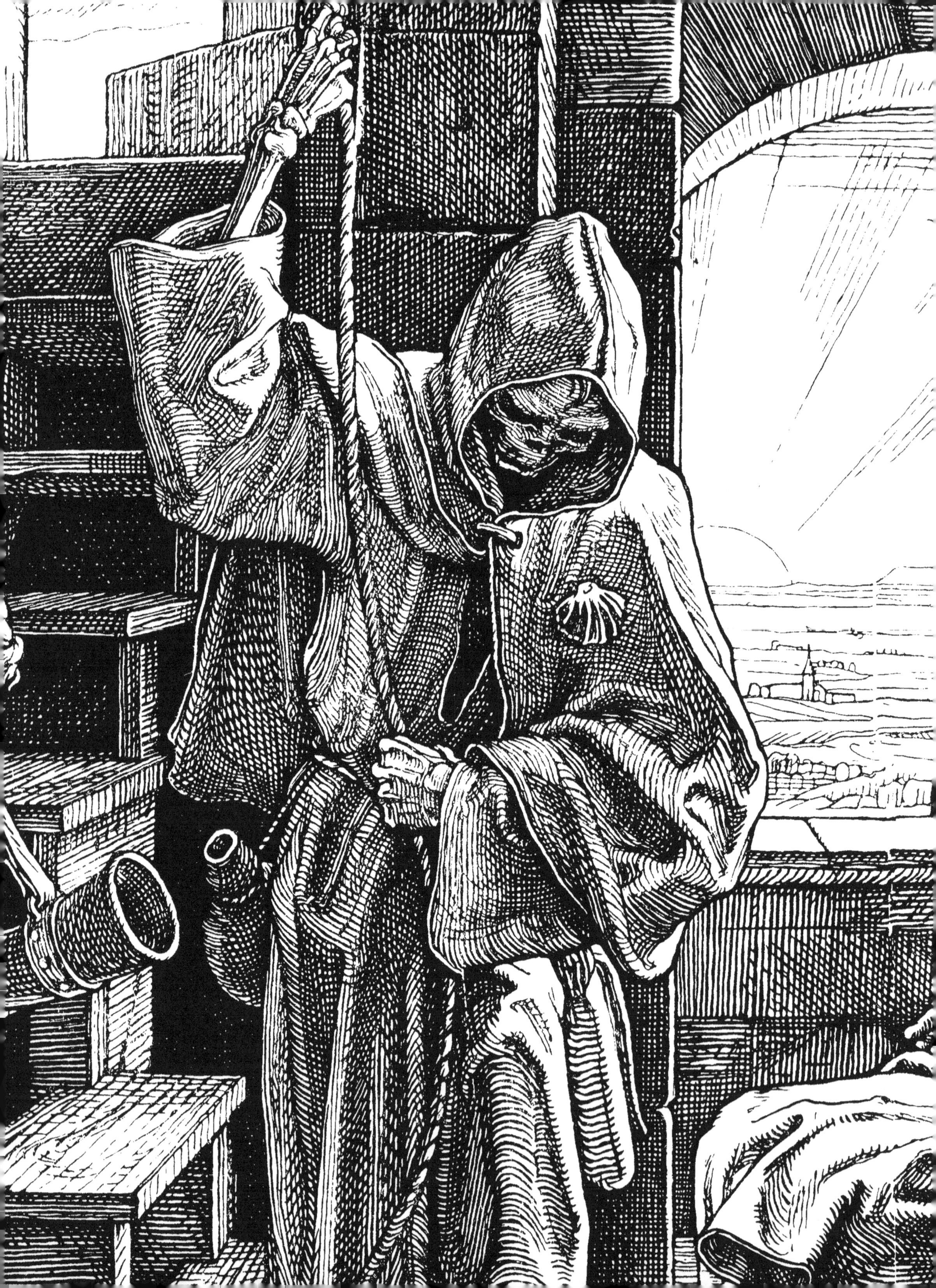

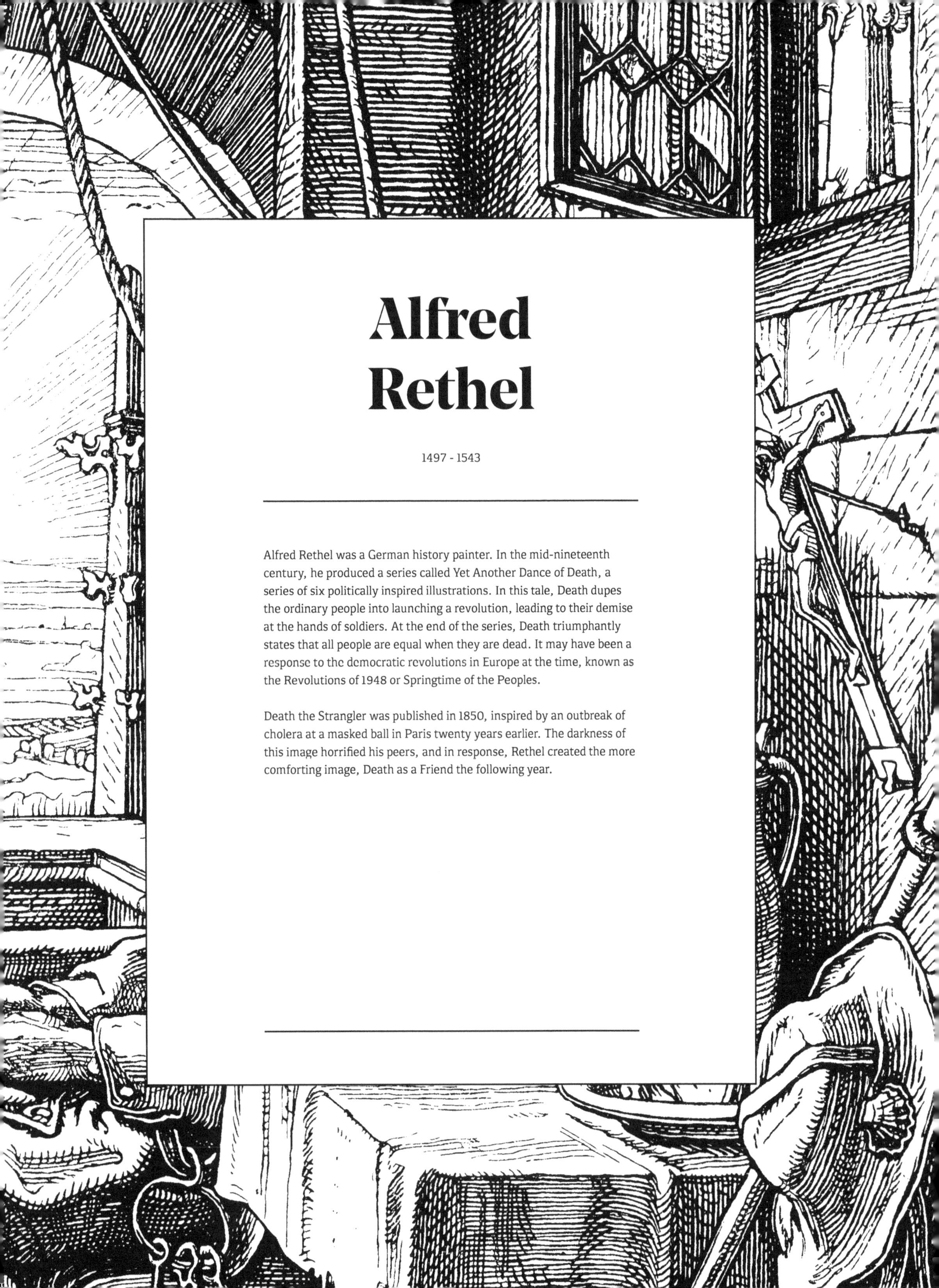

Alfred Rethel

1497 - 1543

Alfred Rethel was a German history painter. In the mid-nineteenth century, he produced a series called Yet Another Dance of Death, a series of six politically inspired illustrations. In this tale, Death dupes the ordinary people into launching a revolution, leading to their demise at the hands of soldiers. At the end of the series, Death triumphantly states that all people are equal when they are dead. It may have been a response to the democratic revolutions in Europe at the time, known as the Revolutions of 1948 or Springtime of the Peoples.

Death the Strangler was published in 1850, inspired by an outbreak of cholera at a masked ball in Paris twenty years earlier. The darkness of this image horrified his peers, and in response, Rethel created the more comforting image, Death as a Friend the following year.

01

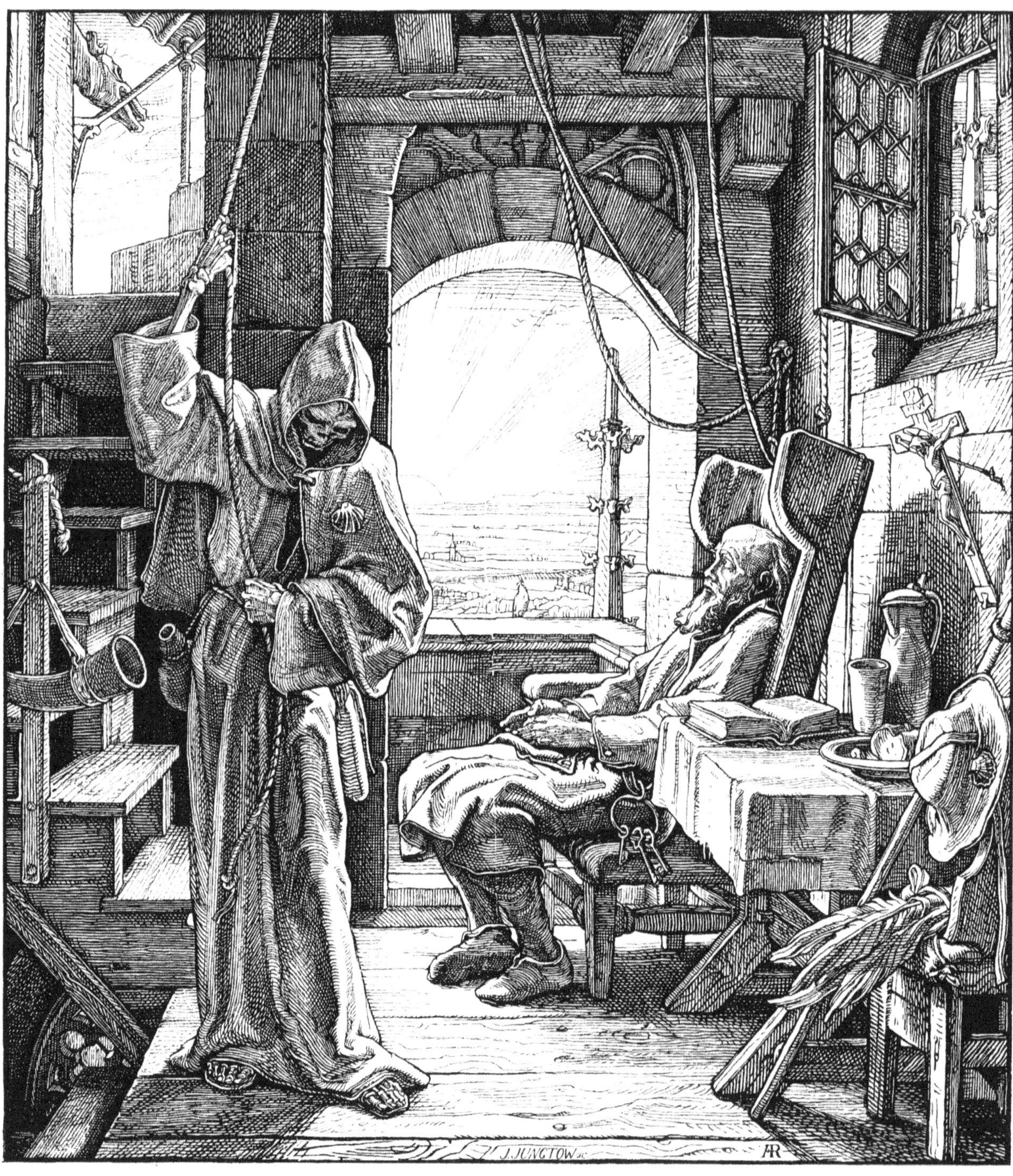

01. Dance of Death, Death as a Friend, Alfred
Rethel, 1850.

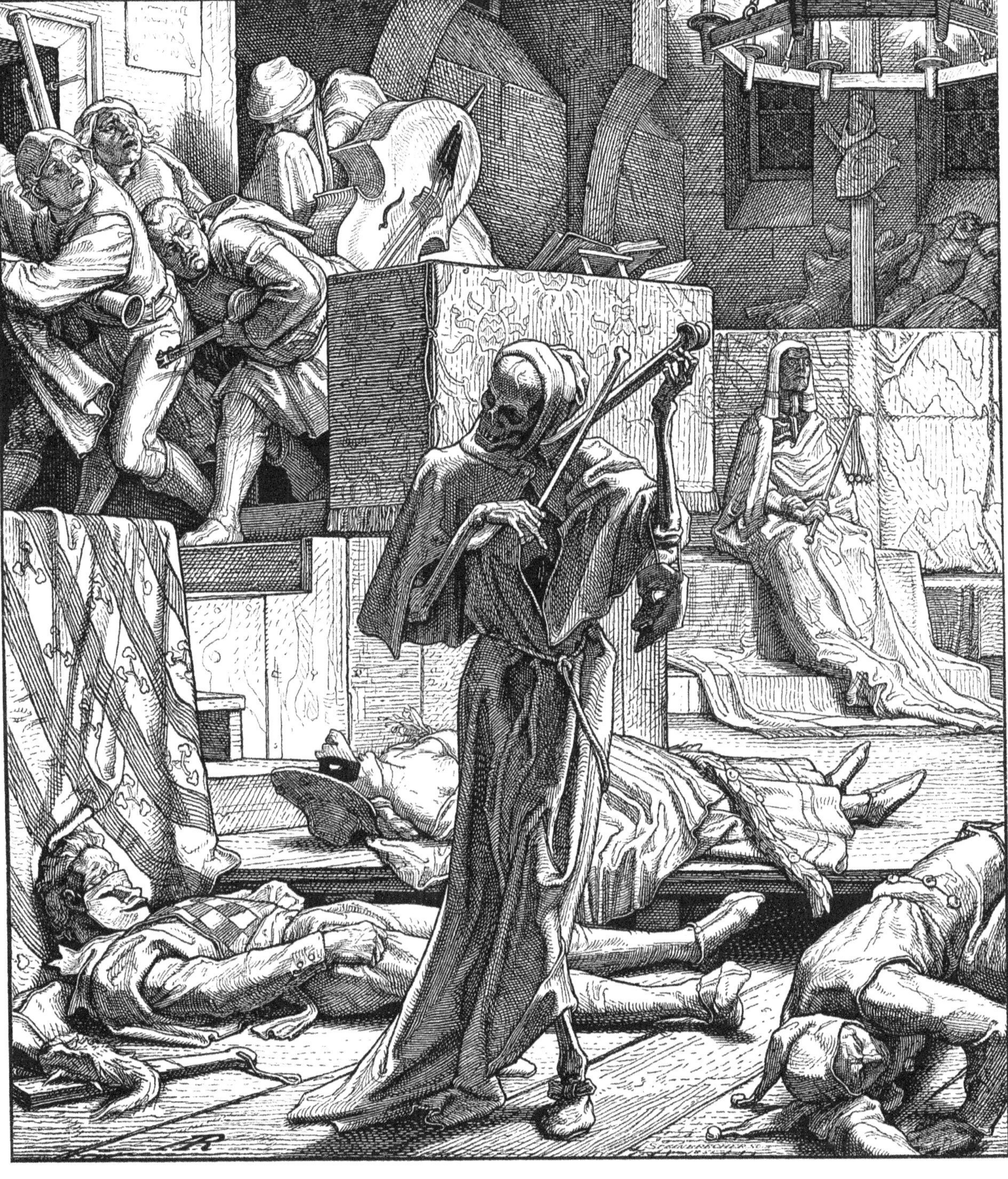

02. Dance of Death, Death as a Strangler, Alfred
Rethel, 1850

03

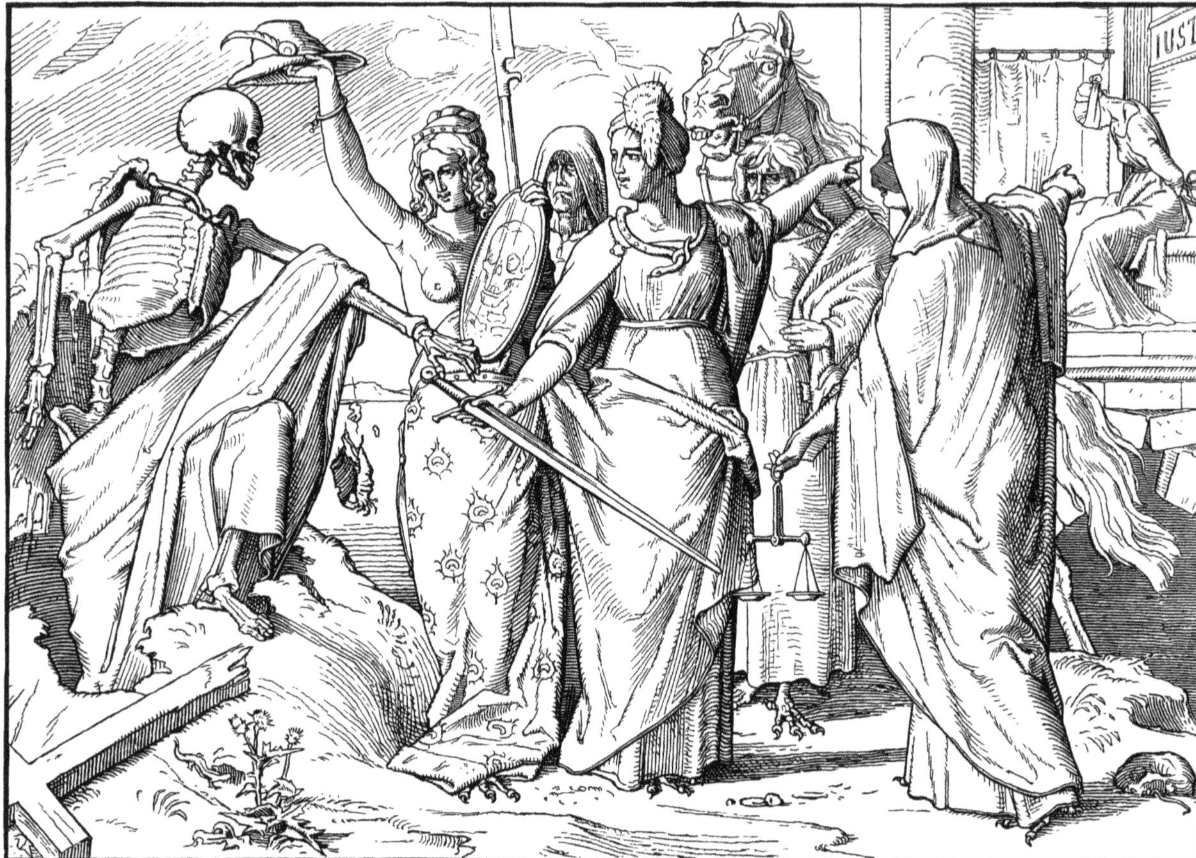

04

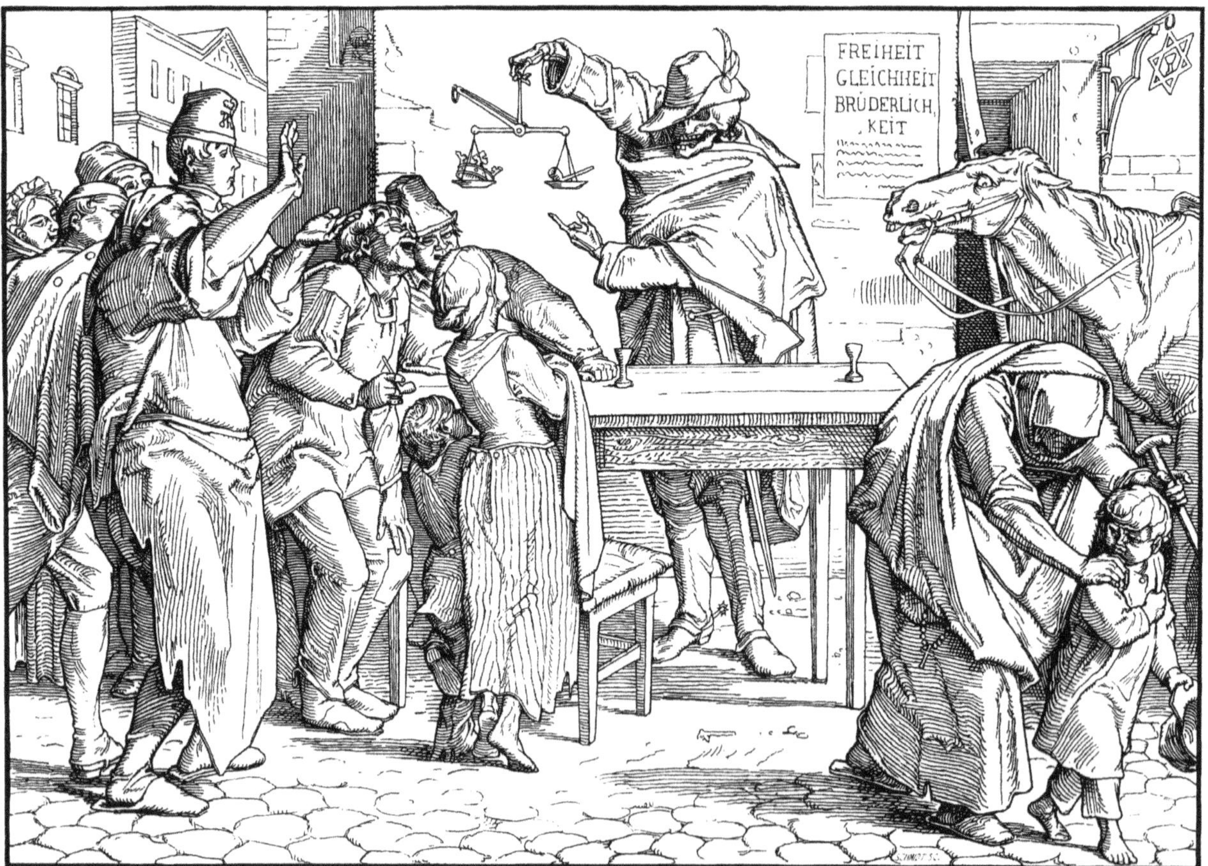

03. Death Rises from the Grave, Alfred Rethel,
1849.

04. Death in front of the Tavern, Alfred Rethel,
1849.

05

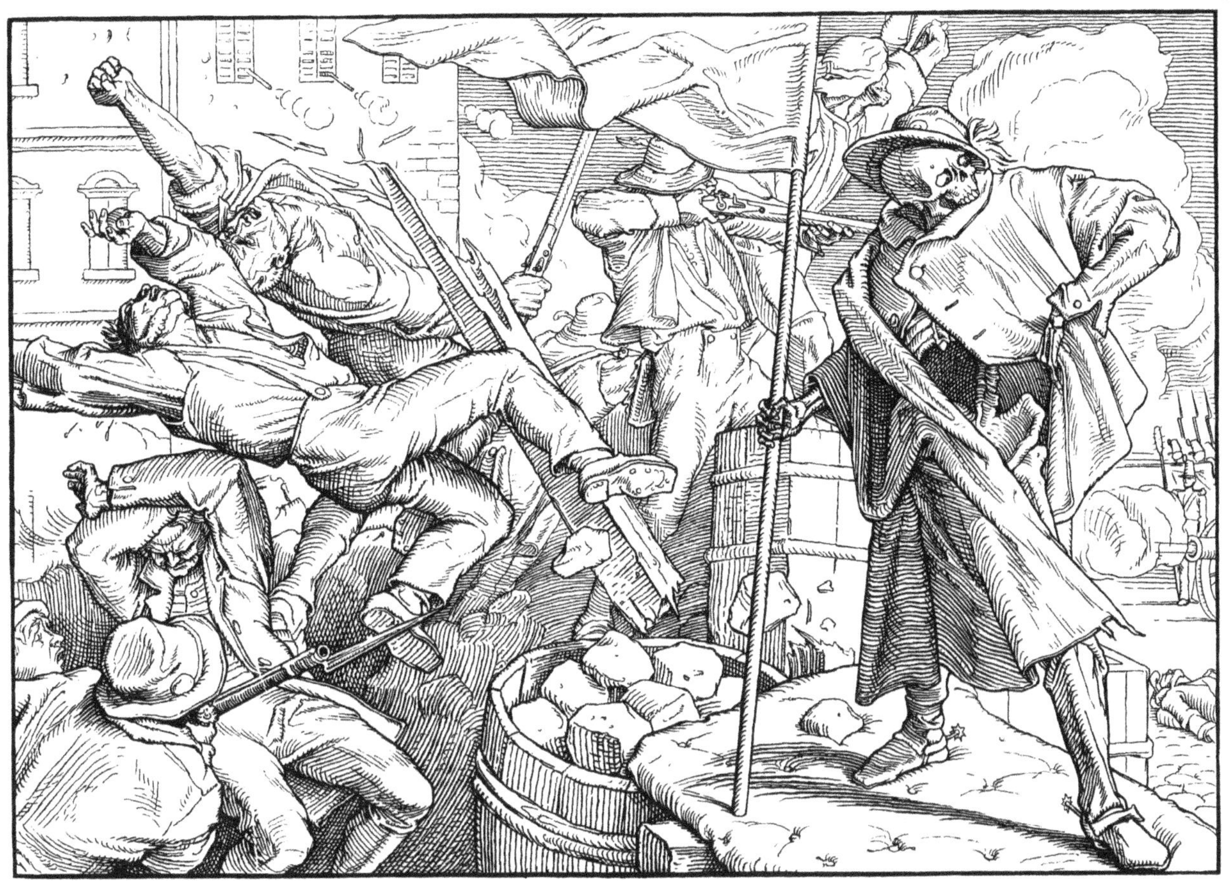

06

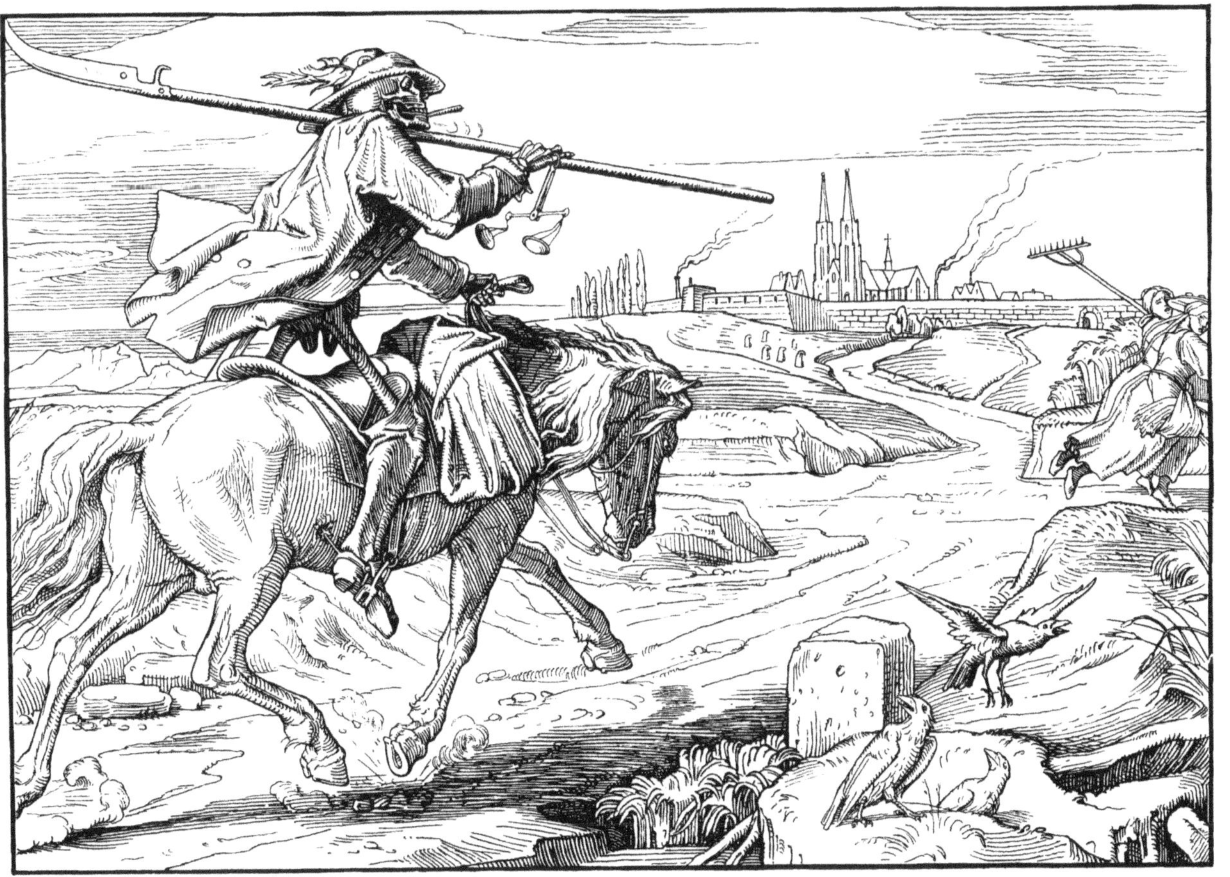

05. Death on the Barricade, Alfred Rethel, 1849.   06. Death Rides to Town, Alfred Rethel, 1849.

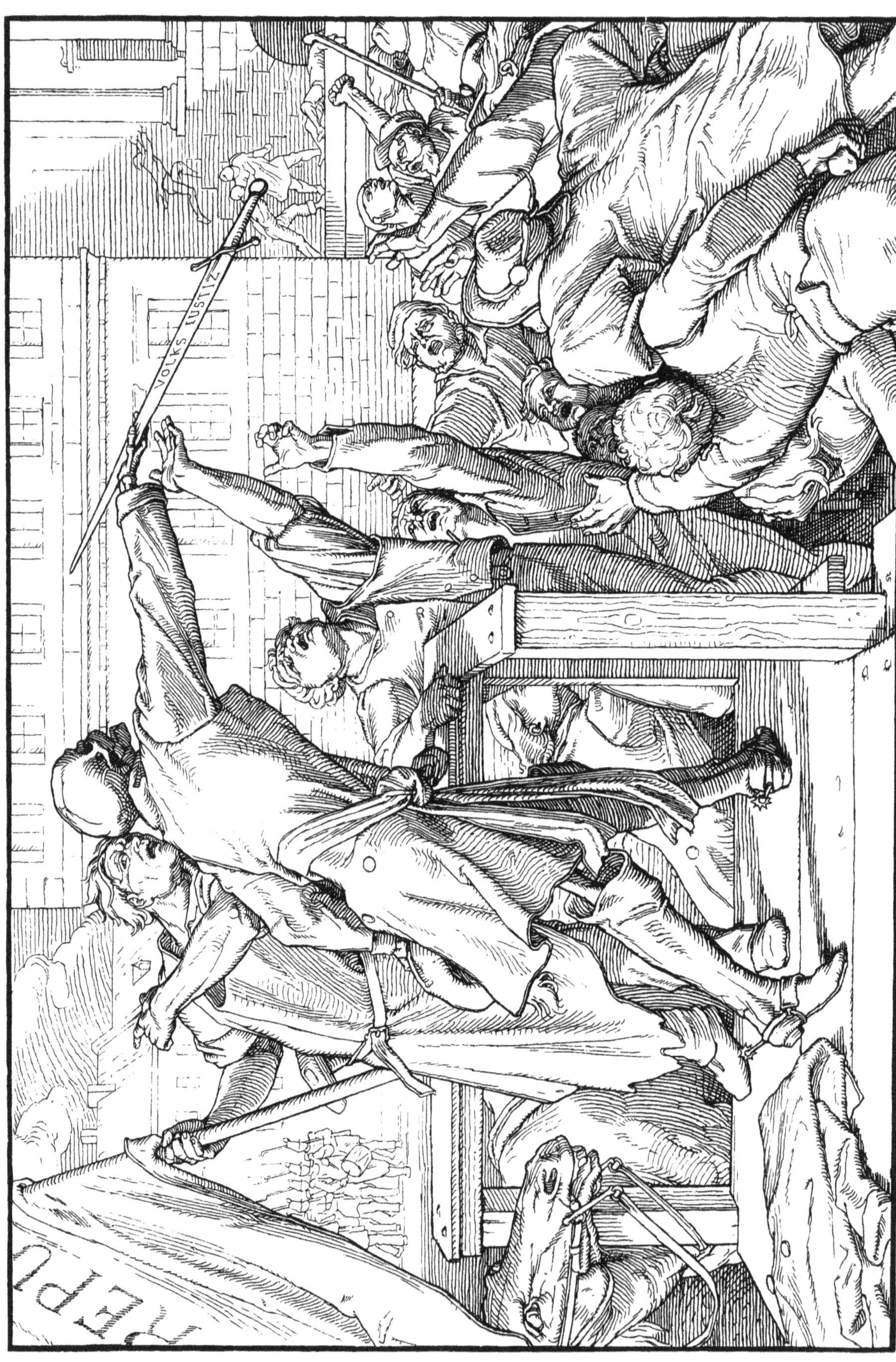

07. Death Delivers the Sword to the People,
Alfred Rethel, 1849.

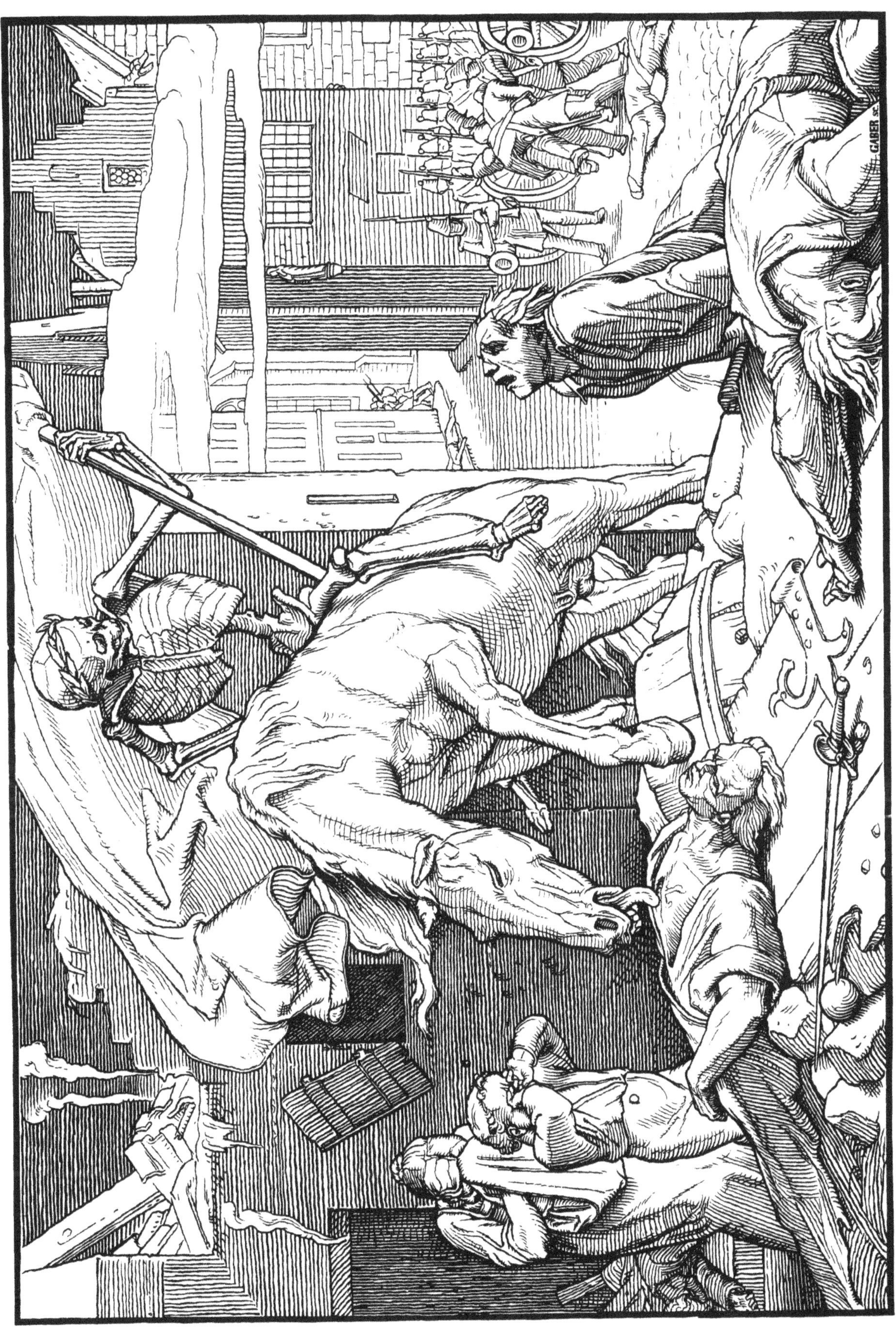

08. Death as Victor, Alfred Rethel, 1849.

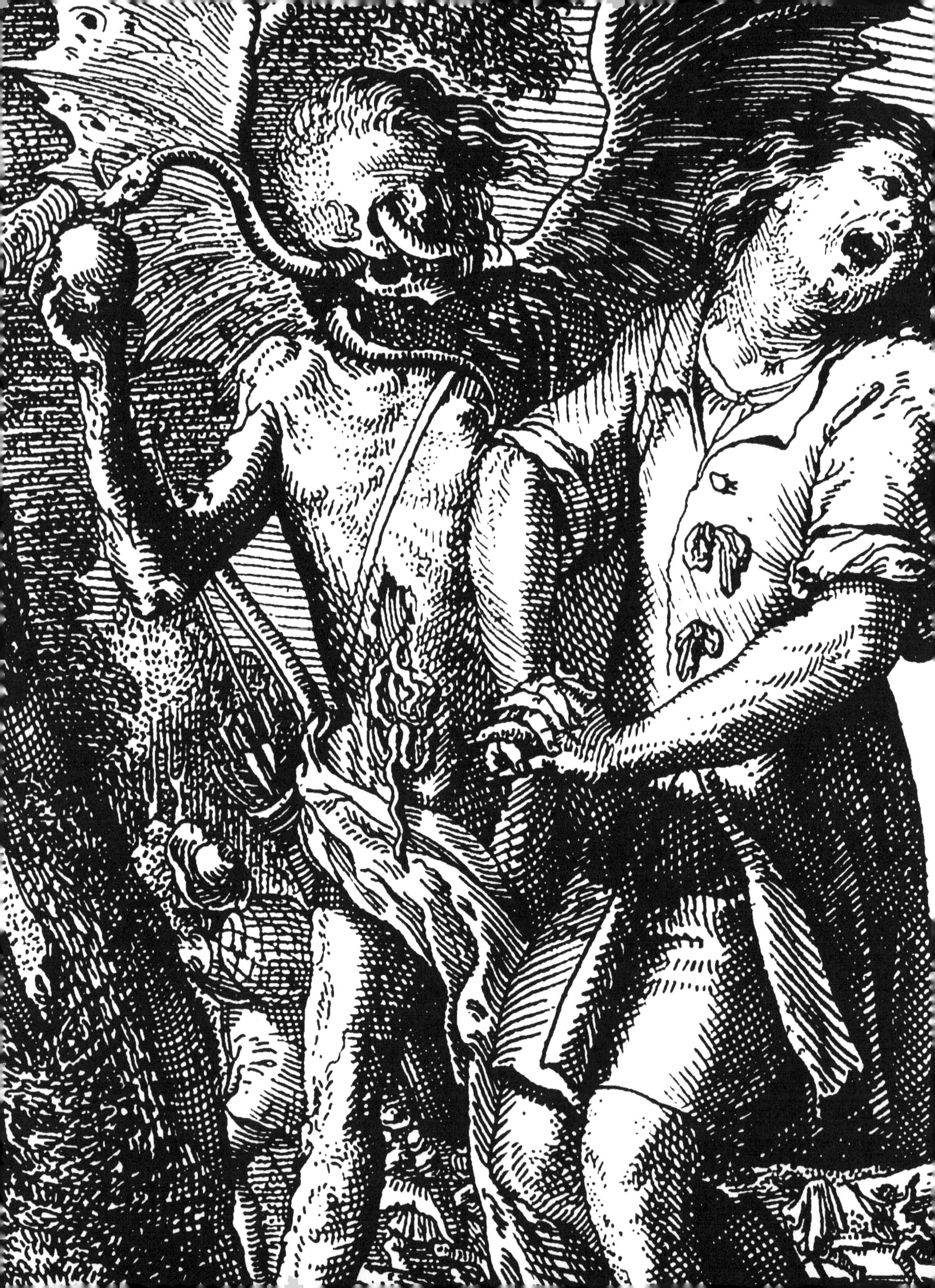

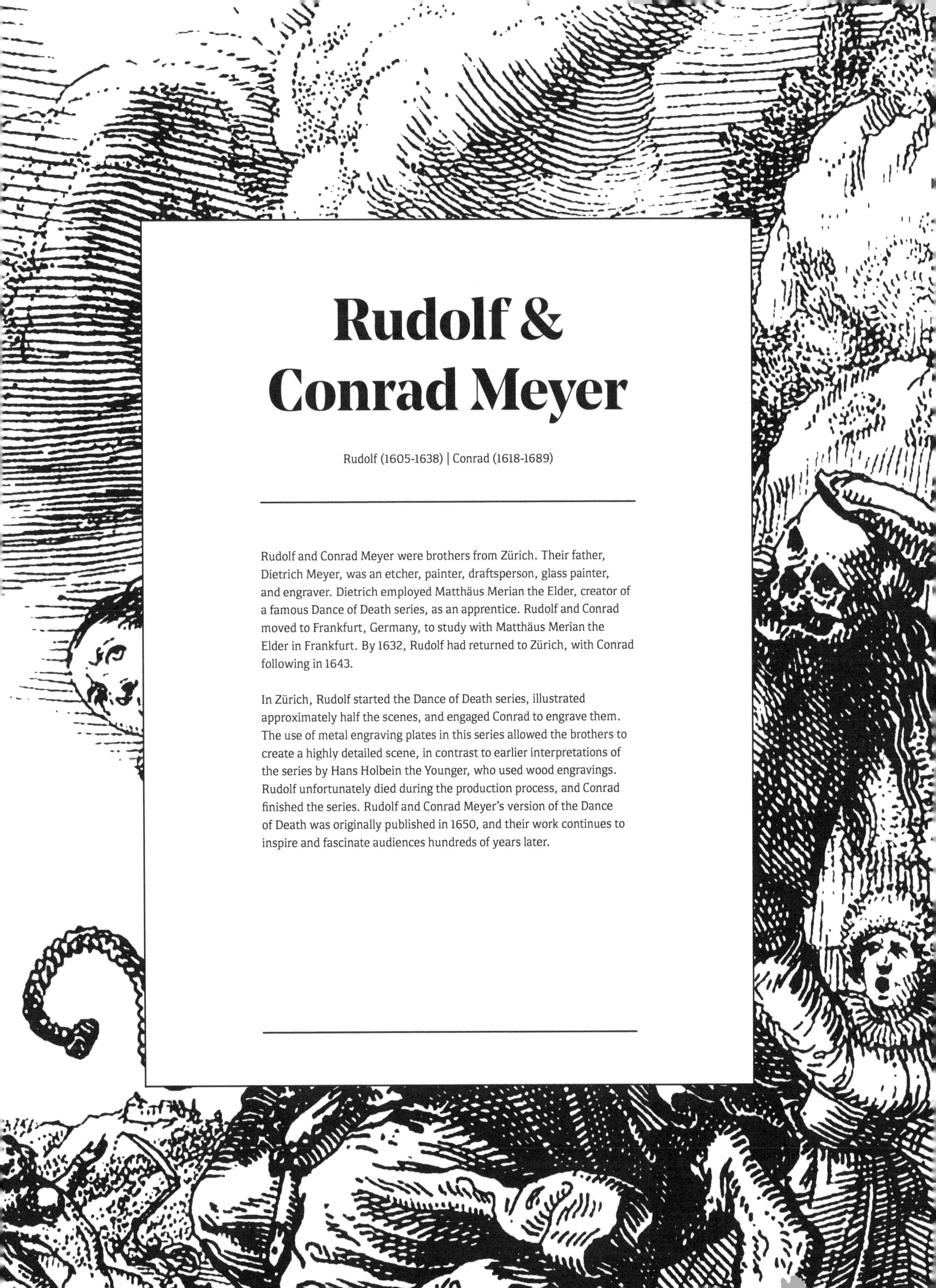

Rudolf & Conrad Meyer

Rudolf (1605-1638) | Conrad (1618-1689)

Rudolf and Conrad Meyer were brothers from Zürich. Their father, Dietrich Meyer, was an etcher, painter, draftsperson, glass painter, and engraver. Dietrich employed Matthäus Merian the Elder, creator of a famous Dance of Death series, as an apprentice. Rudolf and Conrad moved to Frankfurt, Germany, to study with Matthäus Merian the Elder in Frankfurt. By 1632, Rudolf had returned to Zürich, with Conrad following in 1643.

In Zürich, Rudolf started the Dance of Death series, illustrated approximately half the scenes, and engaged Conrad to engrave them. The use of metal engraving plates in this series allowed the brothers to create a highly detailed scene, in contrast to earlier interpretations of the series by Hans Holbein the Younger, who used wood engravings. Rudolf unfortunately died during the production process, and Conrad finished the series. Rudolf and Conrad Meyer's version of the Dance of Death was originally published in 1650, and their work continues to inspire and fascinate audiences hundreds of years later.

09

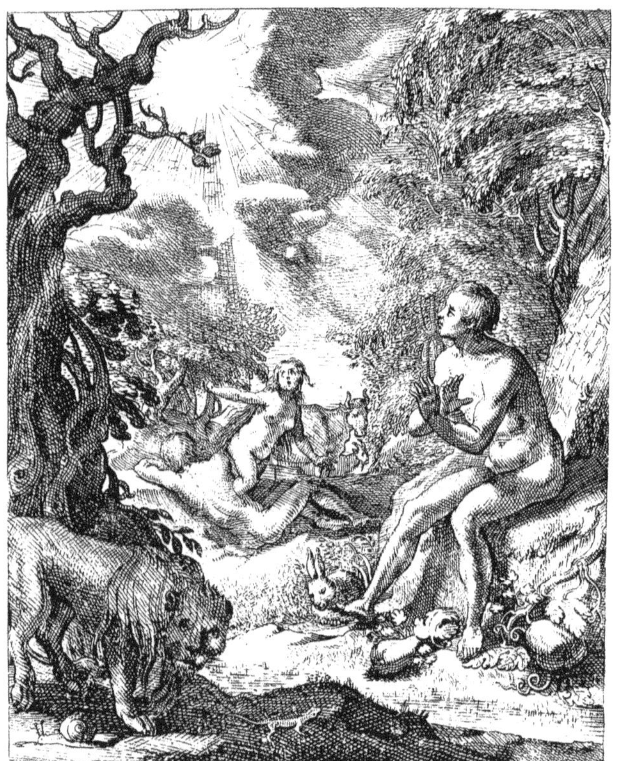

10

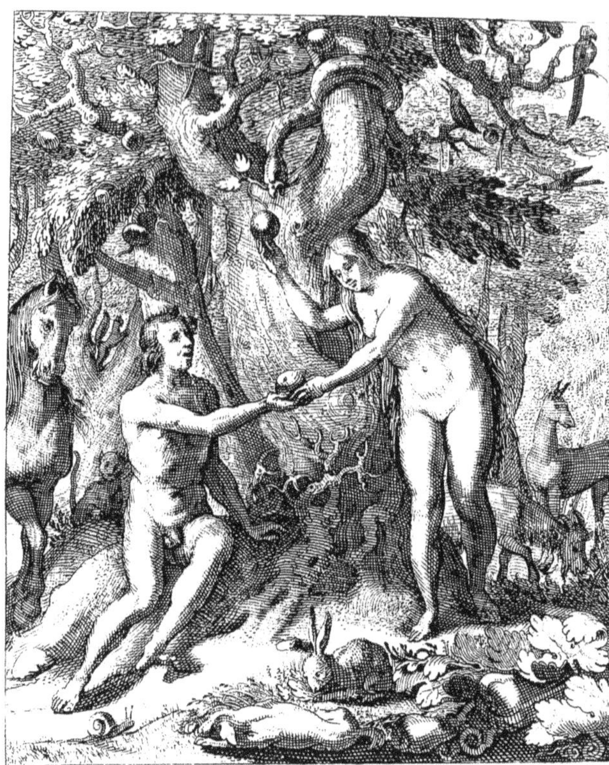

11

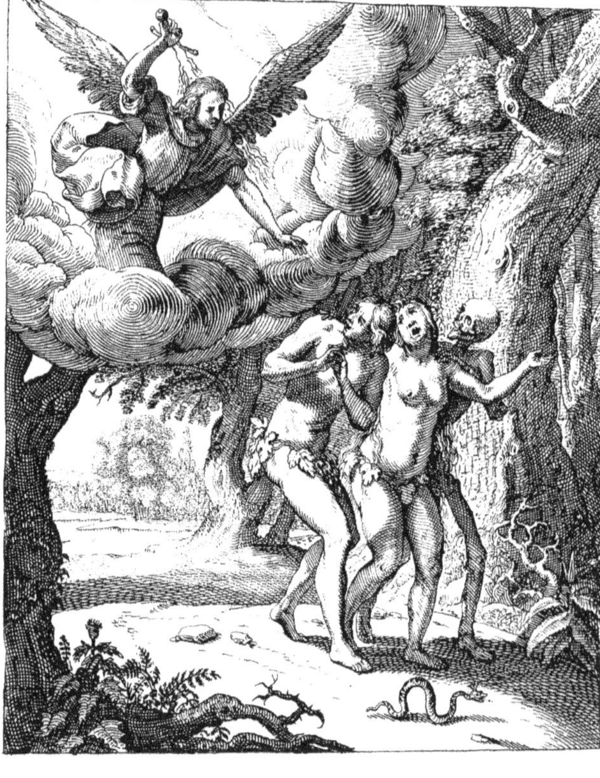

12

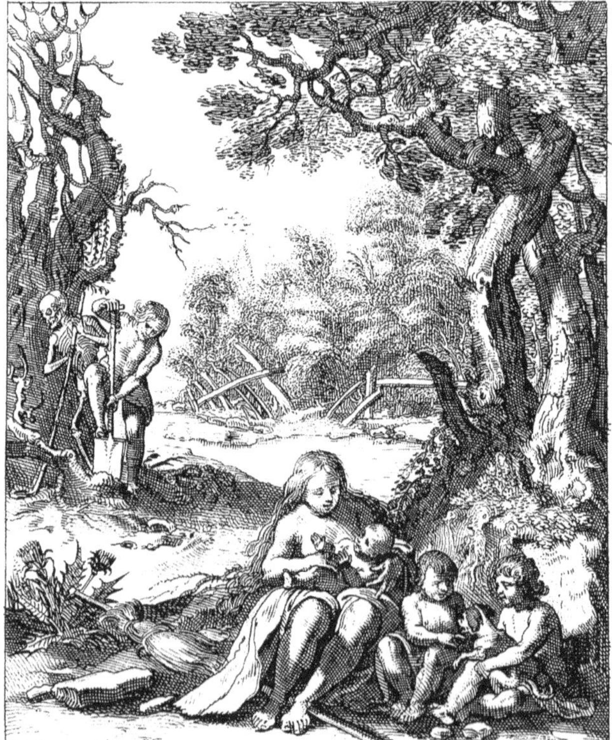

09. Creation of Adam and Eve, Rudolf Meyer, 1650.

10. The Temptation, Rudolf Meyer, 1650.

11. Expulsion from Paradise, Rudolf Meyer, 1650.

12. Misery of Man, Rudolf Meyer, 1650.

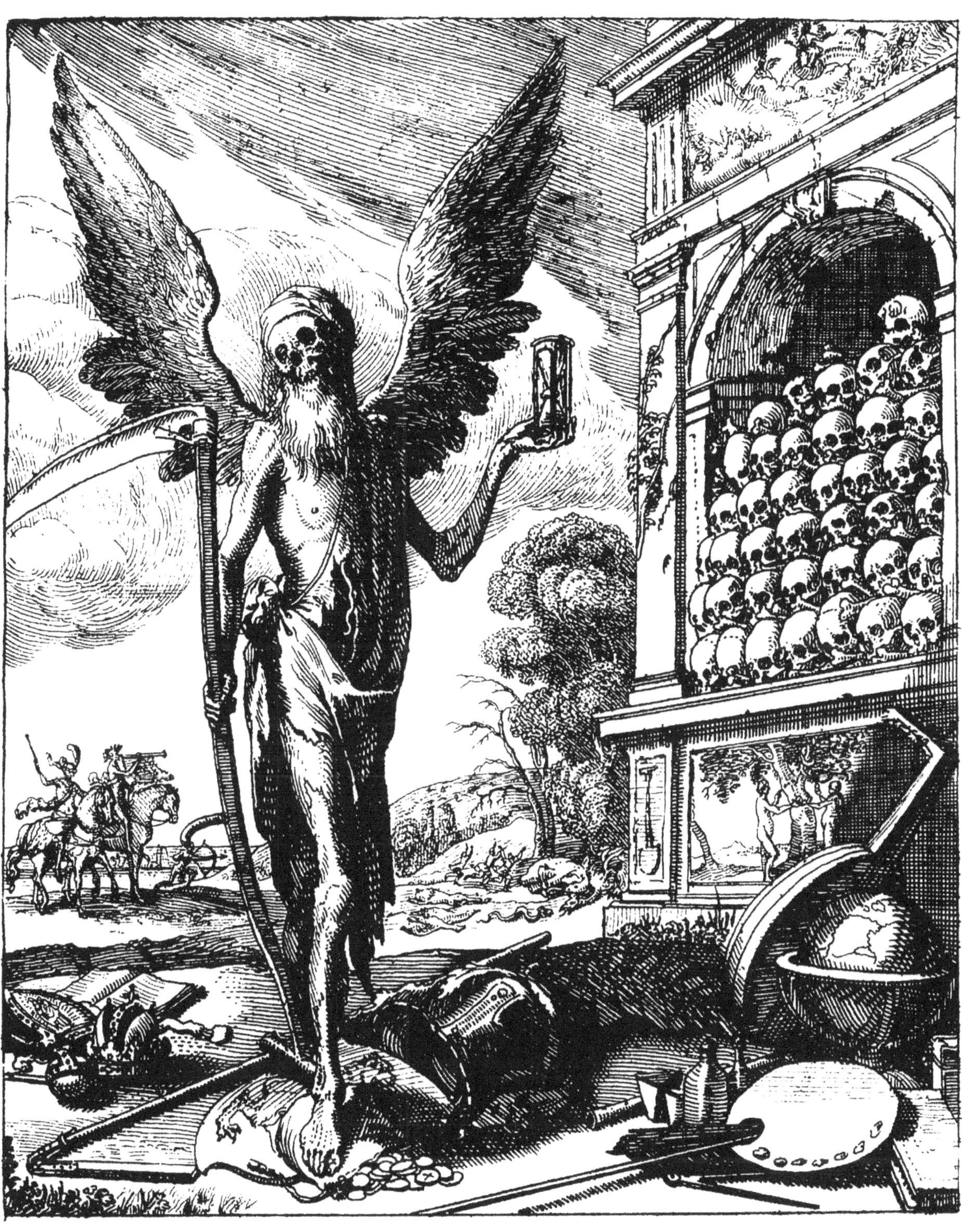

13. Victory Cries of Death, Conrad Meyer, after
Rudolf Meyer, 1650.

14

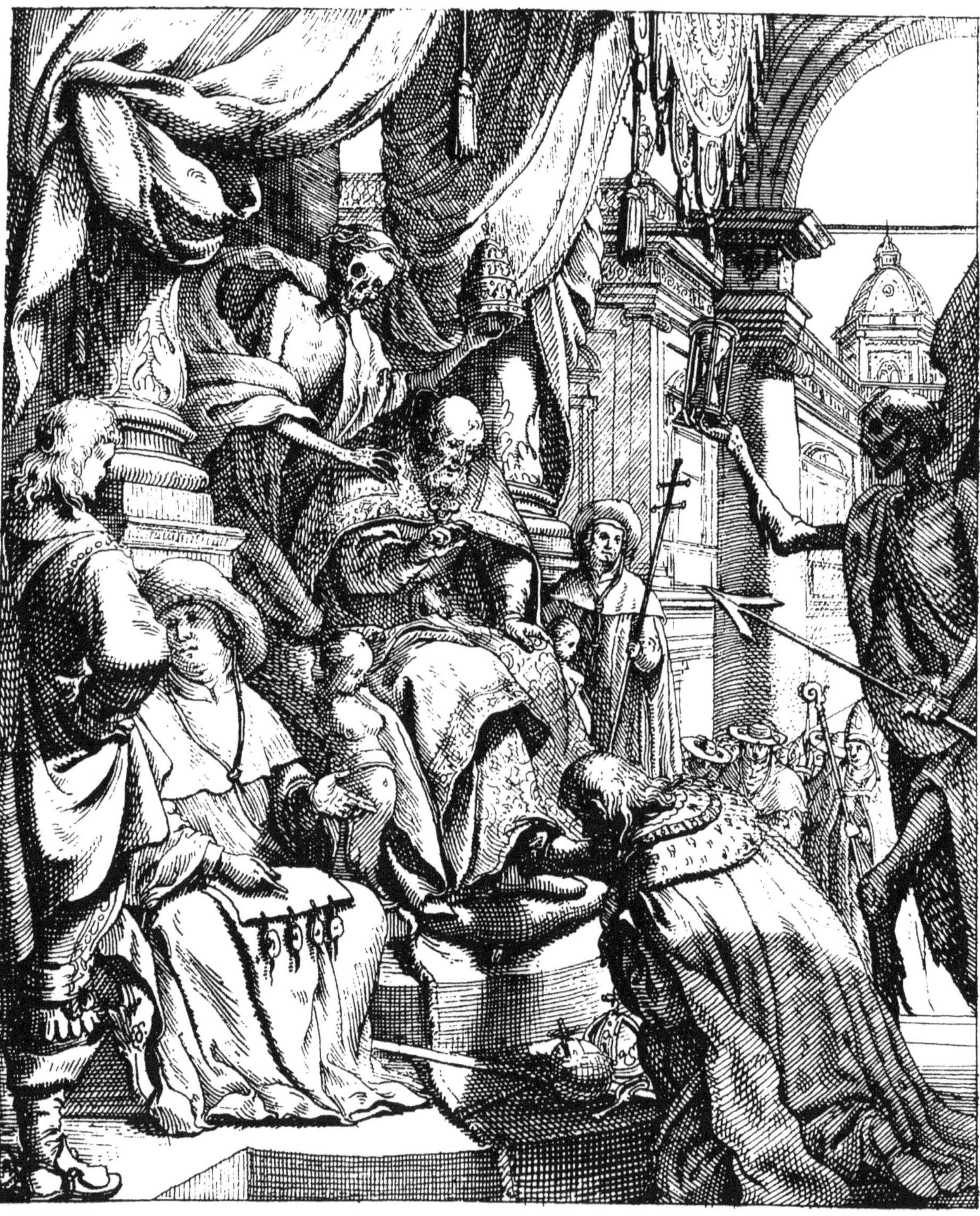

14. Pope and Death, Rudolf Meyer, 1650

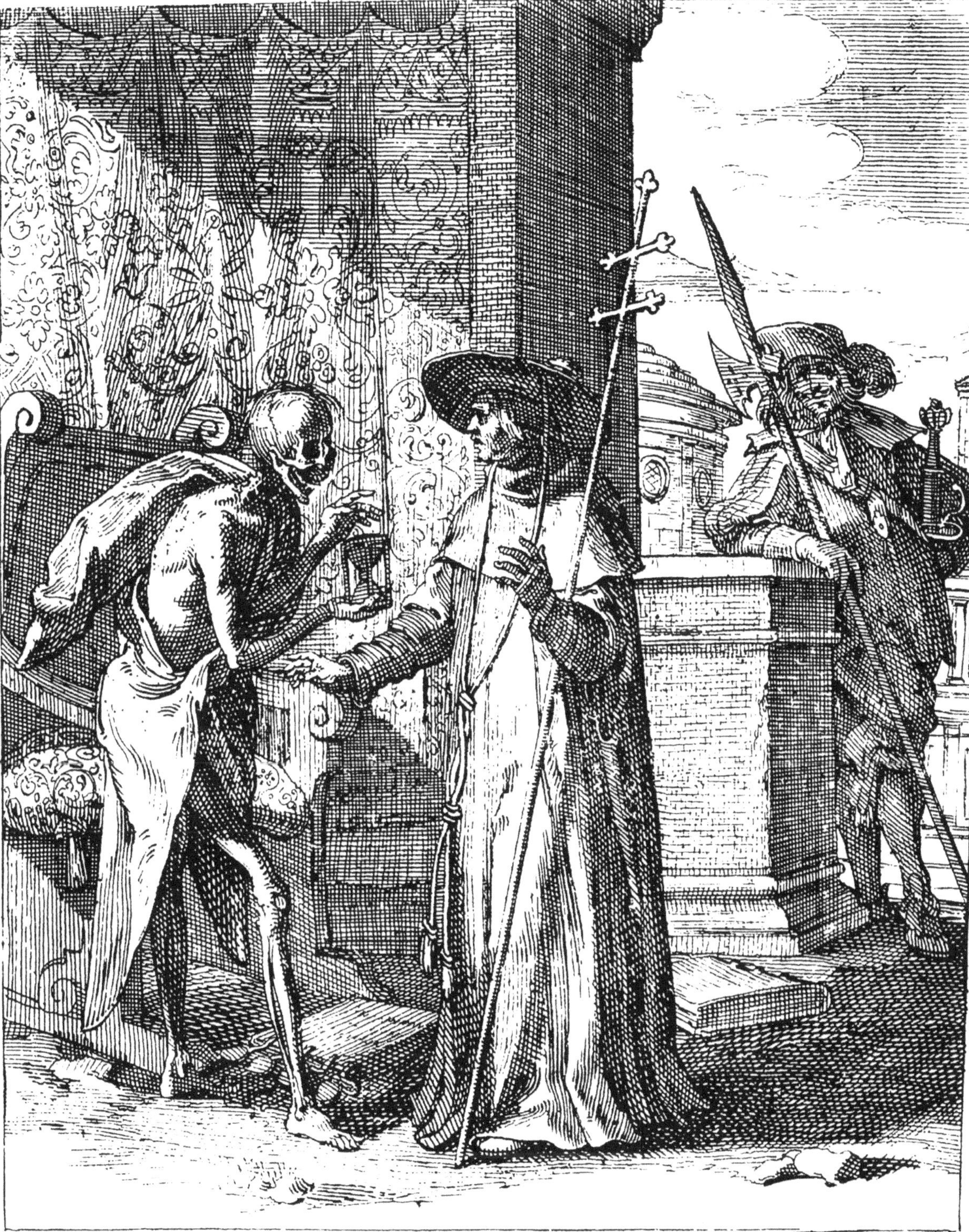

15. Cardinal and Death, Rudolf Meyer, 1650

16

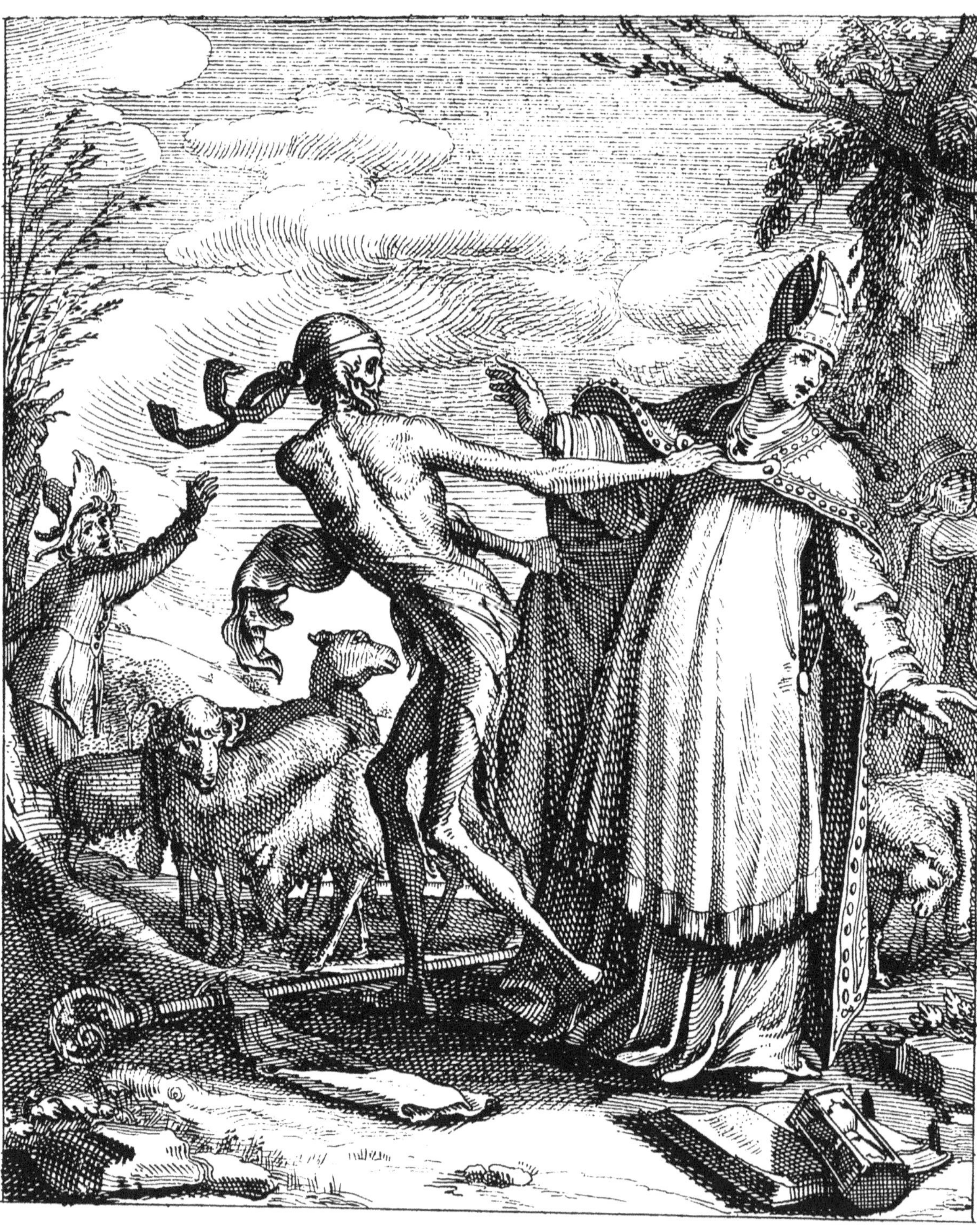

16. Bishop and Death, Rudolf Meyer, 1650

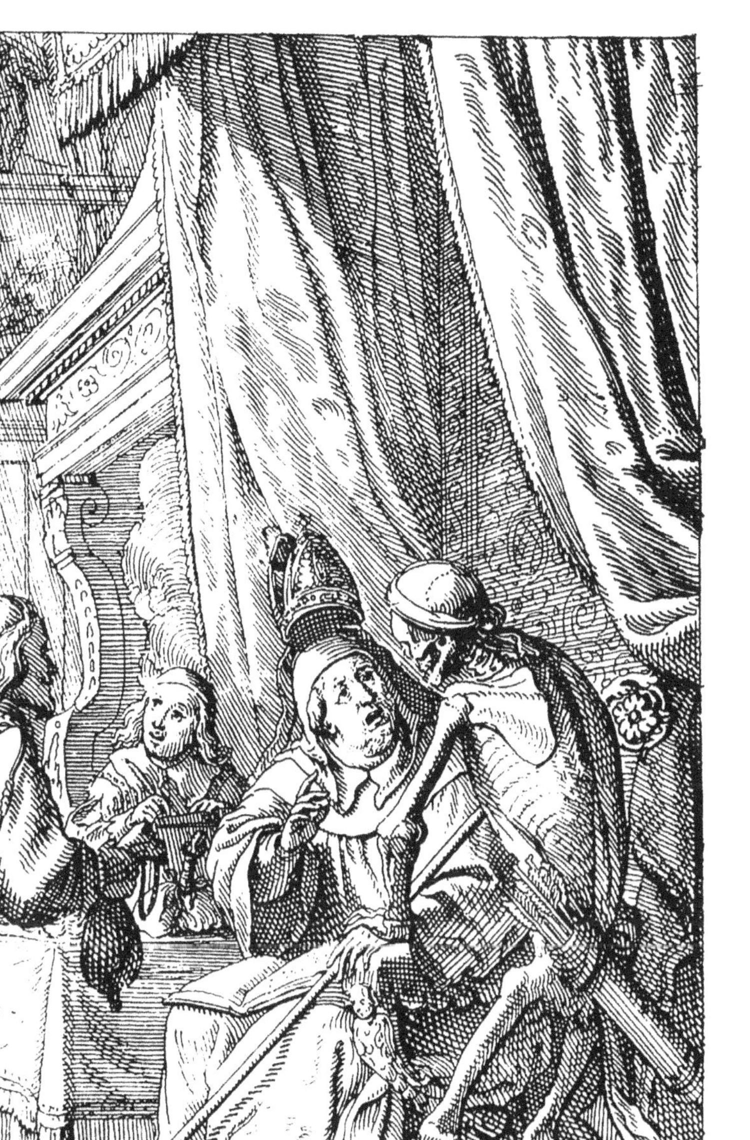

17. Abbot and Death, Rudolf Meyer, 1650

18

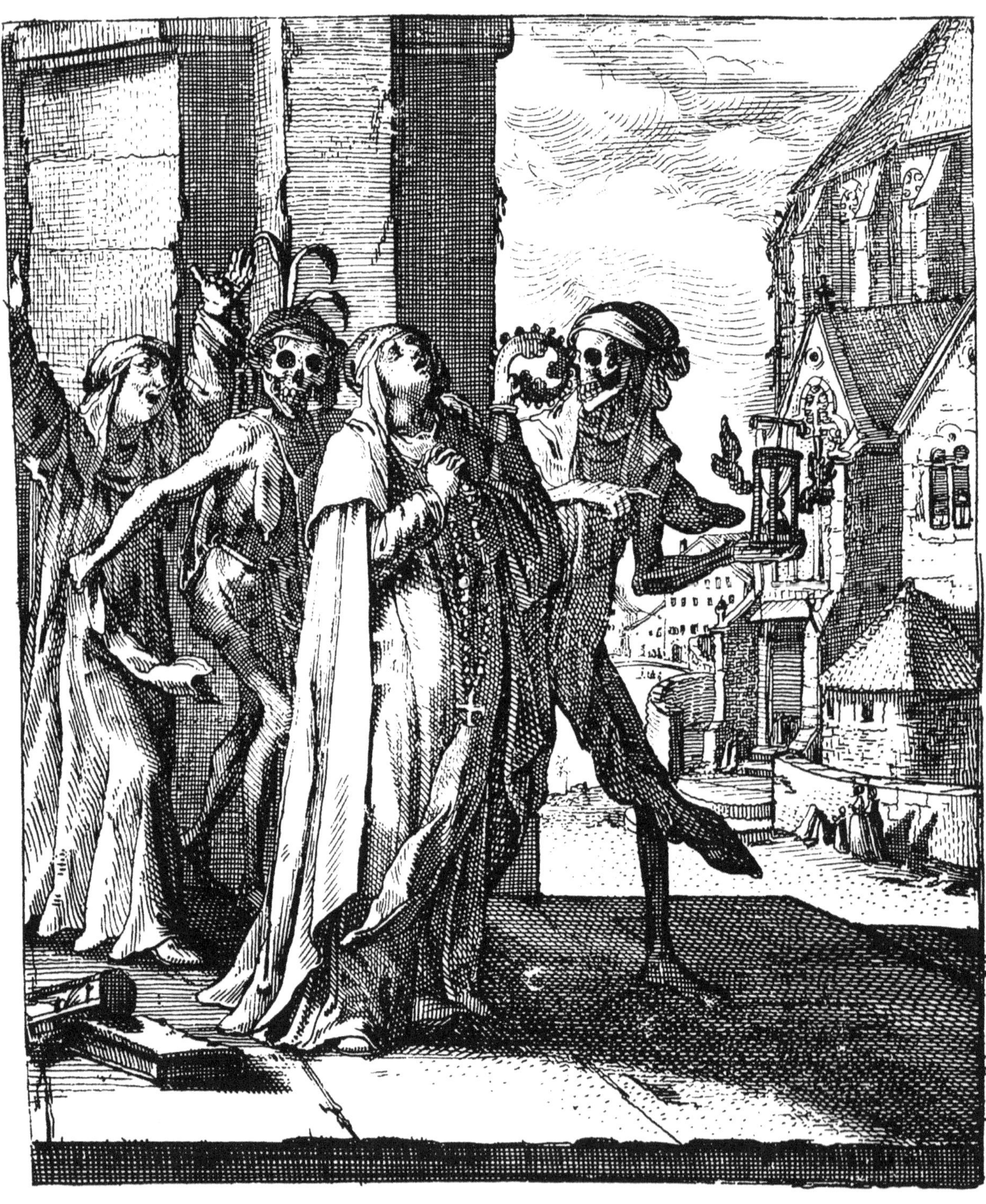

18. Abbess and Death, Rudolf Meyer, 1650

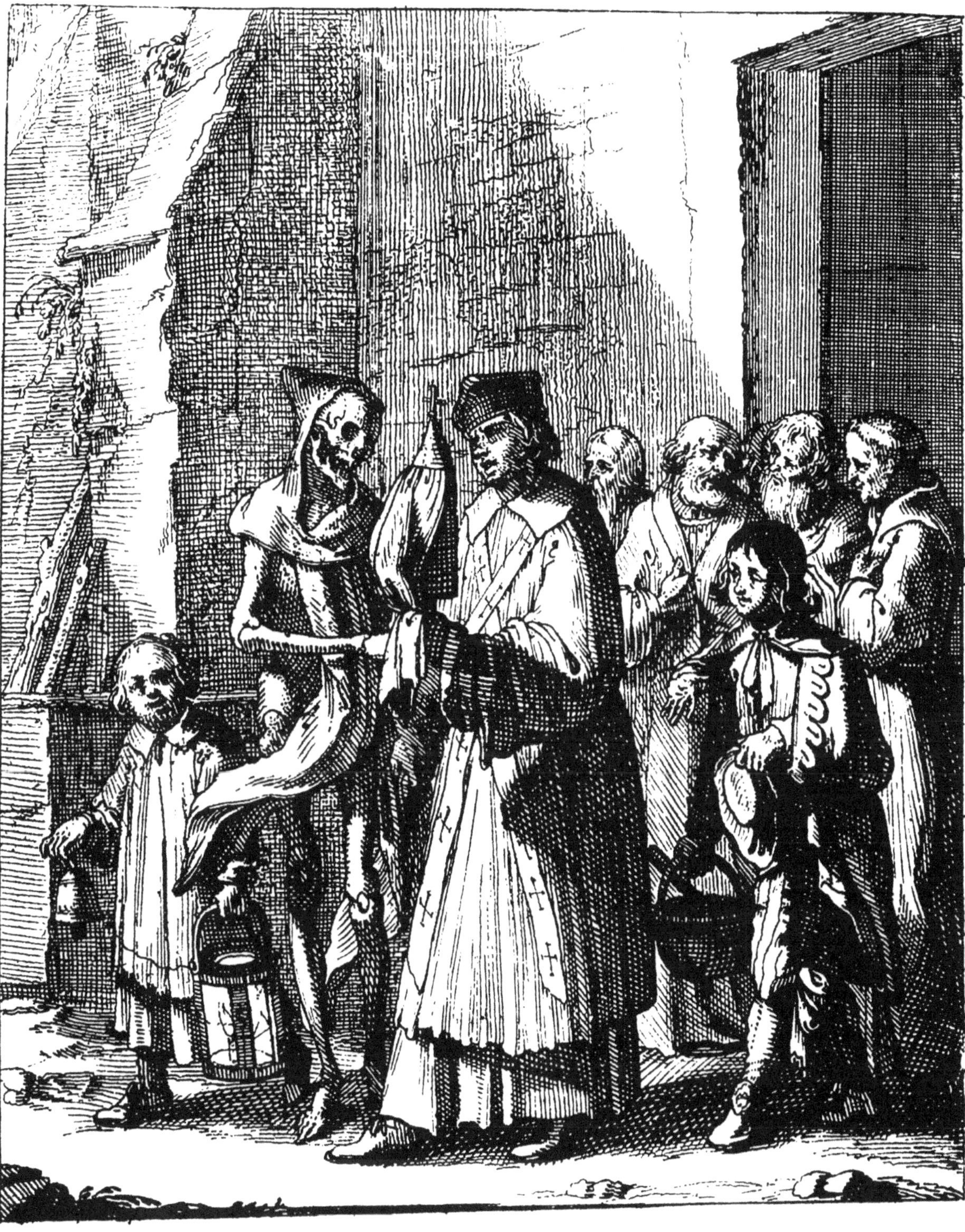

19. Priest and Death, Rudolf Meyer, 1650

20

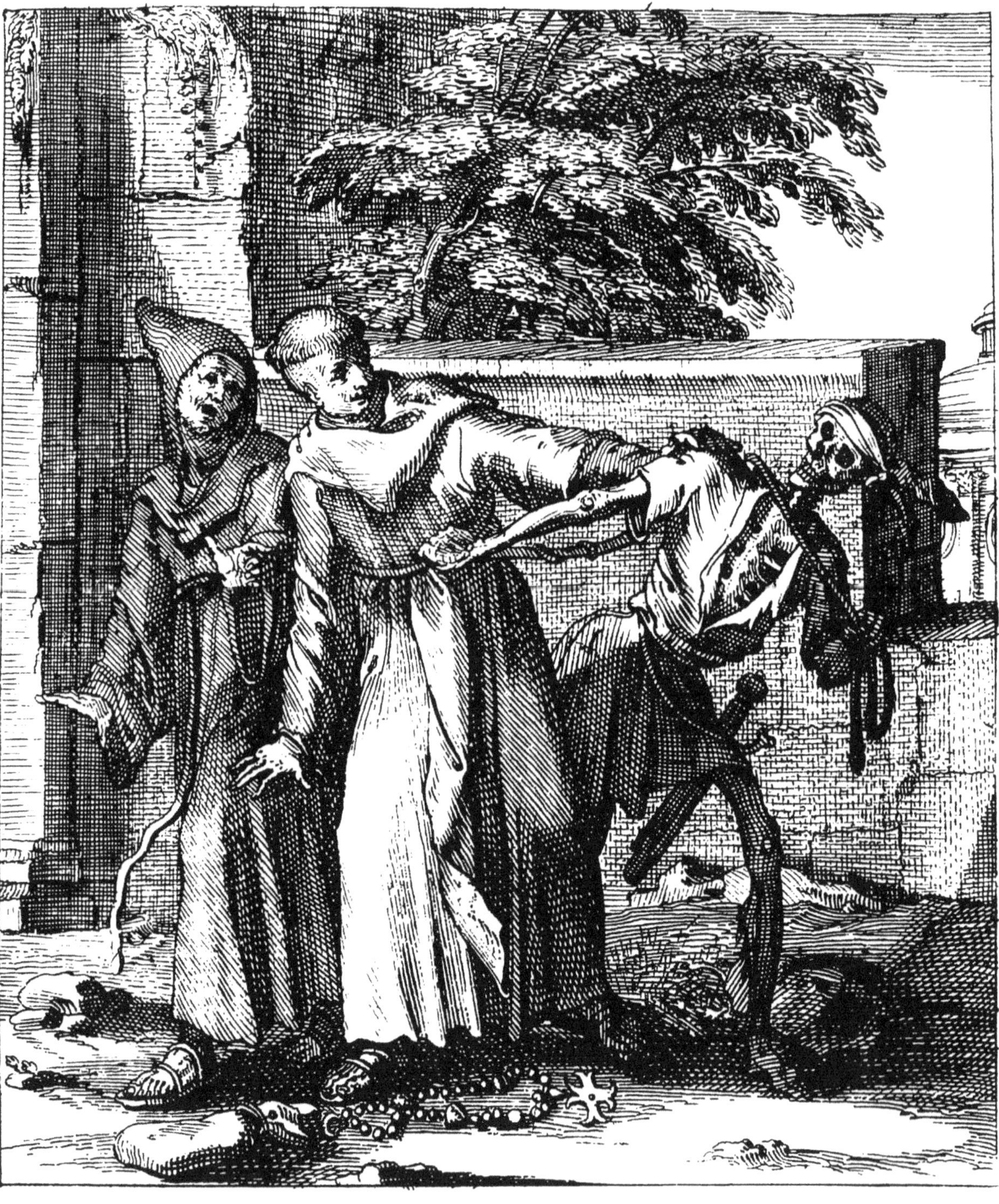

20. Monk and Death, Rudolf Meyer, 1650

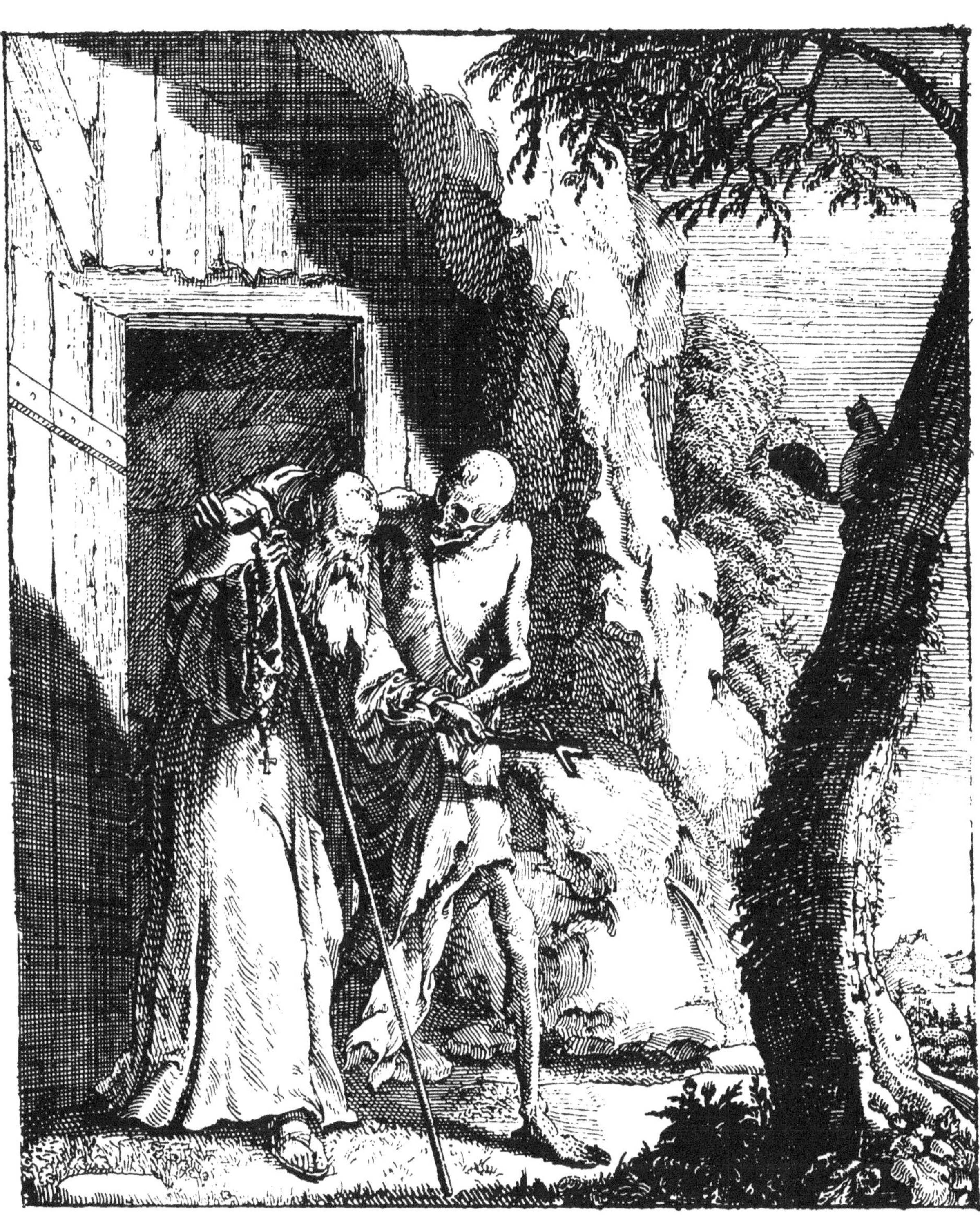

21. Hermit and Death, Conrad Meyer, 1650

22

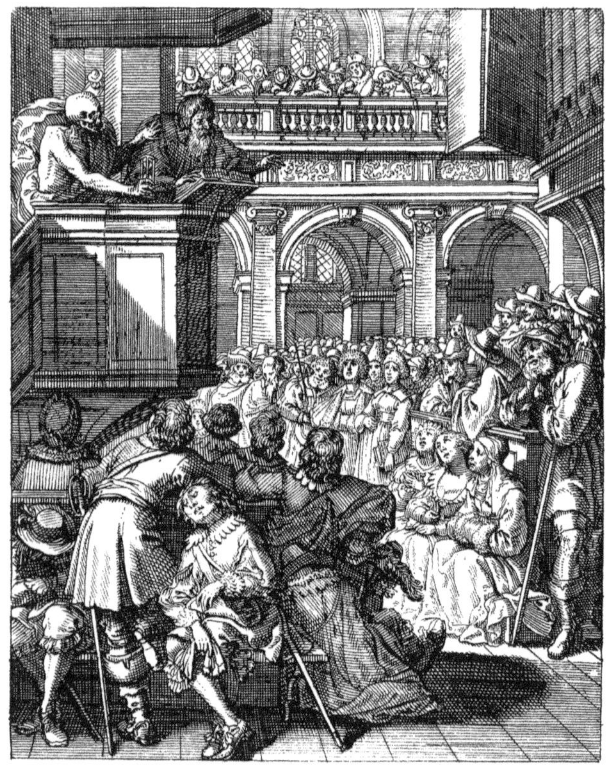

23

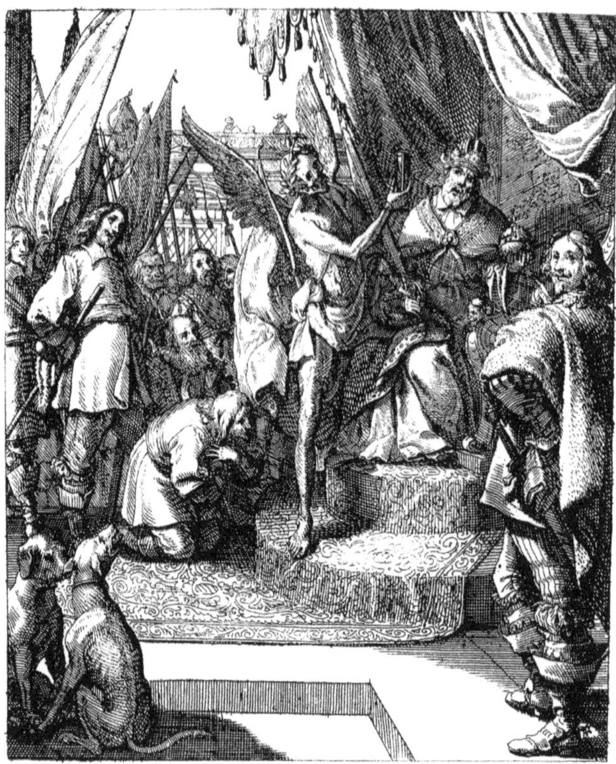

24

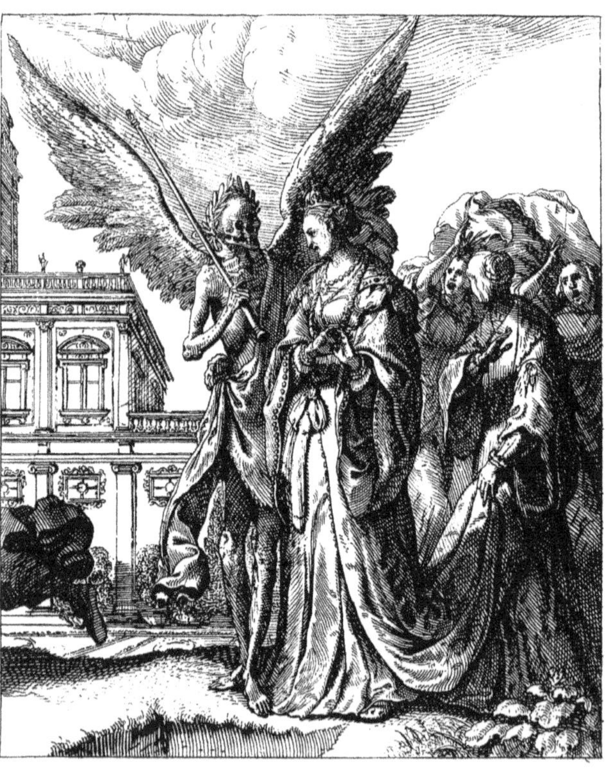

25

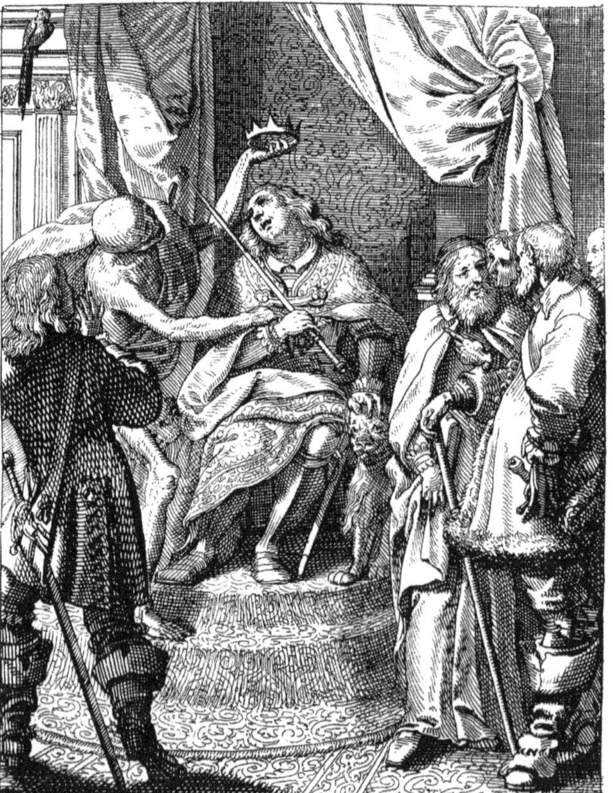

22. Preacher and Death, Rudolf Meyer, 1650.   23. Emperor and Death, Rudolf Meyer, 1650.   24. Empress and Death, Rudolf Meyer, 1650.   25. King and Death, Rudolf Meyer, 1650.

26

27

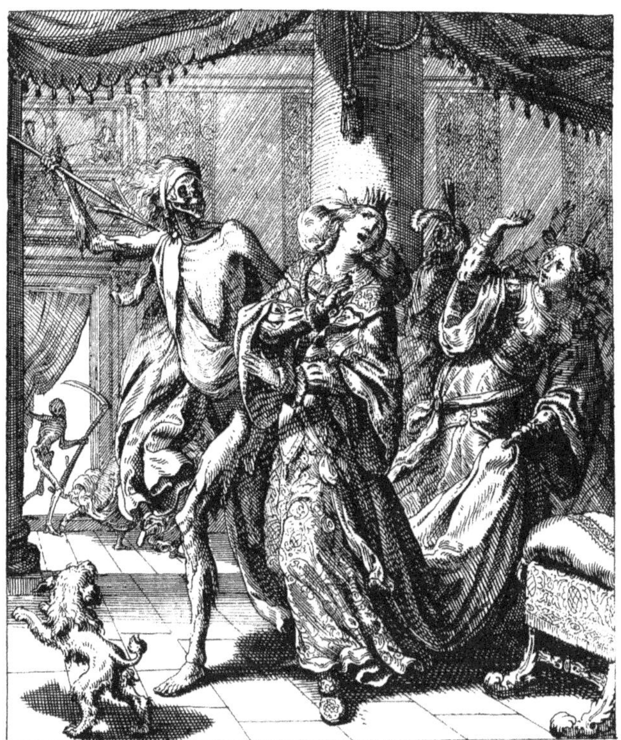

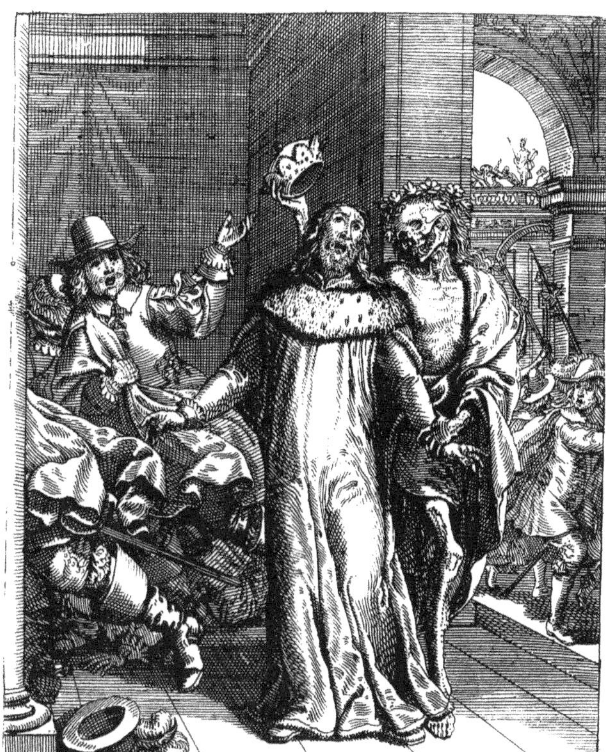

28

29

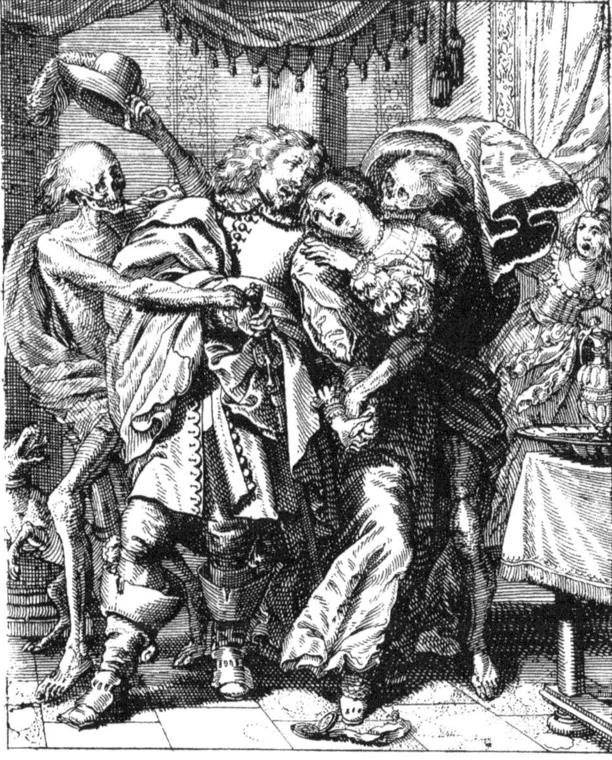

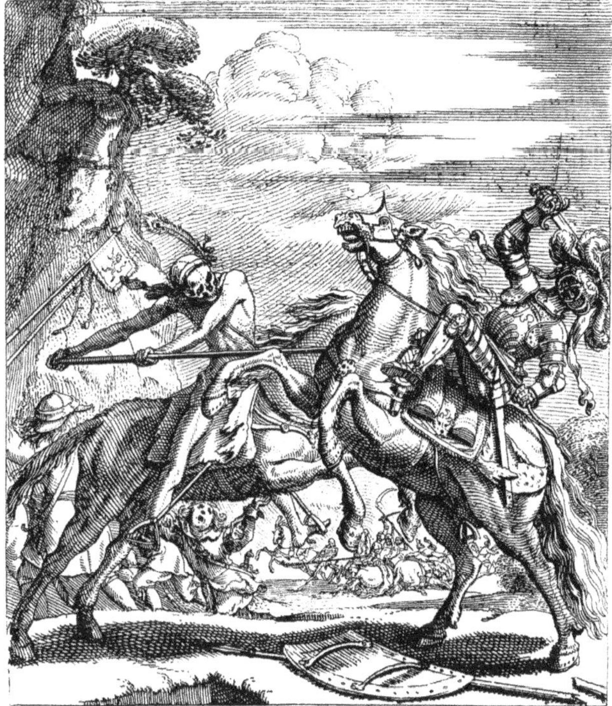

26. Queen and Death, Rudolf Meyer, 1650.

27. Elector and Death, Rudolf Meyer, 1650.

28. Count and Countess and Death, Rudolf Meyer, 1650.

29. Knight and Death, Conrad Meyer, 1650.

30

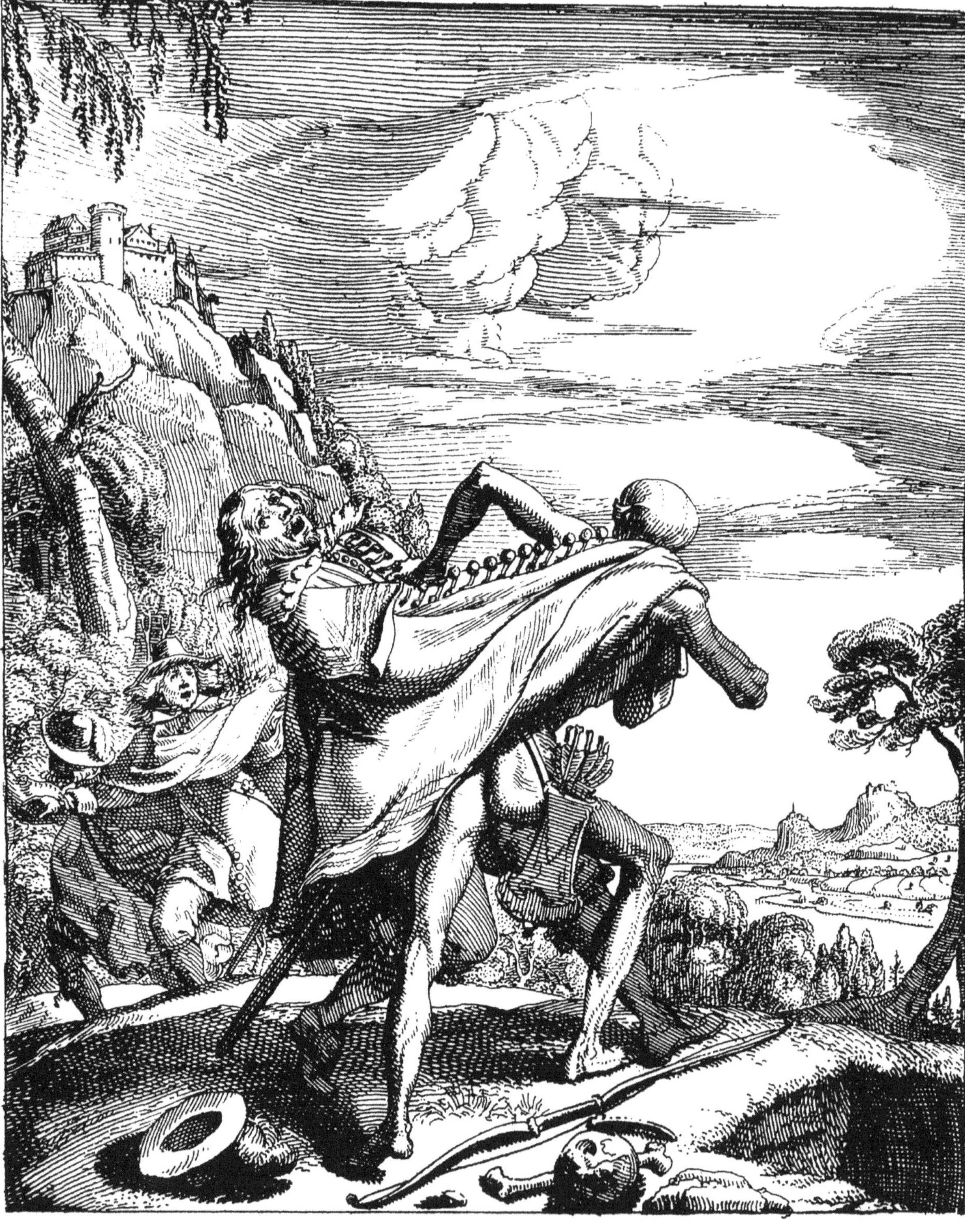

30. Nobleman and Death, Conrad Meyer, 1650

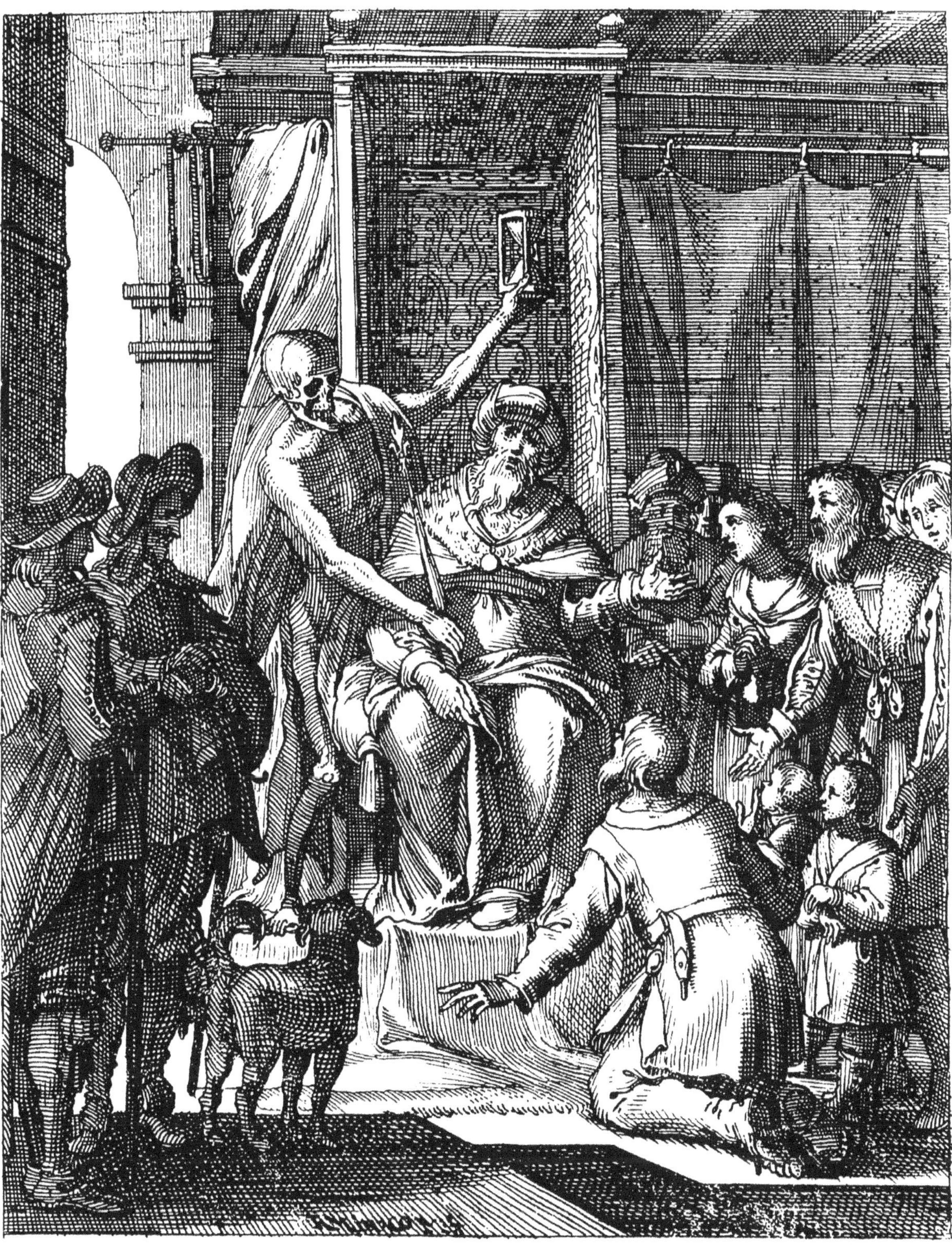

31. Judge and Death, Rudolf Meyer, 1650

32

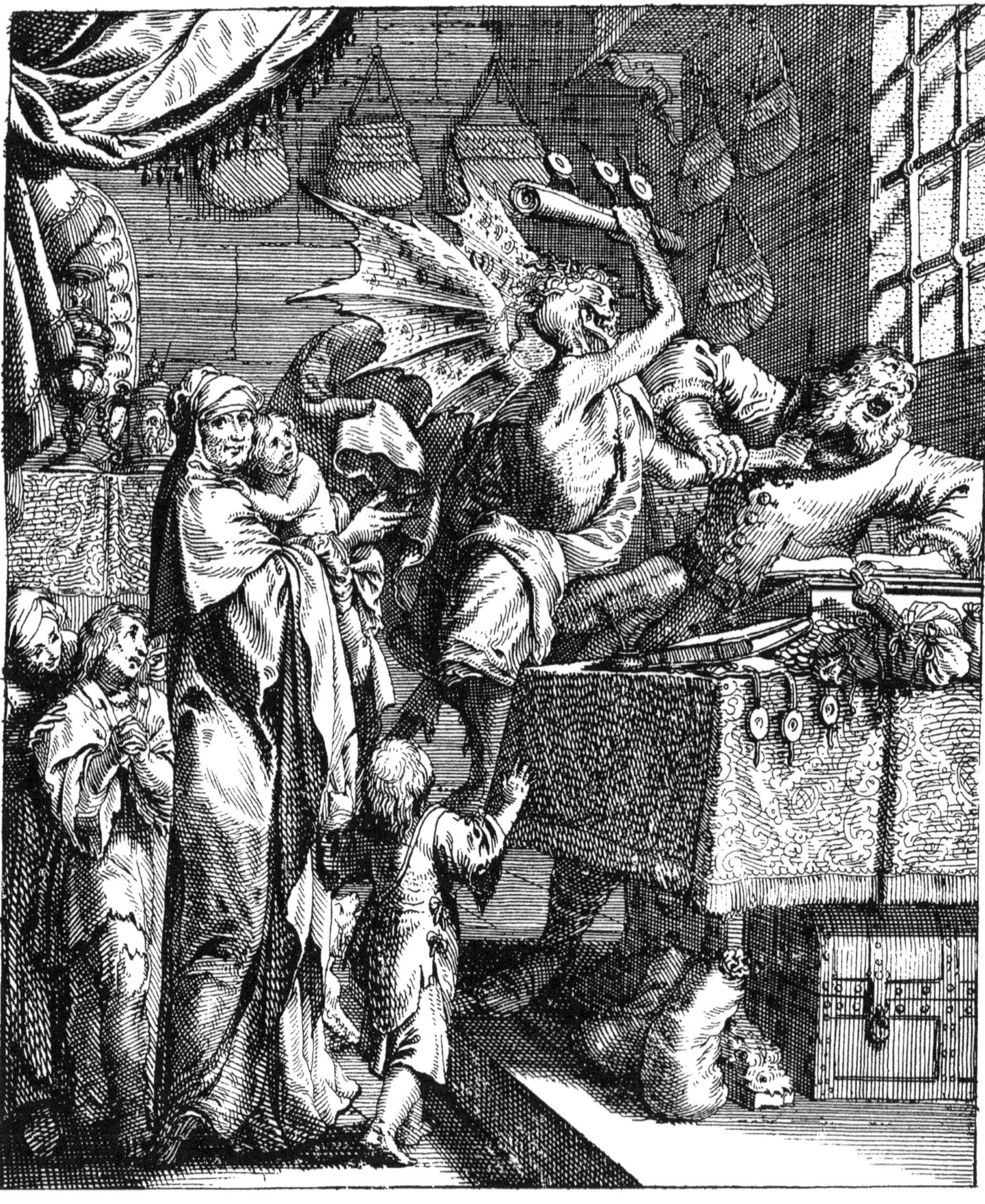

32. Widow, Orphan and bailiff with Death, Conrad
Meyer, after Rudolf Meyer, 1650.

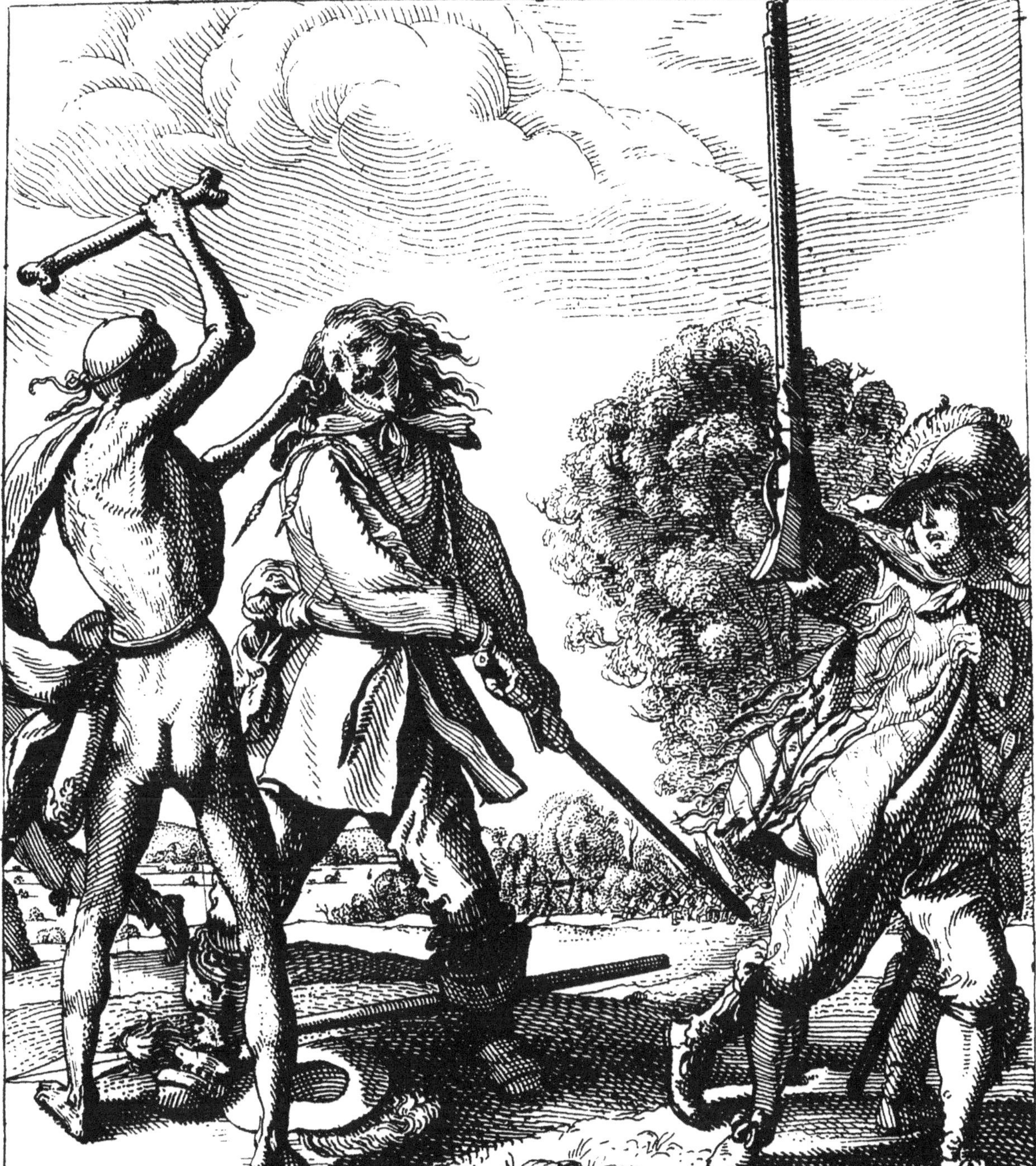

33. Captain and Death, Rudolf Meyer, 1650.

34

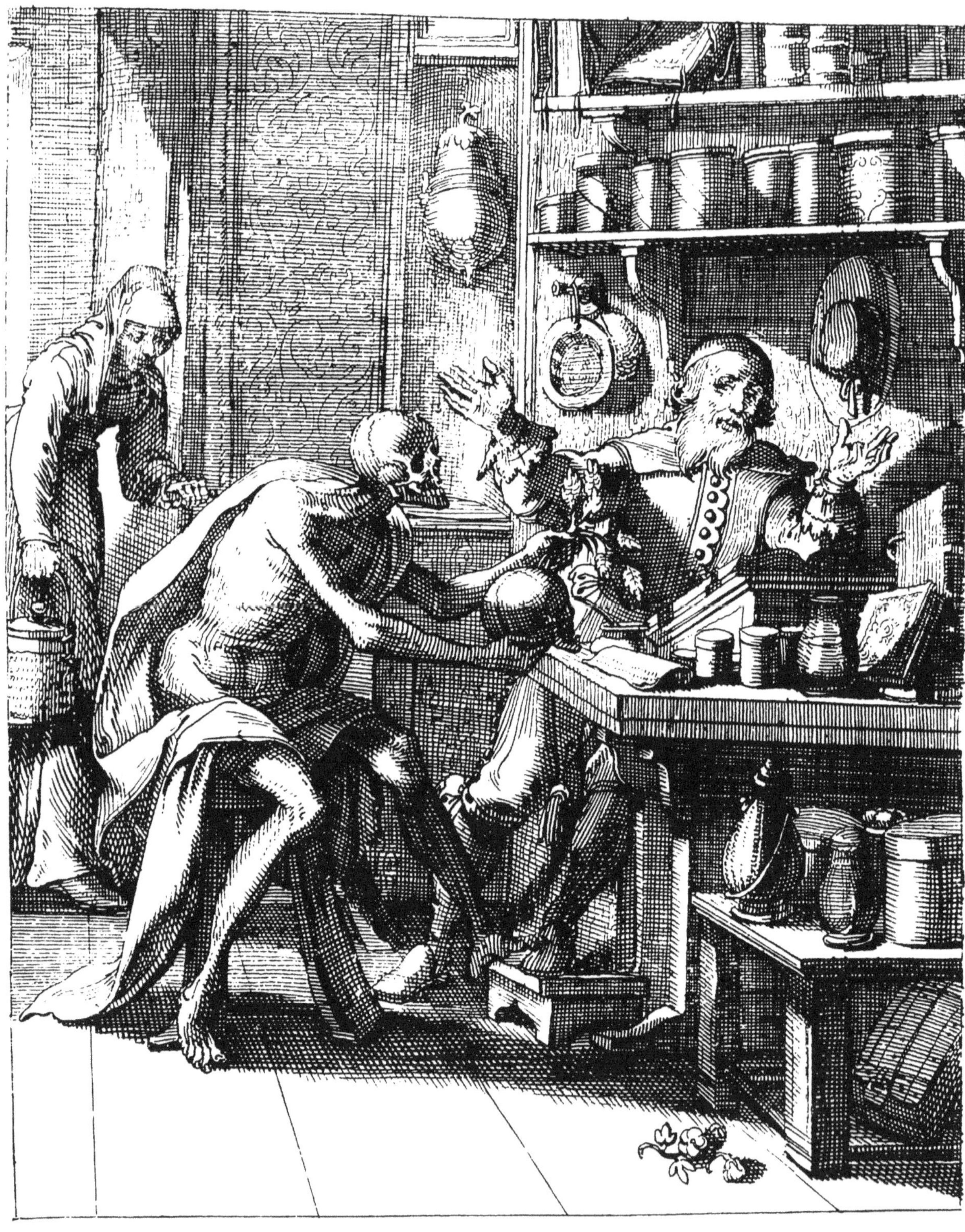

34. Doctor and Death, Conrad Meyer, after Rudolf
Meyer, 1650.

35

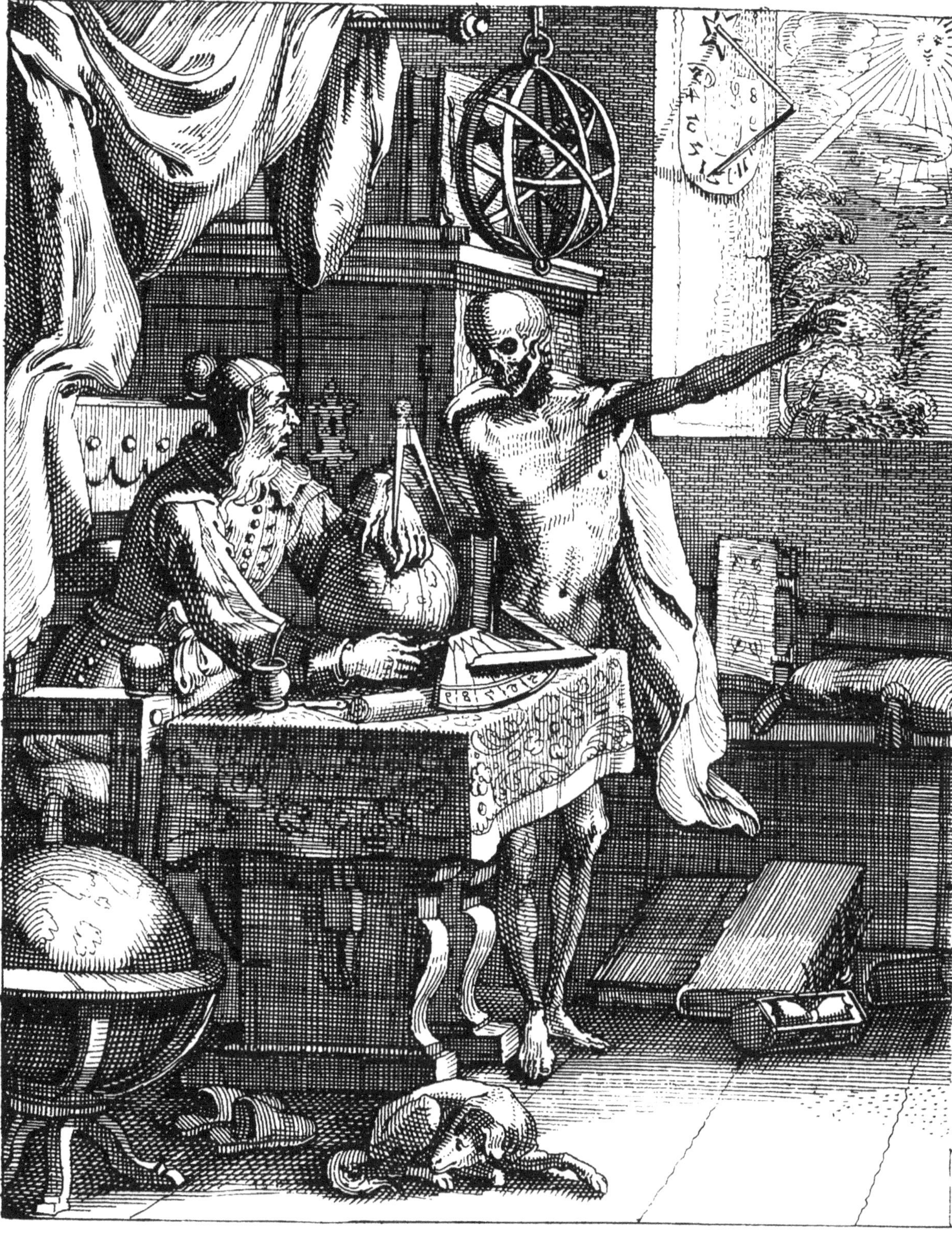

35. Astrologer and Death, Conrad Meyer, 1650.

36

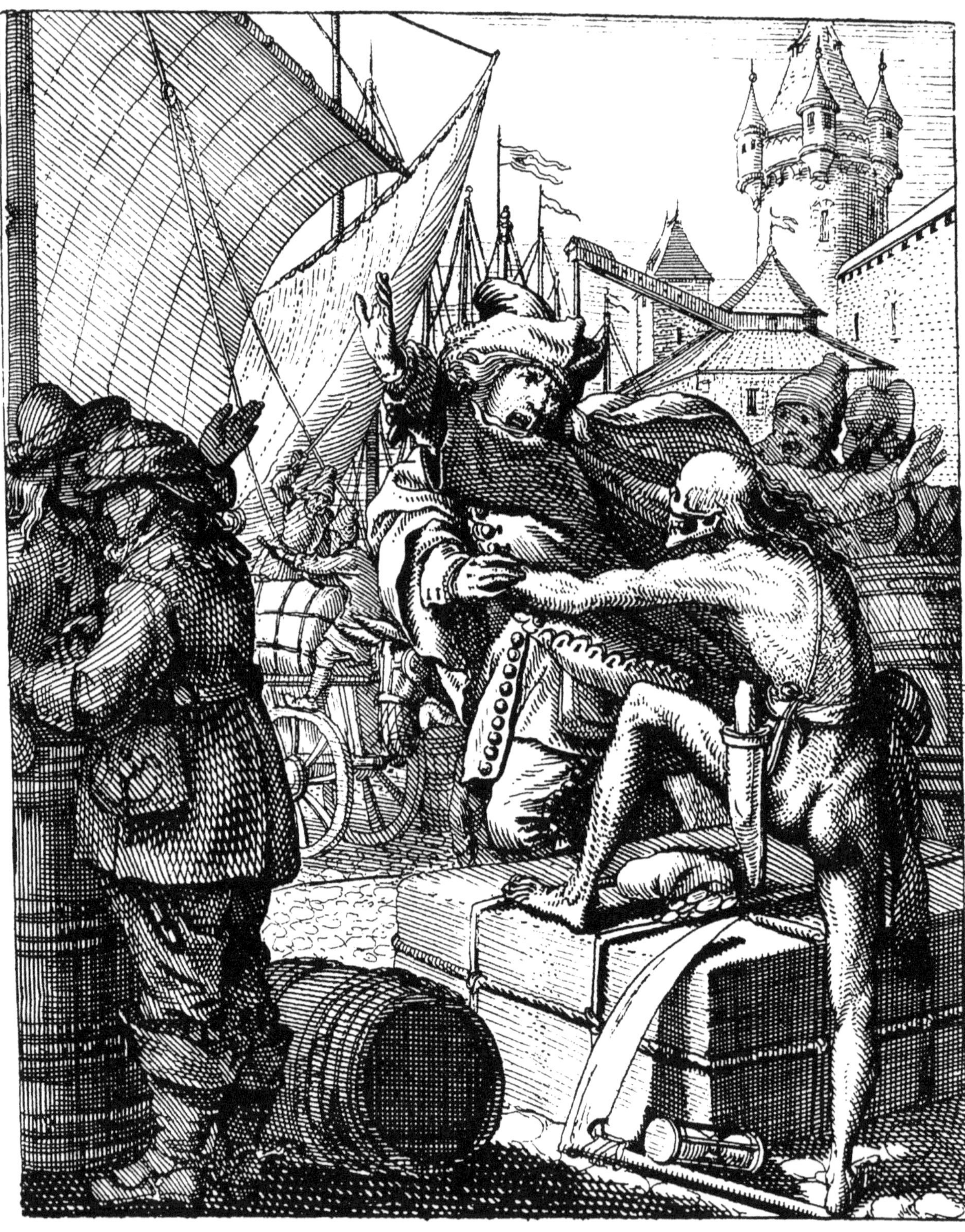

36. Merchant and Death, Conrad Meyer, 1650.

37

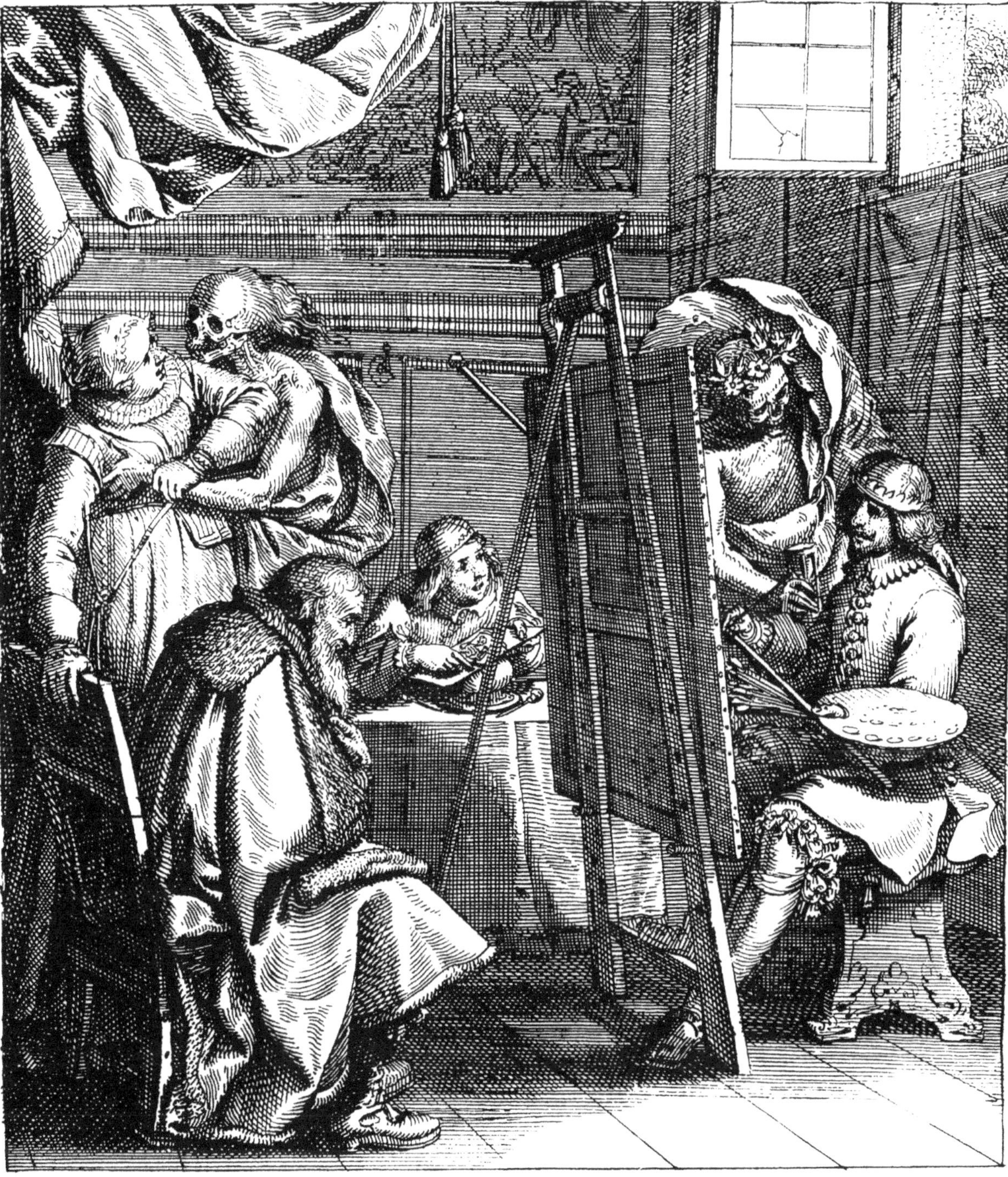

37. Painter and Engraver and Death, Conrad
Meyer, 1650.

38

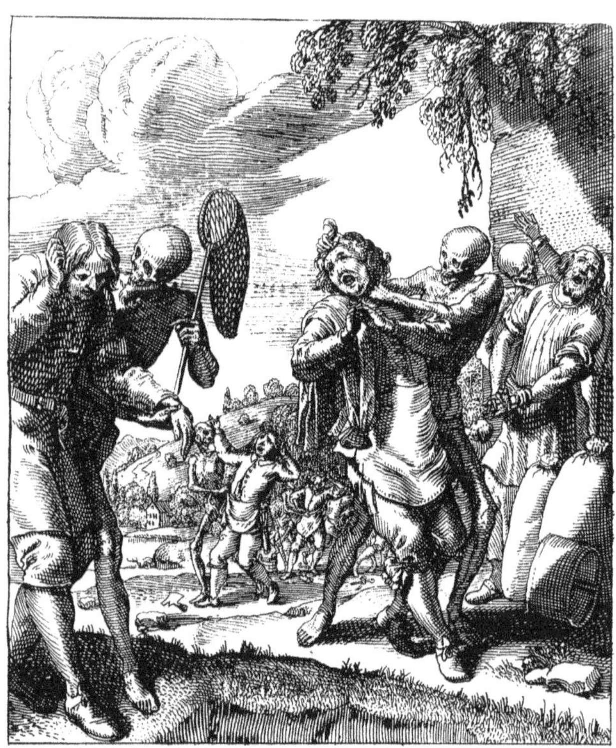

39

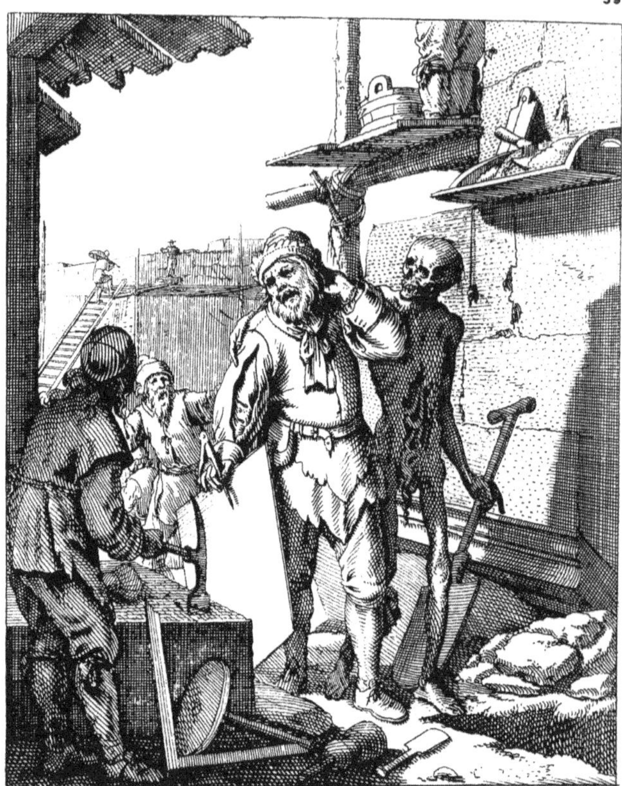

40

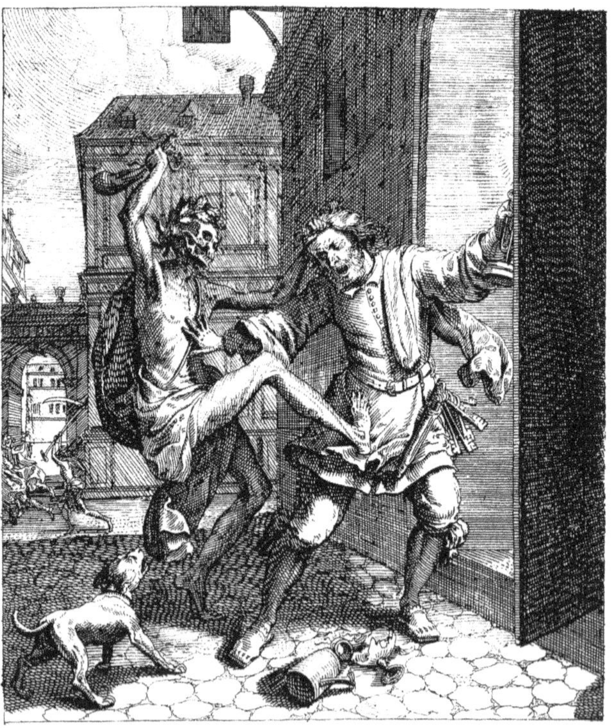

41

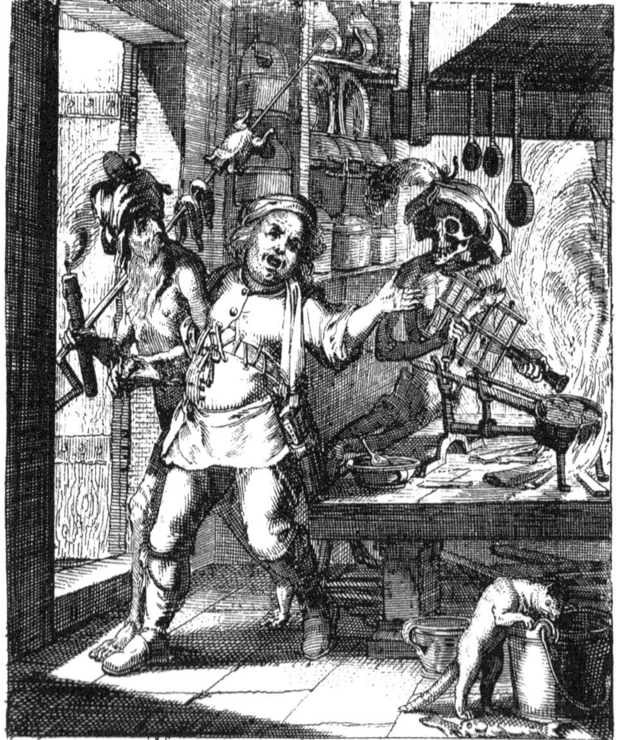

38. Craftsman and Death, Rudolf Meyer, 1650.

39. Builder or Architect and Death, Rudolf Meyer, 1650.

40. Innkeeper and Death, Rudolf Meyer, 1650.

41. Cook and Death, Conrad Meyer, after Rudolf Meyer, 1650.

42

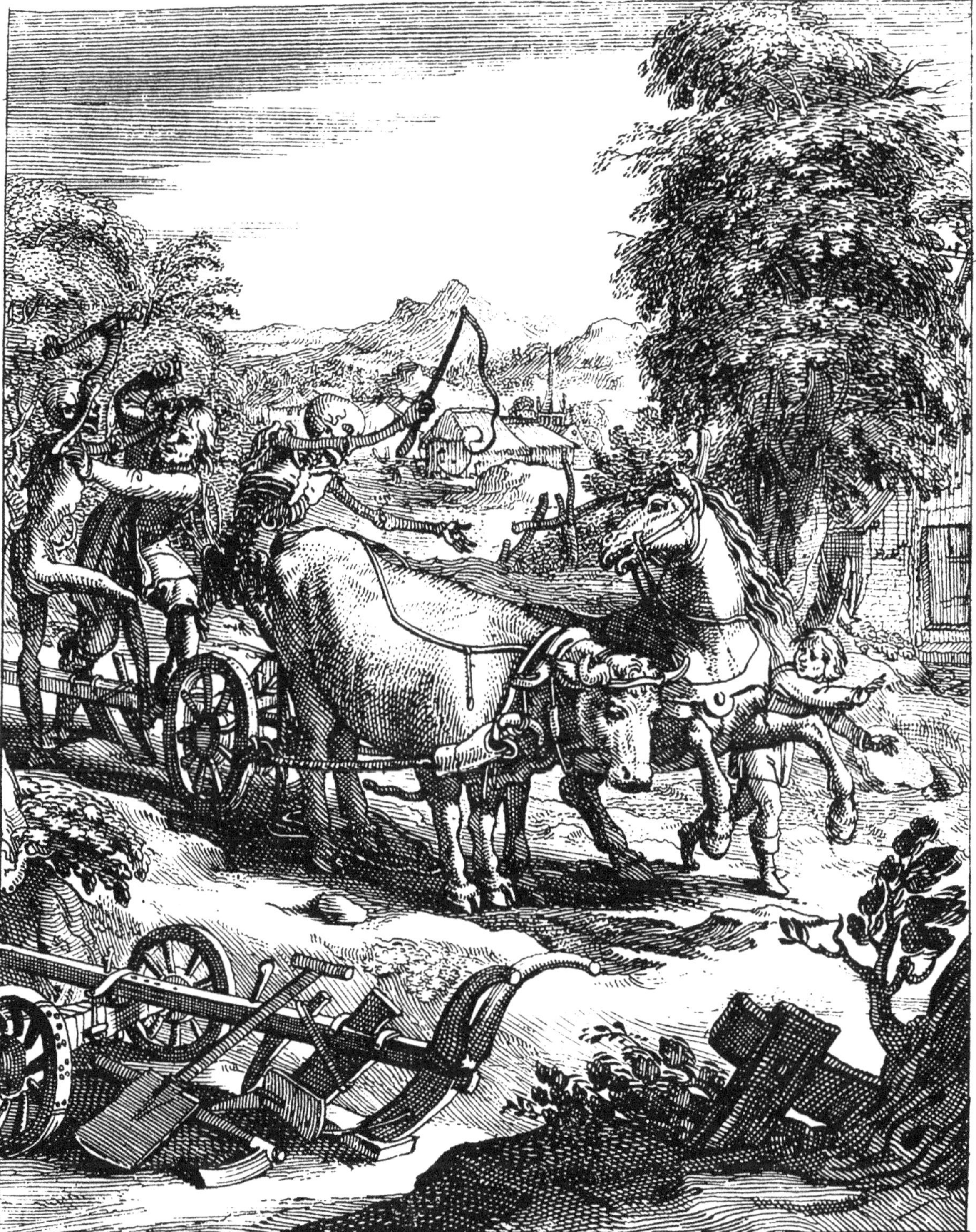

THE DANCE OF DEATH

42. Peasant and Death, Rudolf Meyer, 1650.

43

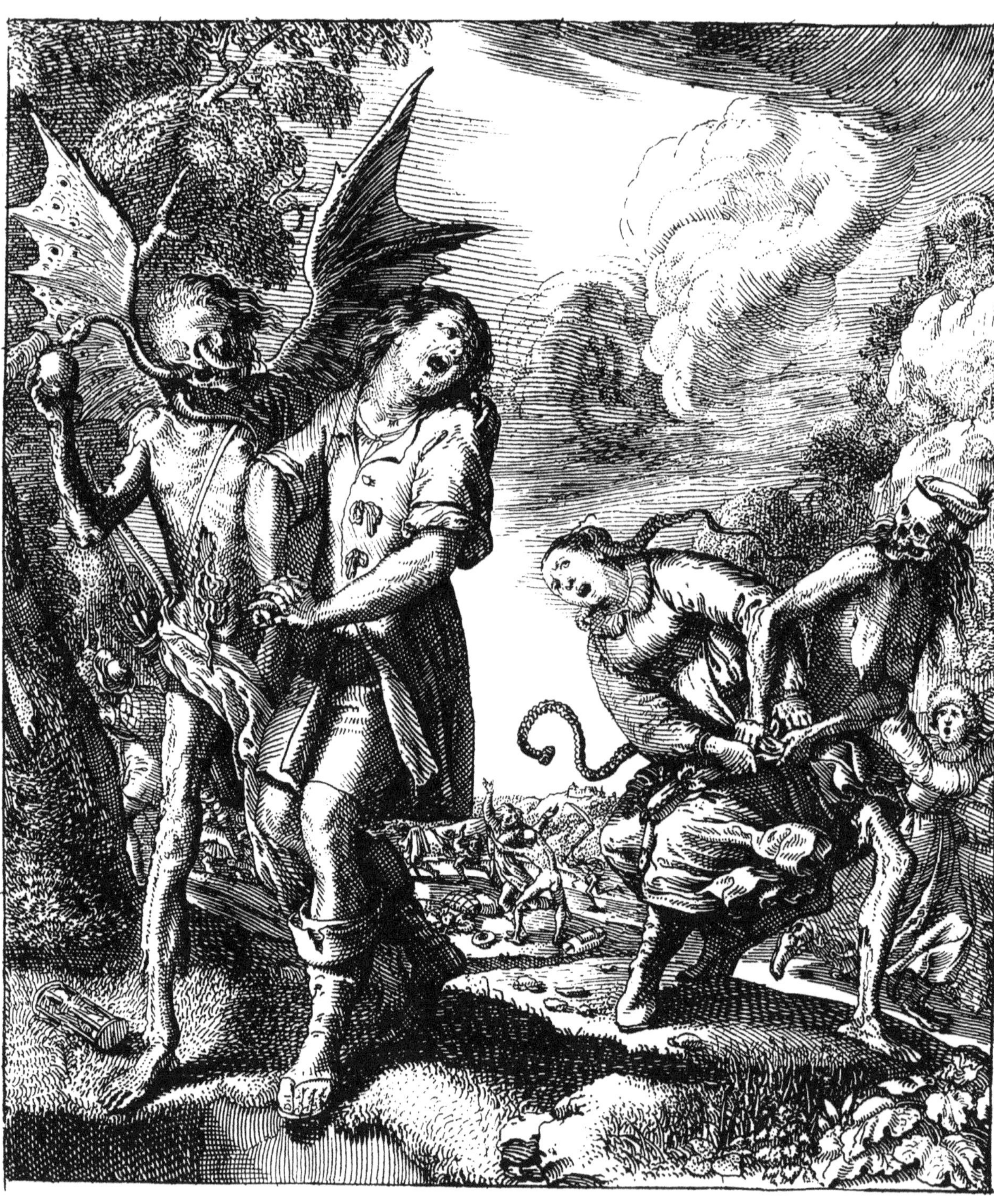

43. Man and Woman and Death, Rudolf Meyer,
1650.

44

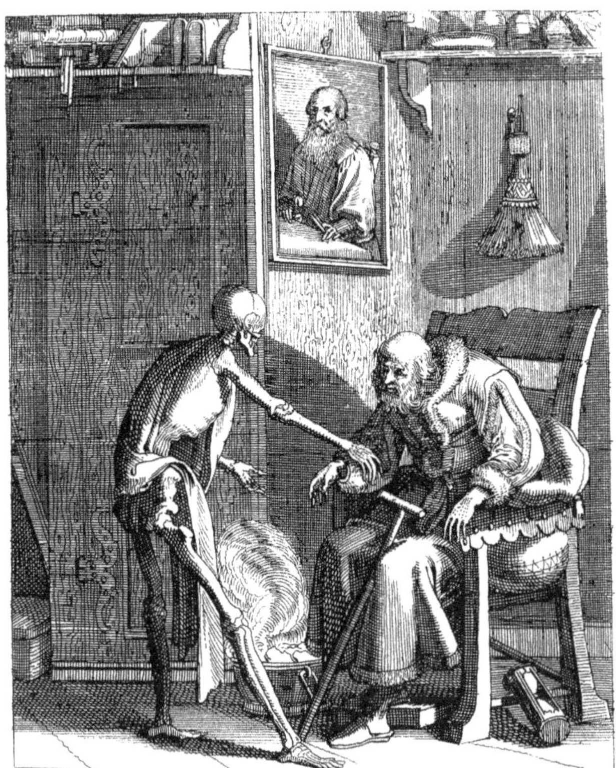

45

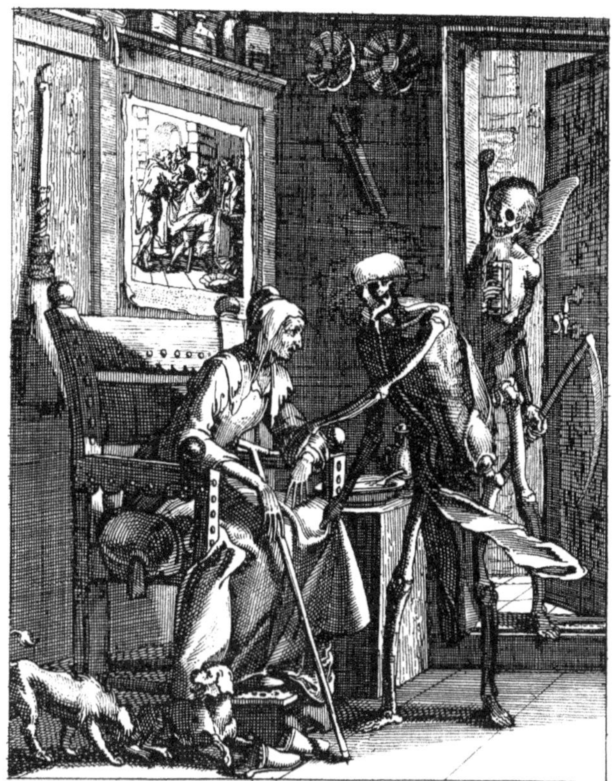

46

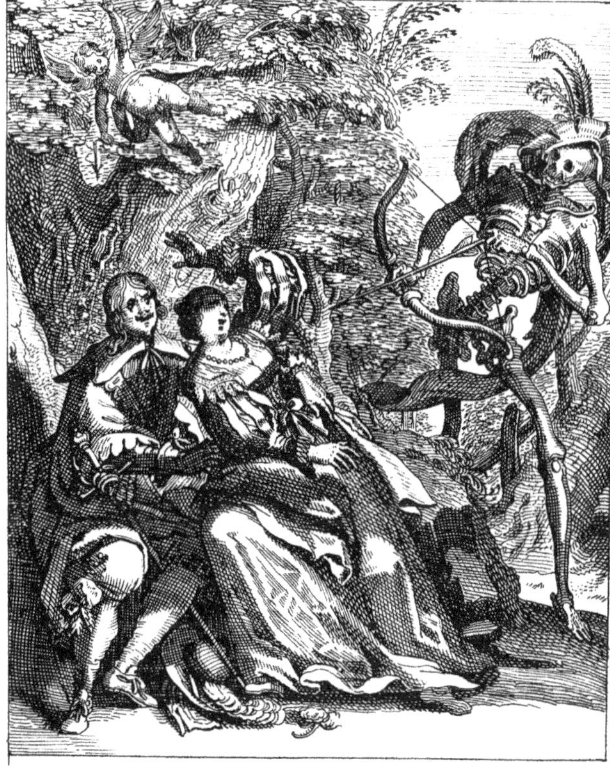

47

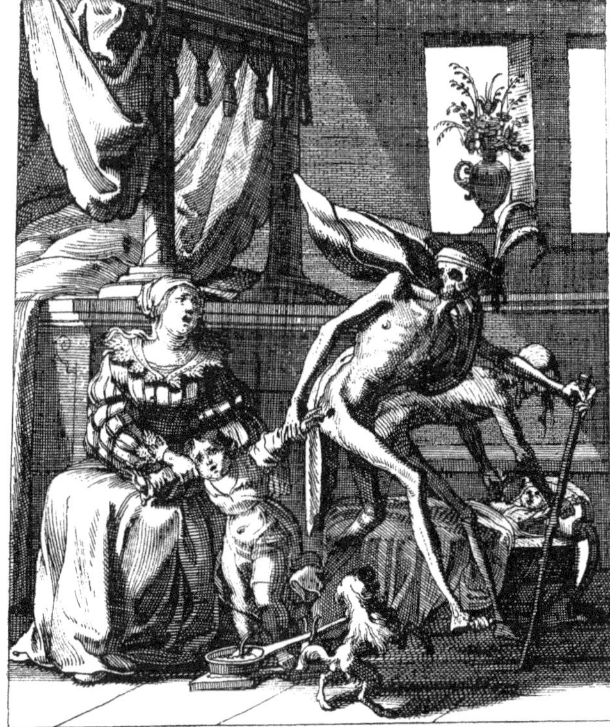

44. Old Man and Death, Rudolf Meyer, 1650.

45. Old Woman and Death, Rudolf Meyer, 1650.

46. Lovers and Death, Rudolf Meyer, 1650.

47. Child and Death 2, Conrad Meyer, after Rudolf Meyer, 1650.

48

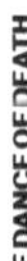

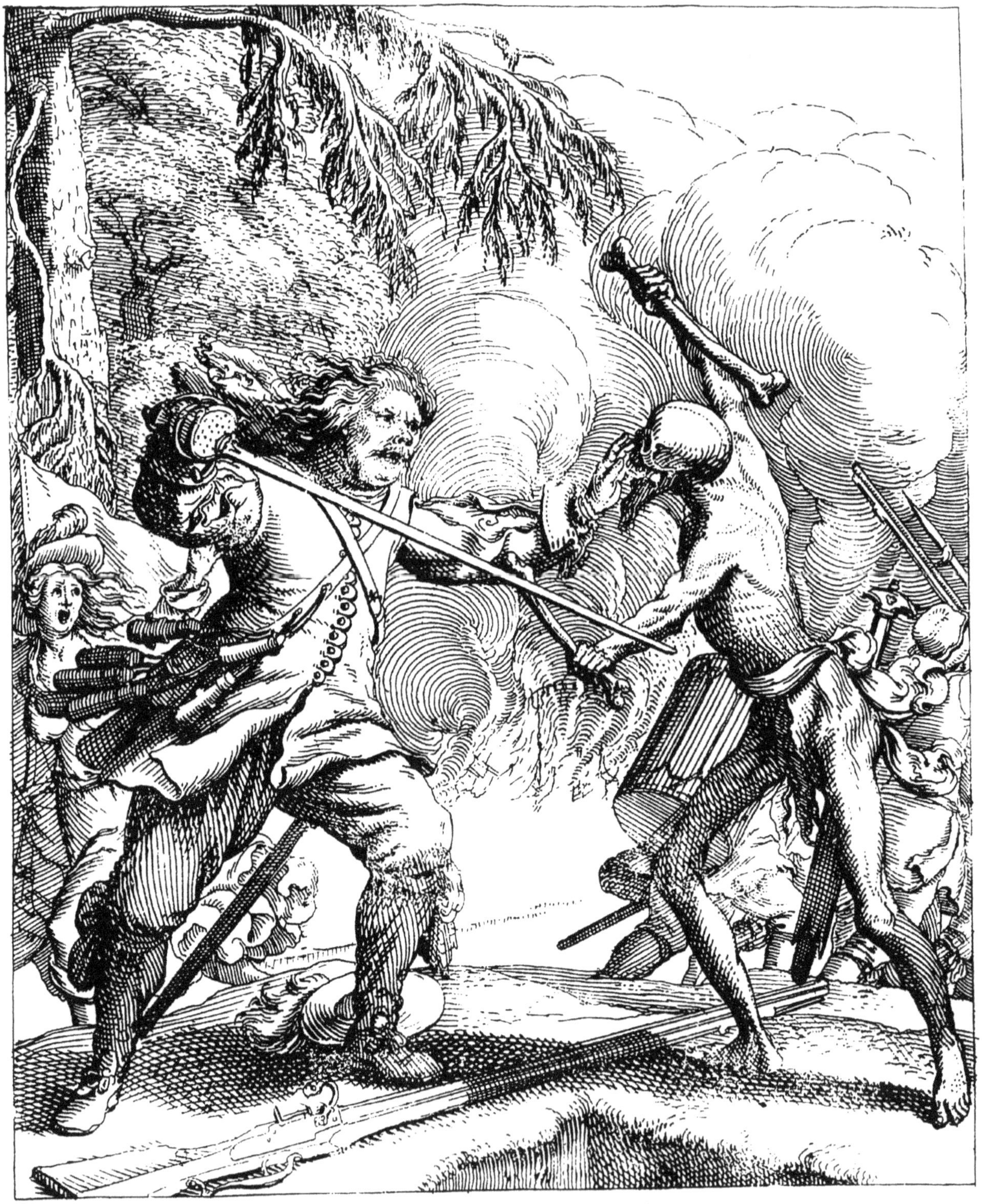

48. Soldier and Death, Rudolf Meyer, 1650.

49

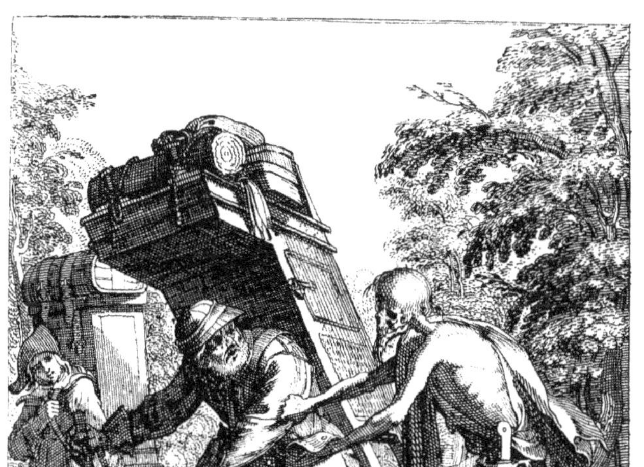

50

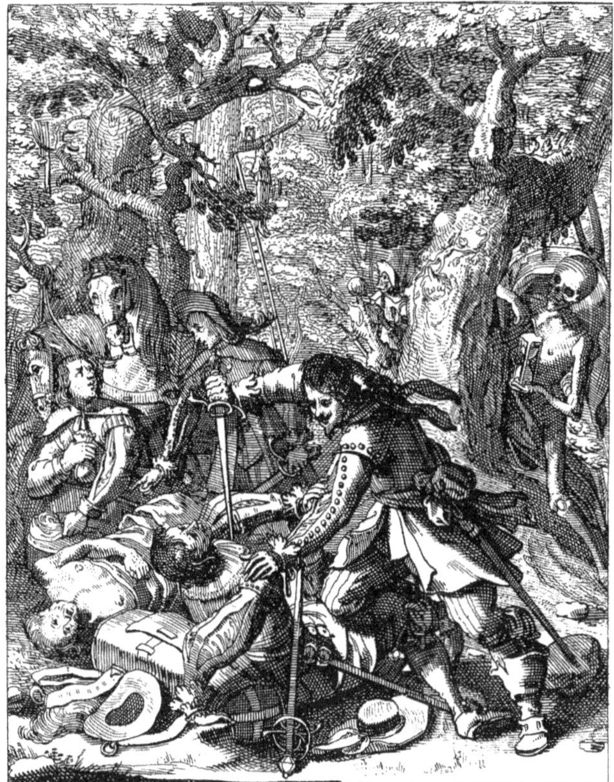

51

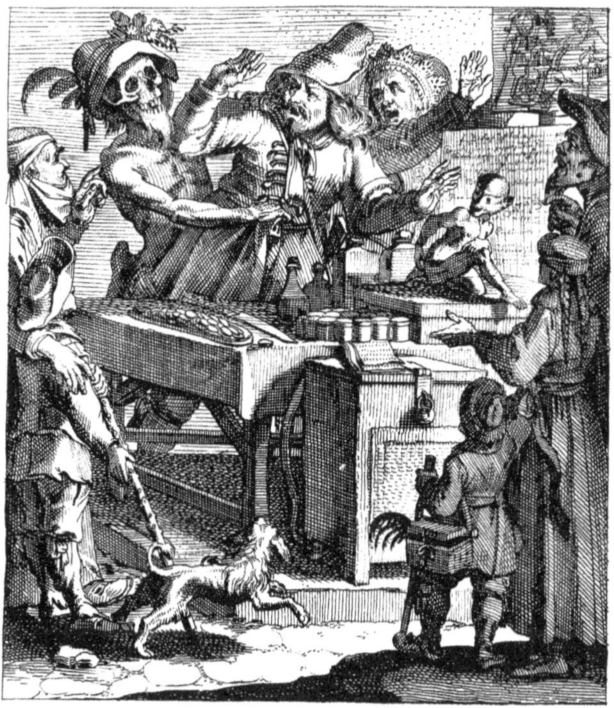

52

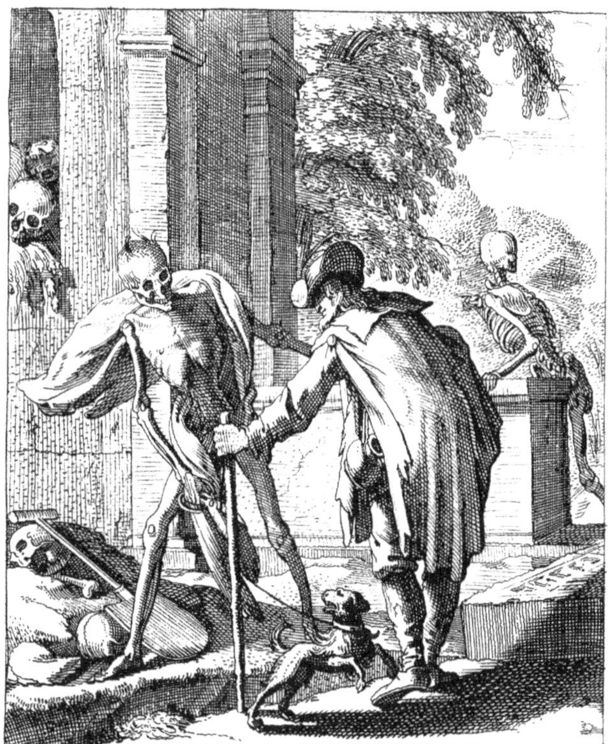

49. Pedlar and Death, Conrad Meyer, 1650.   50. Robber and Death, Conrad Meyer, 1650.   51. Charlatan and Death, Rudolf Meyer, 1650.   52. Blind Man and Death, Rudolf Meyer, 1650.

53

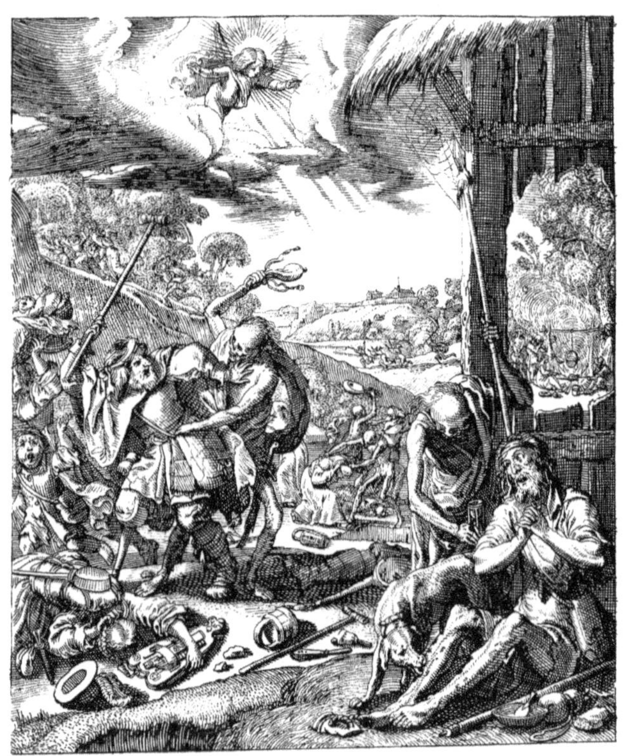

54

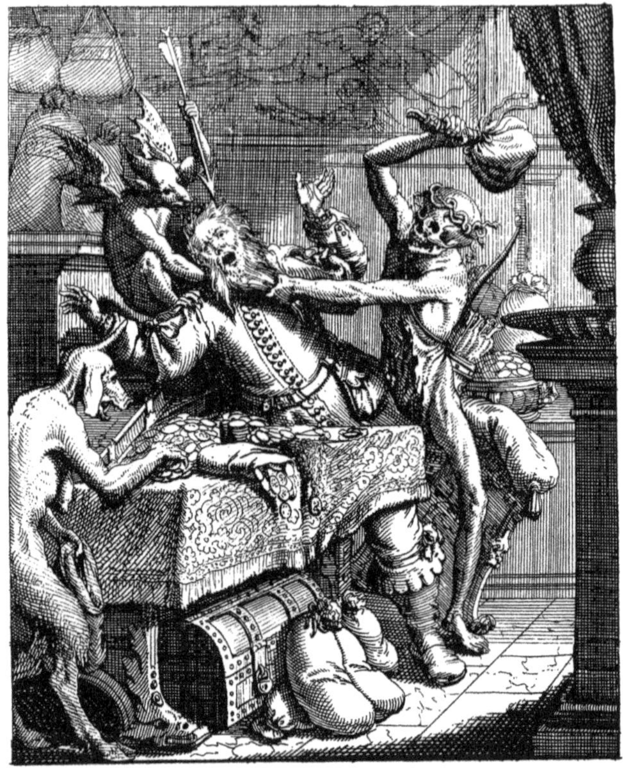

55

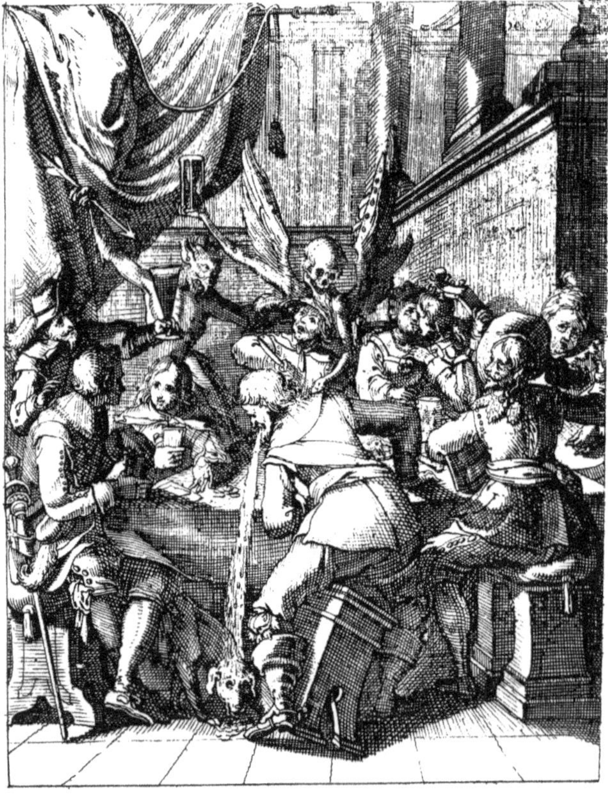

56

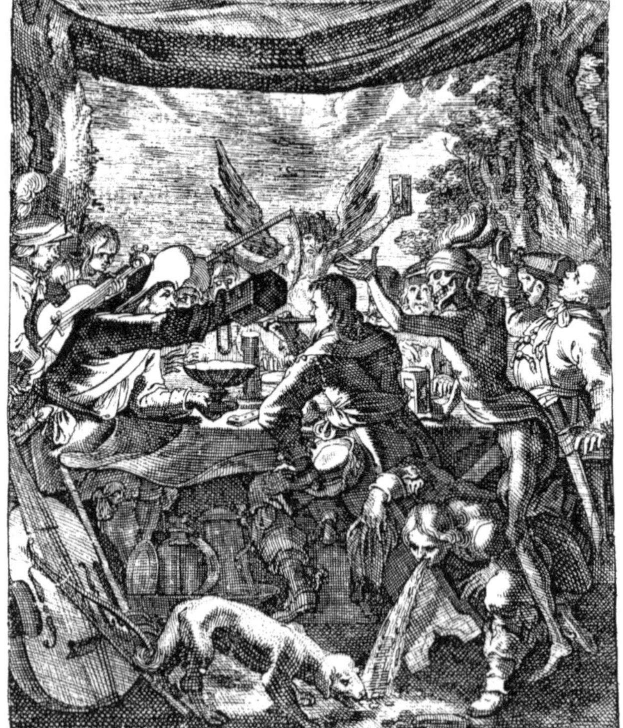

53. Beggars and Death, Rudolf Meyer, 1650.

54. Usurer and Death, Conrad Meyer, 1650.

55. Card Players and Death, Rudolf Meyer, 1650.

56. Drinking Brothers and Death, Rudolf Meyer, 1650.

57

58

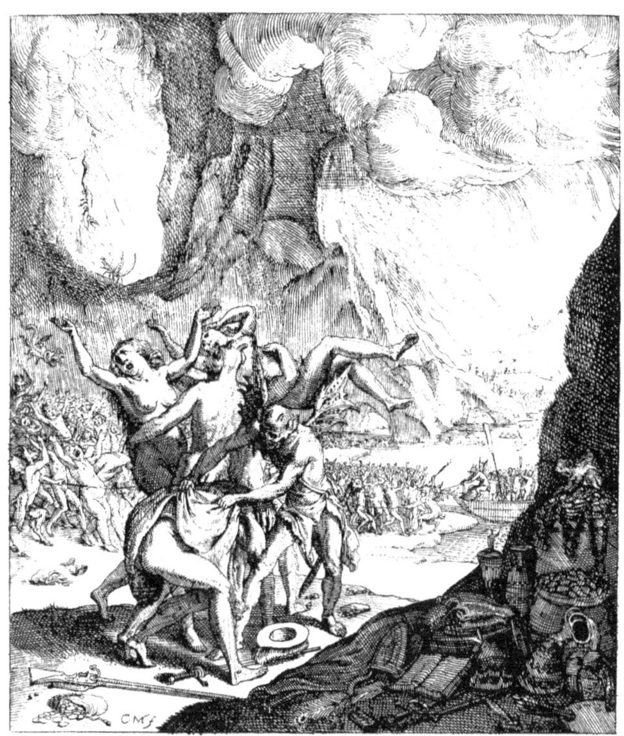

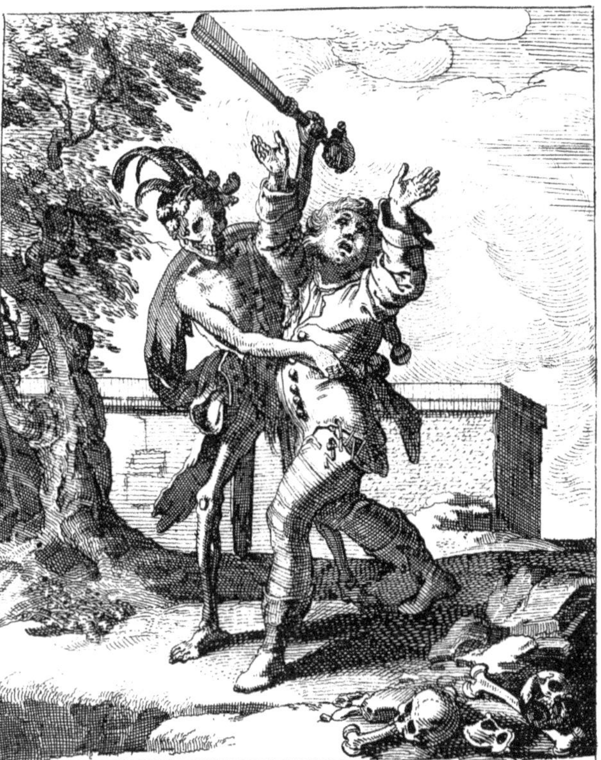

59

60

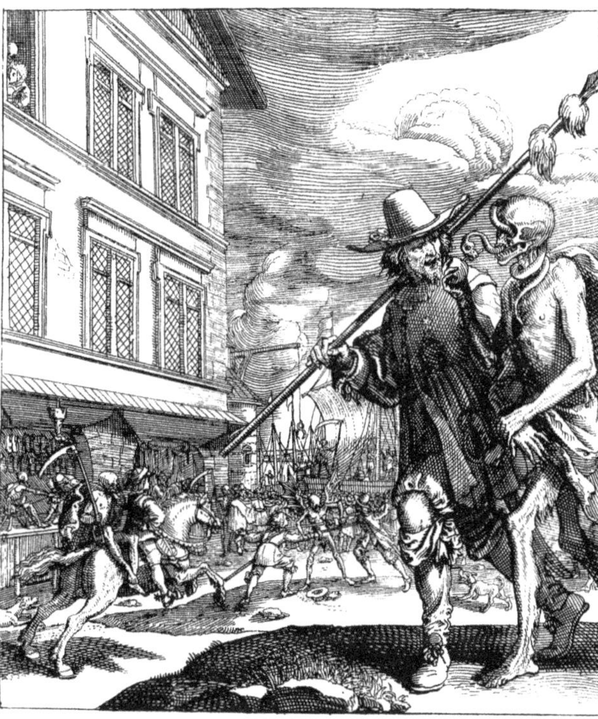

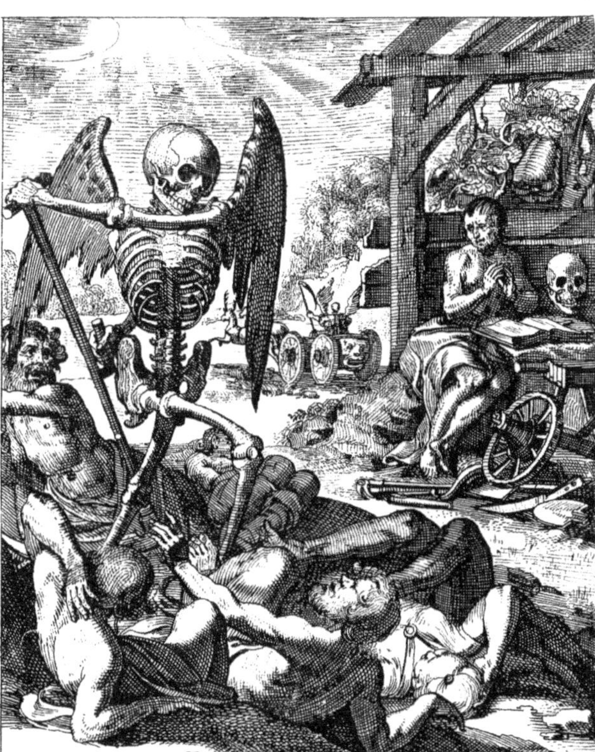

57. Belly Servants (Gluttons), Conrad Meyer, after Rudolph Meyer, 1650.

58. Jester and Death, Rudolf Meyer, 1650.

59. The Certainty of Death, Rudolf Meyer, 1650.

60. Uncertainty of Death, Rudolph Meyer, 1650.

61

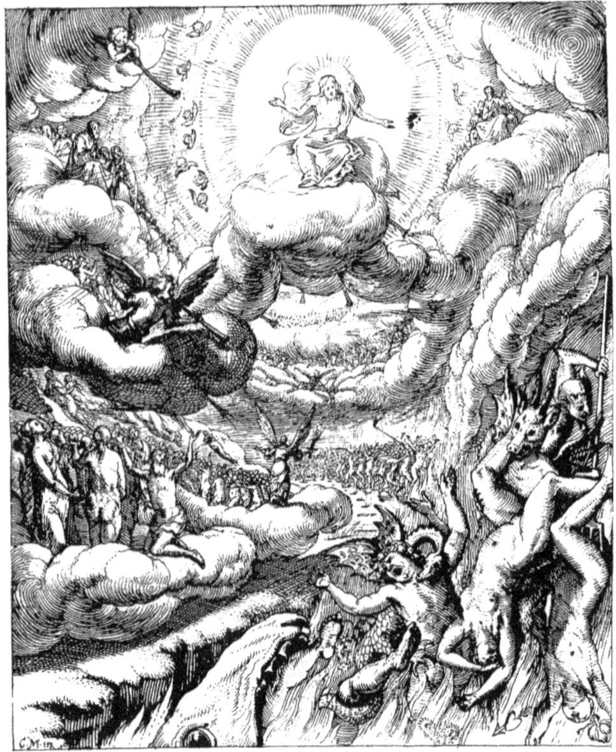

62

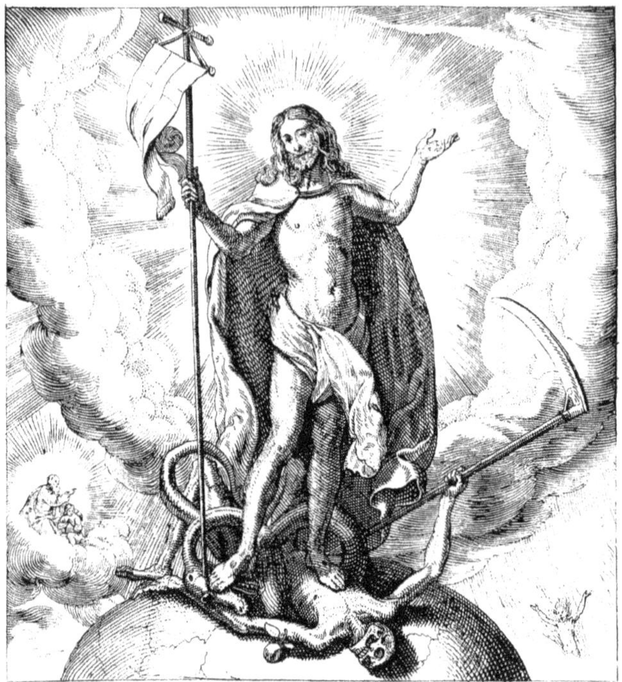

63

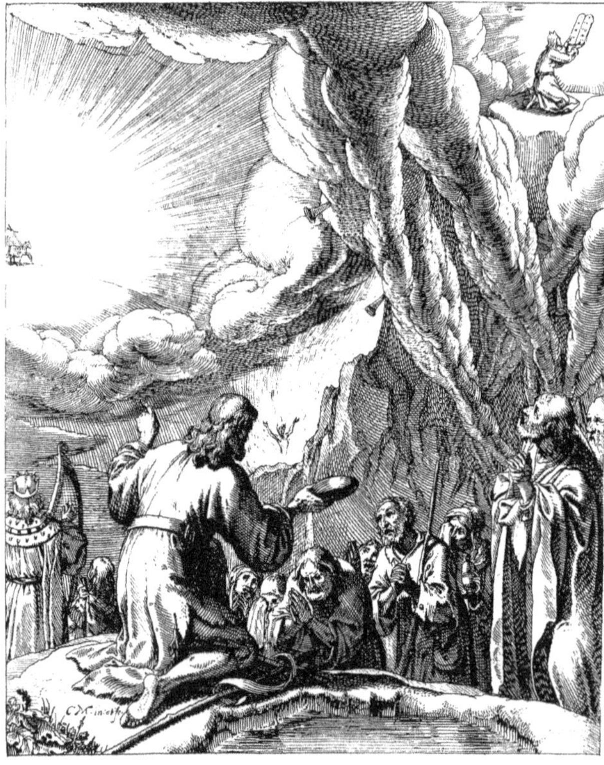

64

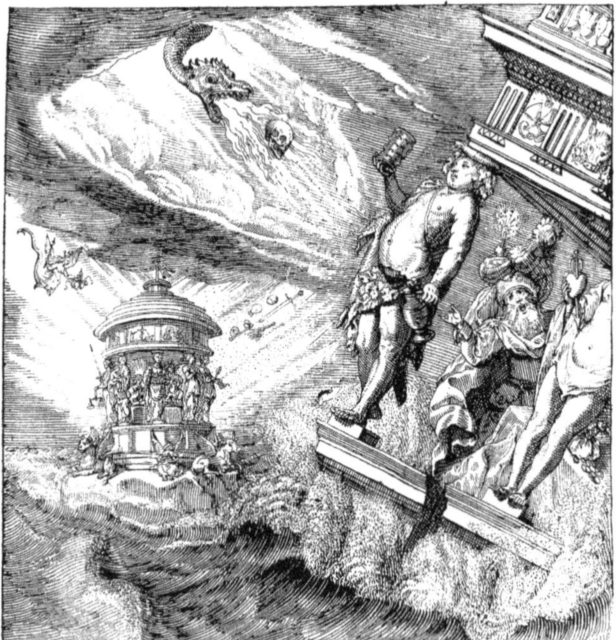

61. The Last Judgement, Conrad Meyer, 1650.

62. Second Coming of Christ, Rudolf Meyer, 1650.

63. Christ Addresses Believers, Conrad Meyer, 1650.

64. The End of the World, Rudolf Meyer, 1650.

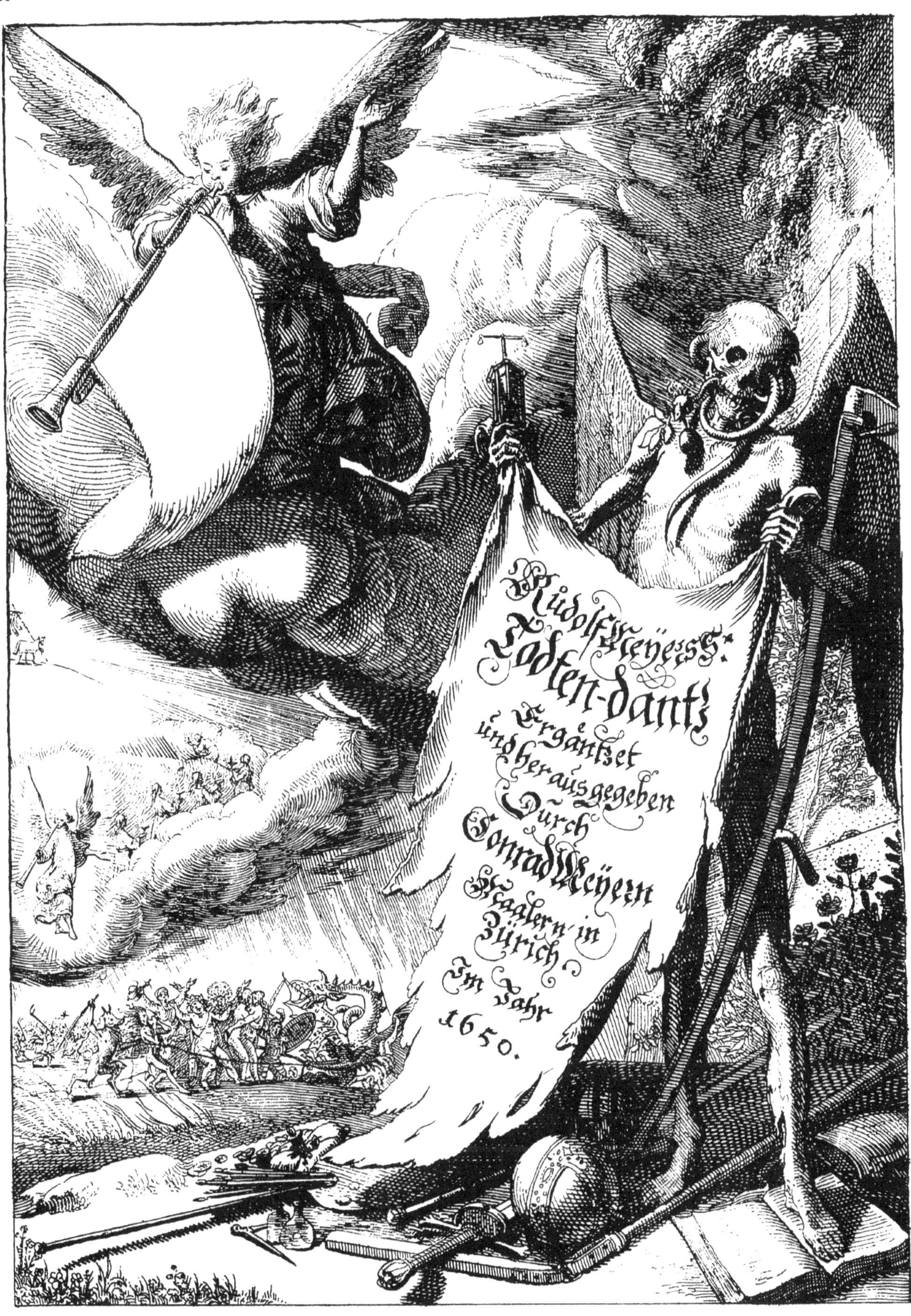

65. Death and Fama (Fama is the memory one
leaves behind after death), Rudolf Meyer, 1650.

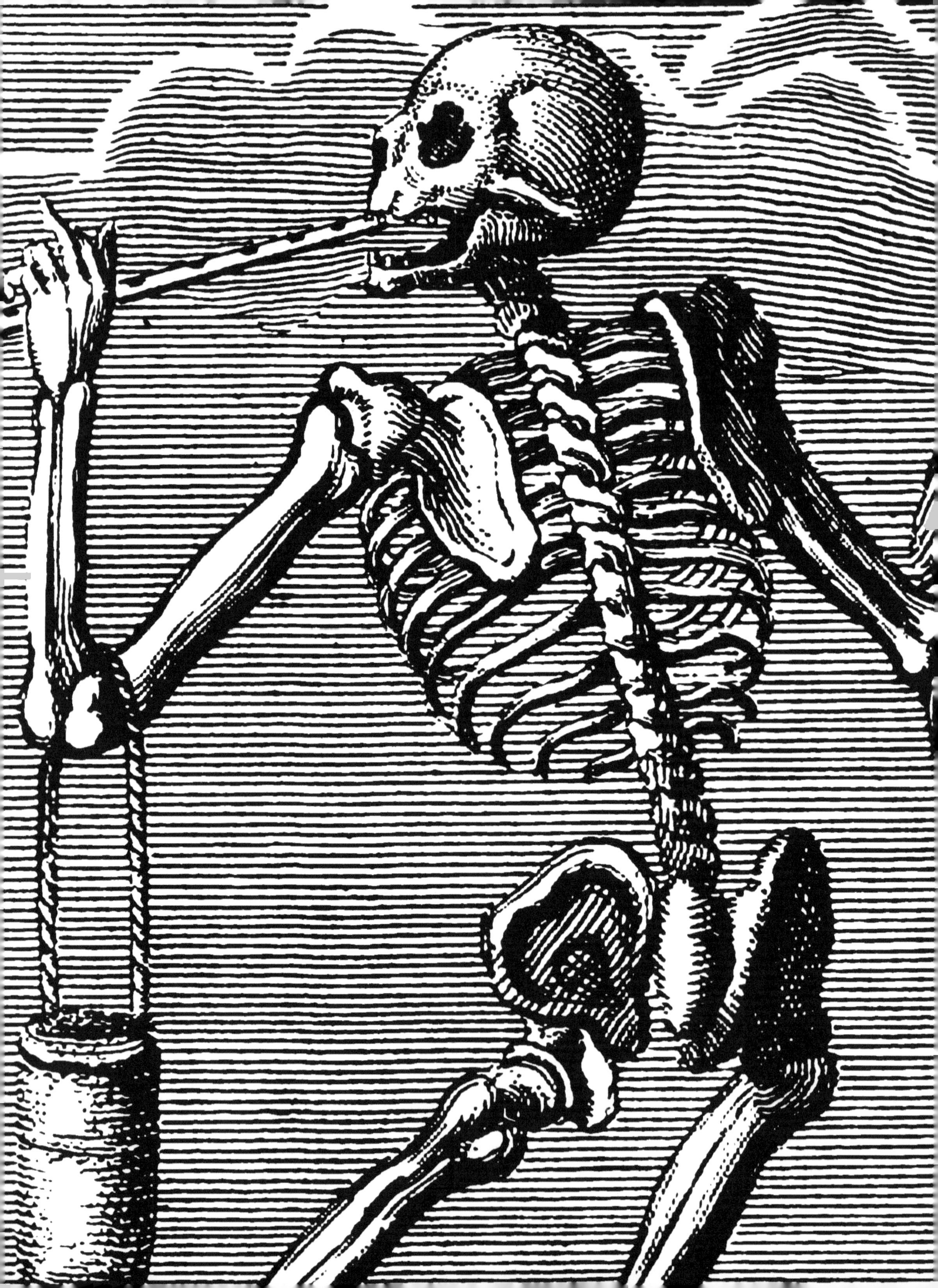

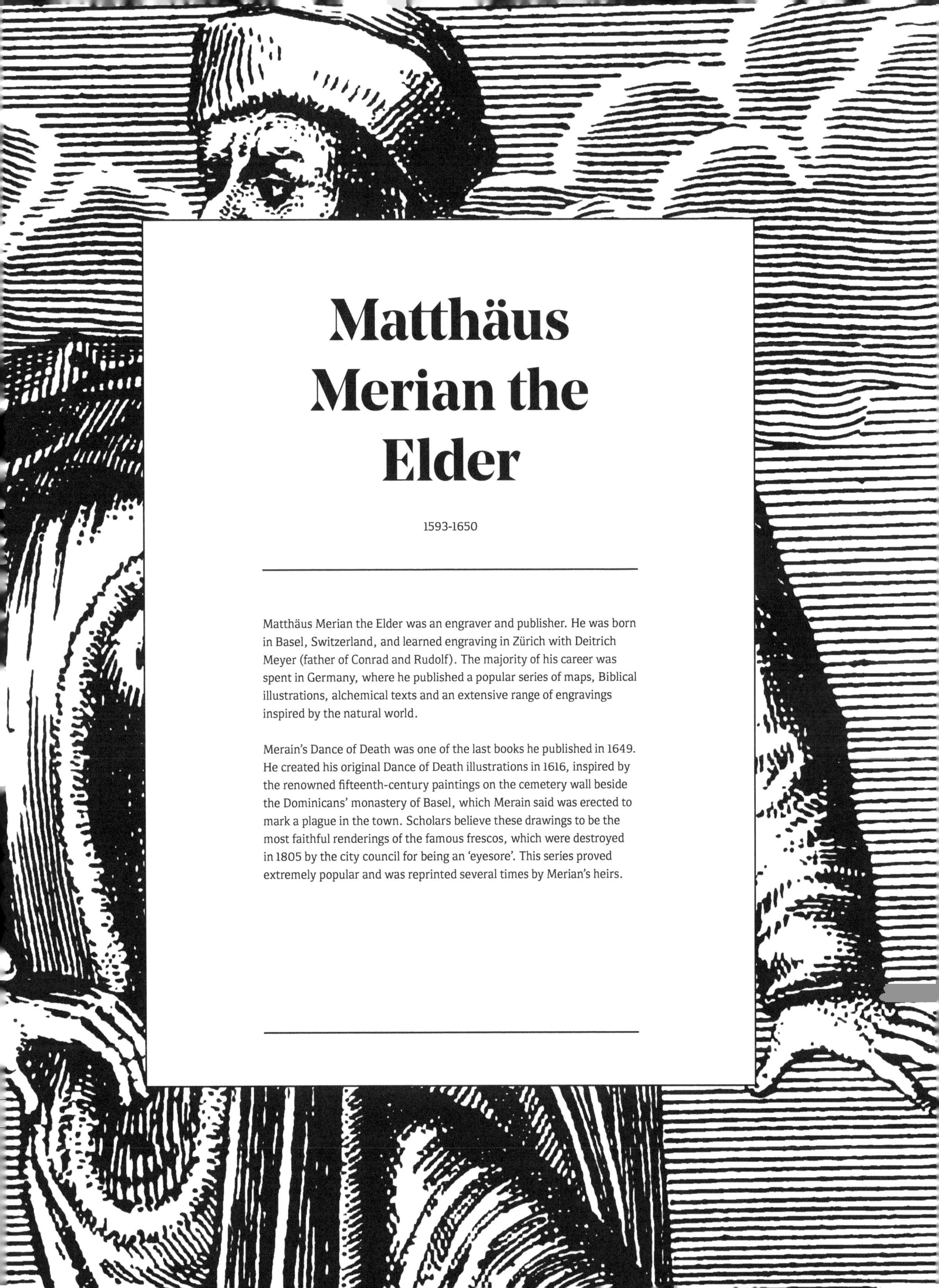

Matthäus Merian the Elder

1593-1650

Matthäus Merian the Elder was an engraver and publisher. He was born in Basel, Switzerland, and learned engraving in Zürich with Deitrich Meyer (father of Conrad and Rudolf). The majority of his career was spent in Germany, where he published a popular series of maps, Biblical illustrations, alchemical texts and an extensive range of engravings inspired by the natural world.

Merain's Dance of Death was one of the last books he published in 1649. He created his original Dance of Death illustrations in 1616, inspired by the renowned fifteenth-century paintings on the cemetery wall beside the Dominicans' monastery of Basel, which Merain said was erected to mark a plague in the town. Scholars believe these drawings to be the most faithful renderings of the famous frescos, which were destroyed in 1805 by the city council for being an 'eyesore'. This series proved extremely popular and was reprinted several times by Merian's heirs.

66

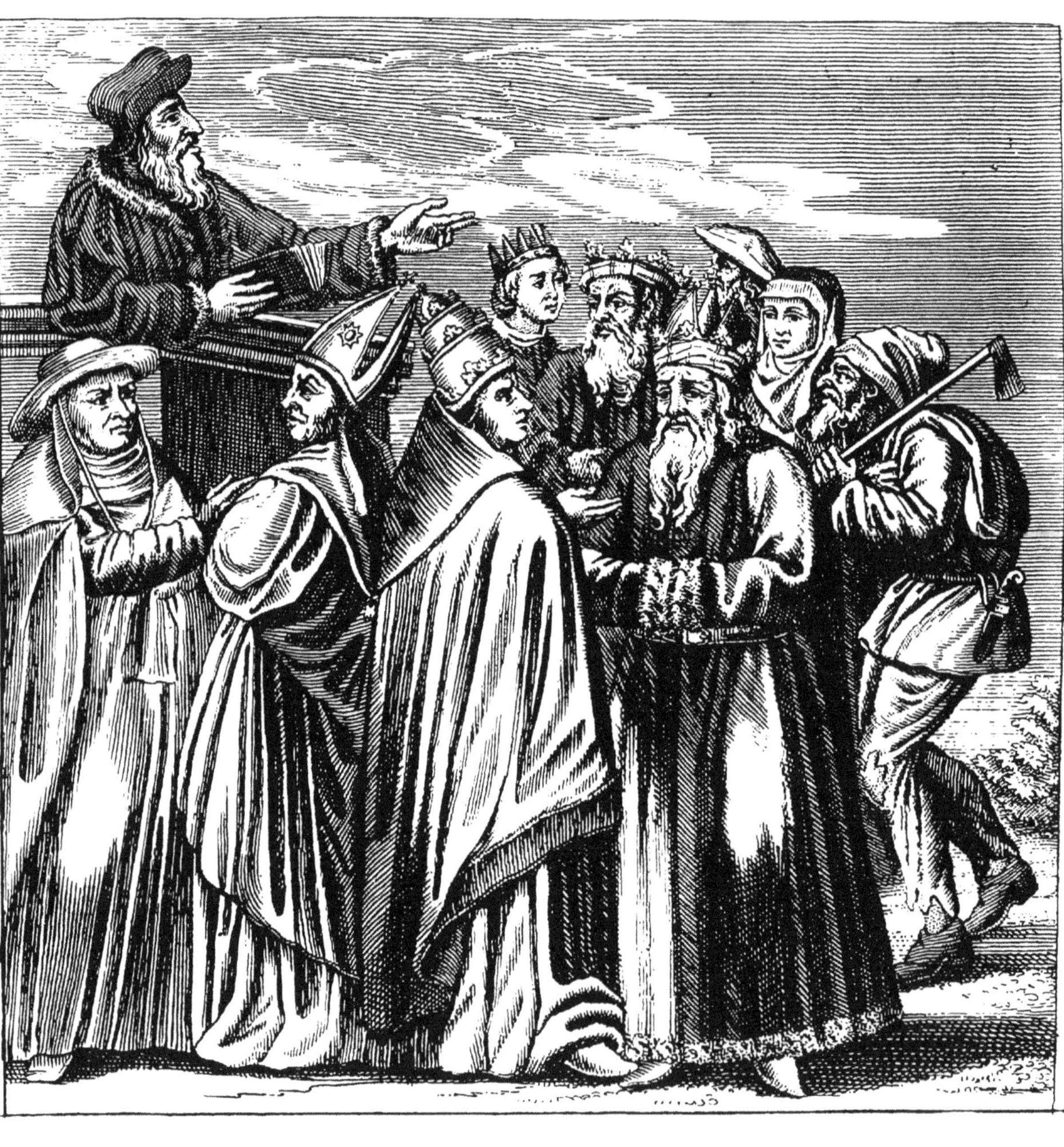

66. Preacher adresses clergy, royalty and
common people, Matthäus Merian the Elder.
1593–1650.

67

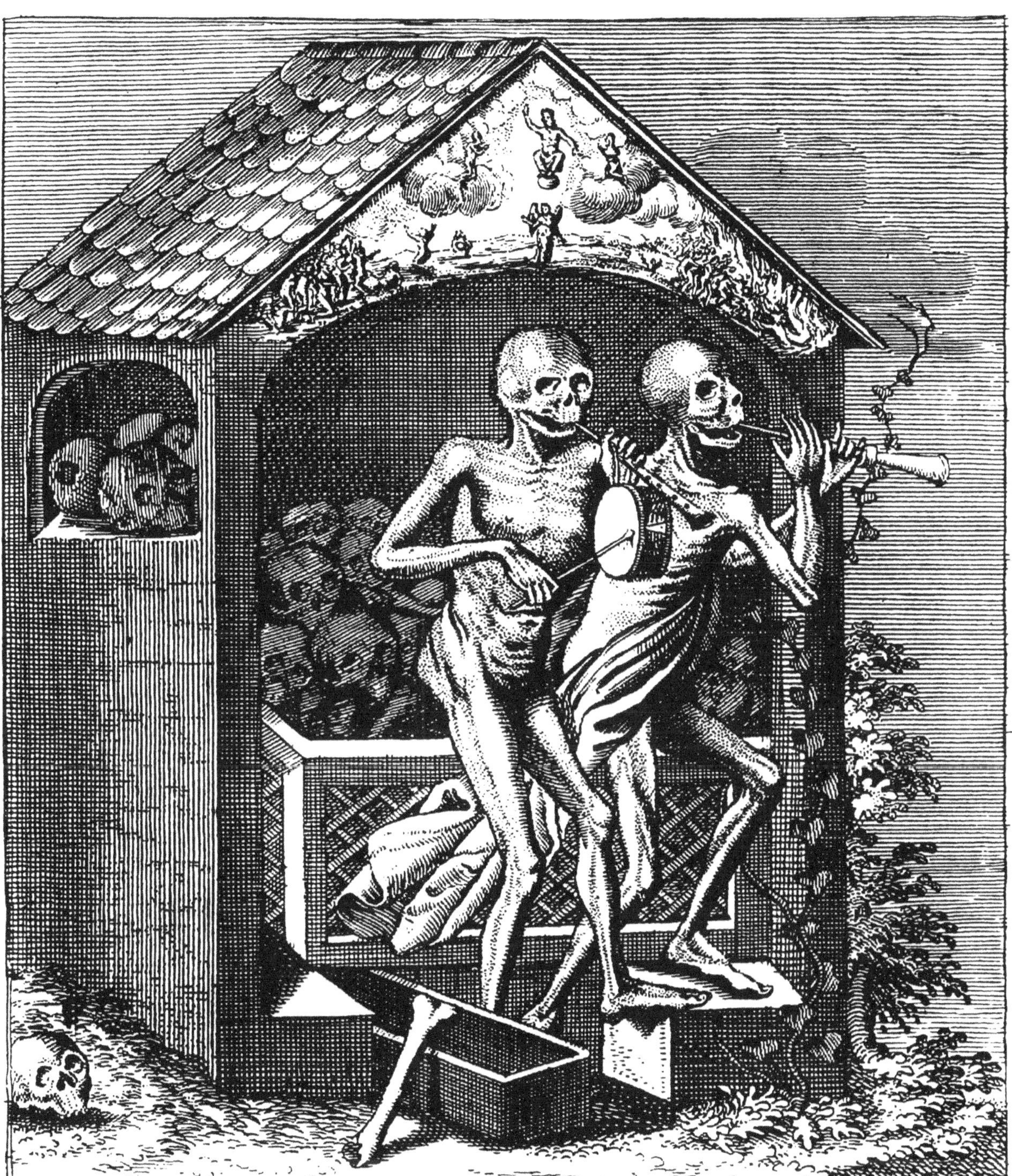

67. The Ossuary, The Dance of the Dead,
Matthäus Merian the Elder. 1593–1650.

68

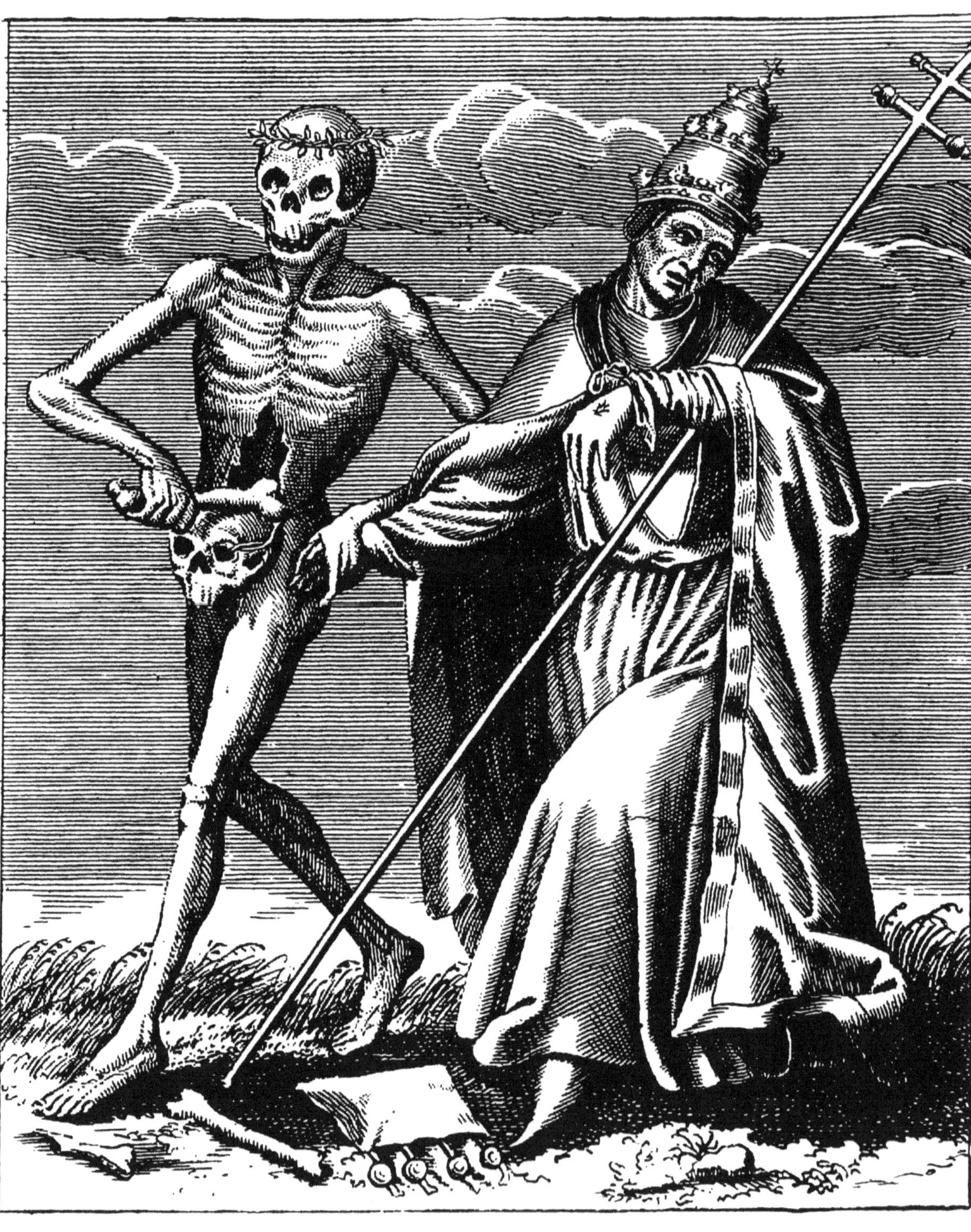

68. Death and the Pope, Matthäus Merian the
Elder. 1593–1650.

69

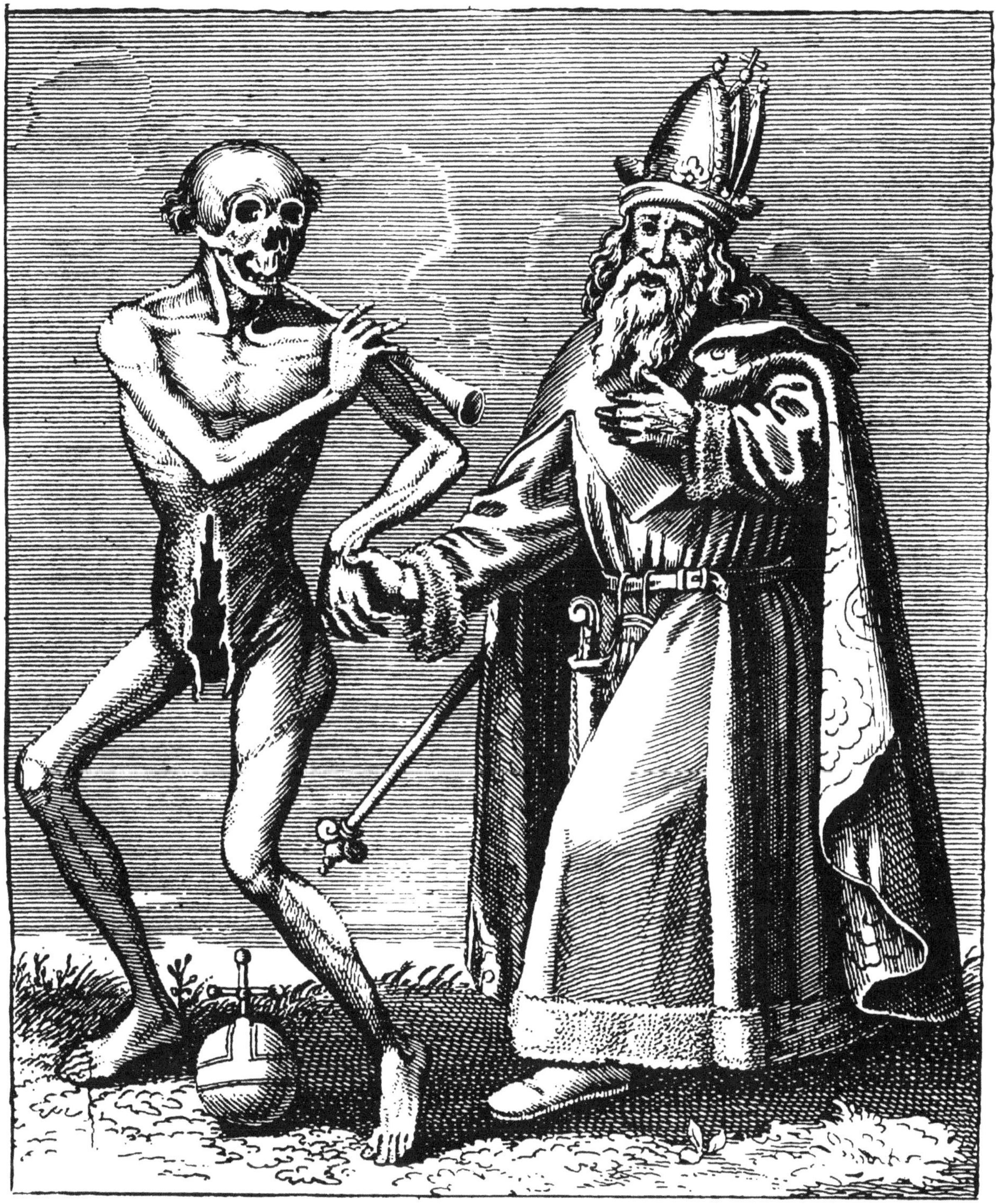

69. Death and the Emperor, Matthäus Merian the
Elder. 1593–1650.

70

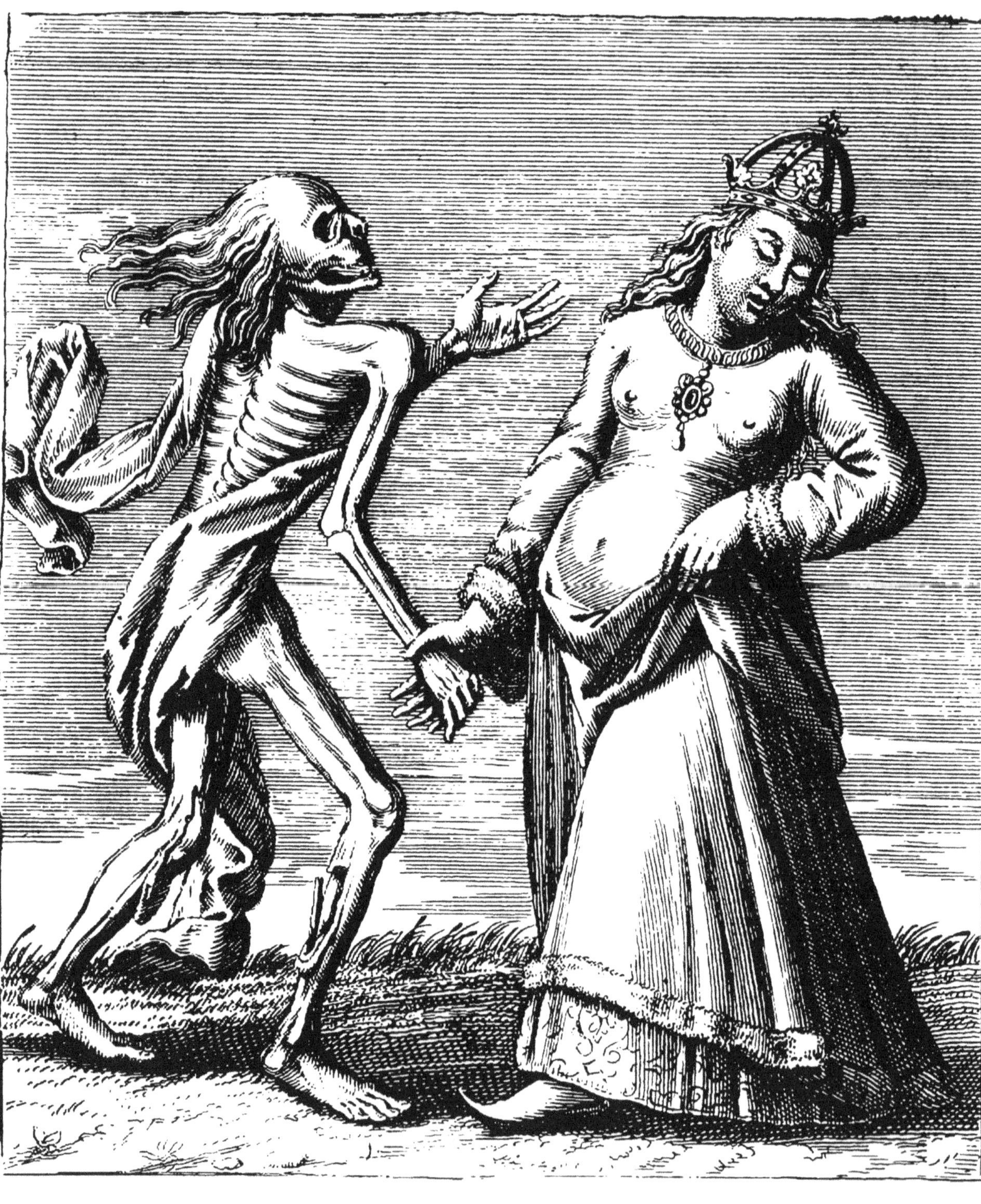

70. Death and the Empress, Matthäus Merian the
Elder. 1593–1650.

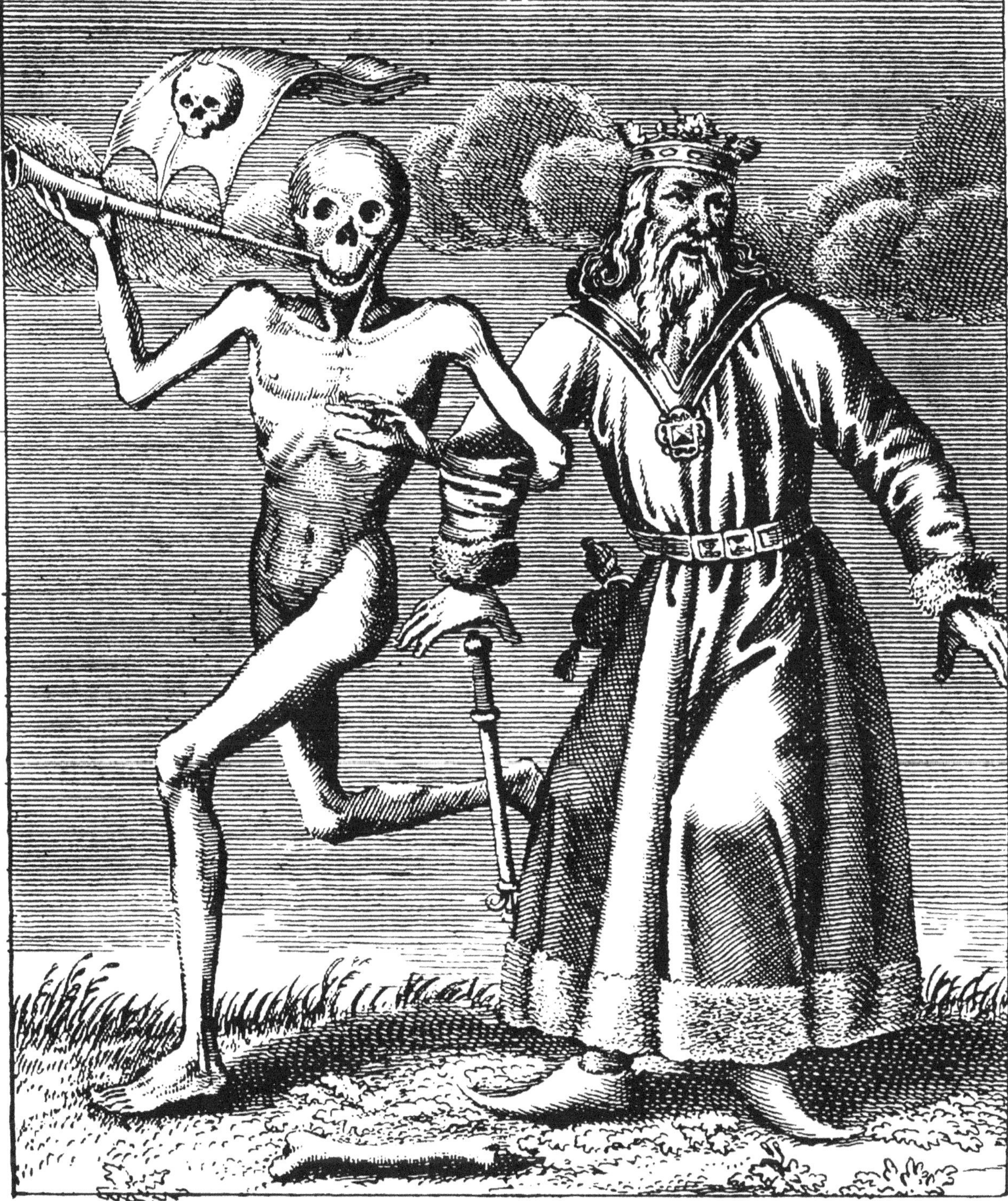

71. Death and the King, Matthâus Merian the
Elder. 1593–1650.

72

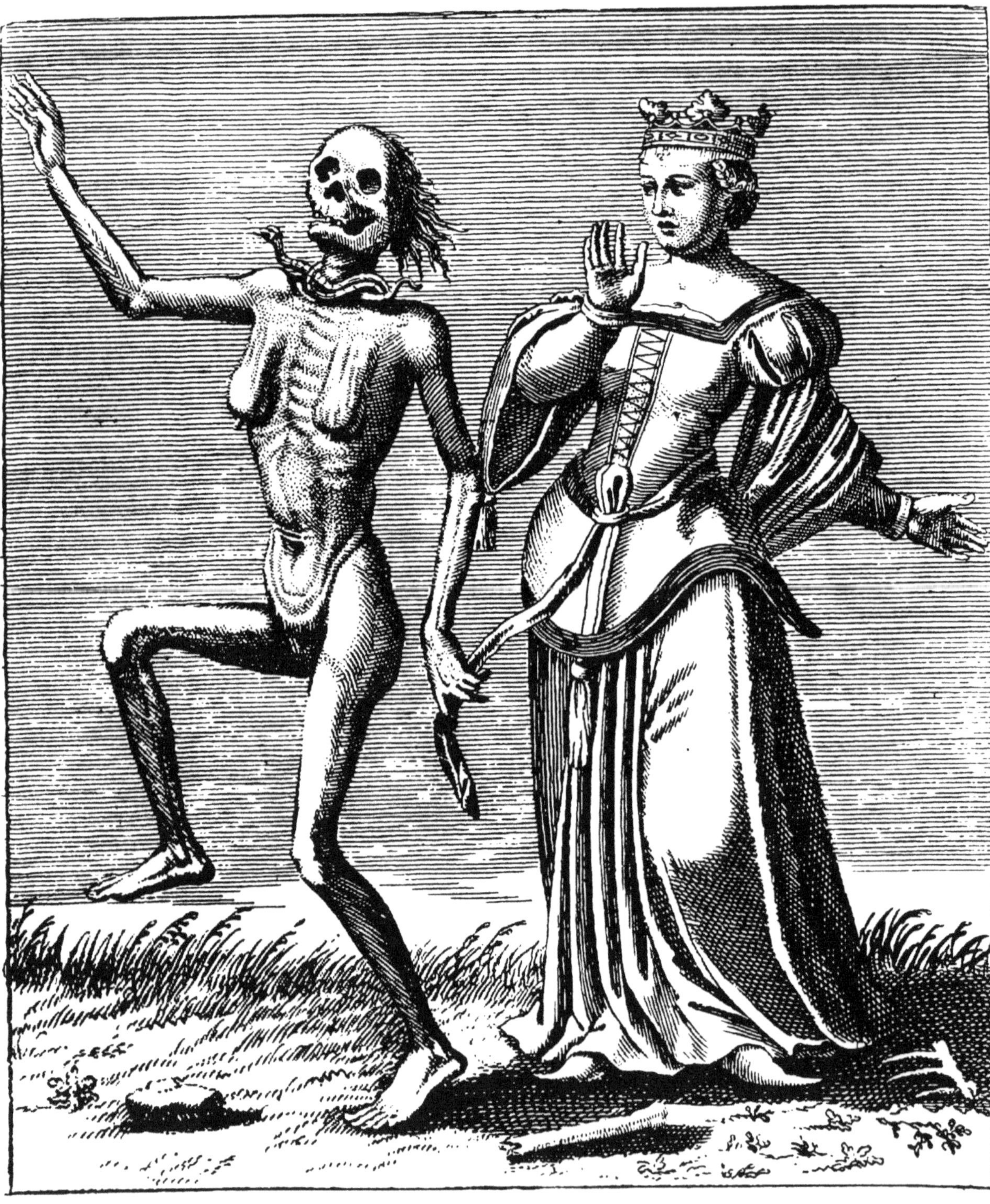

72. Death and the Queen, Matthäus Merian the
Elder. 1593–1650.

73

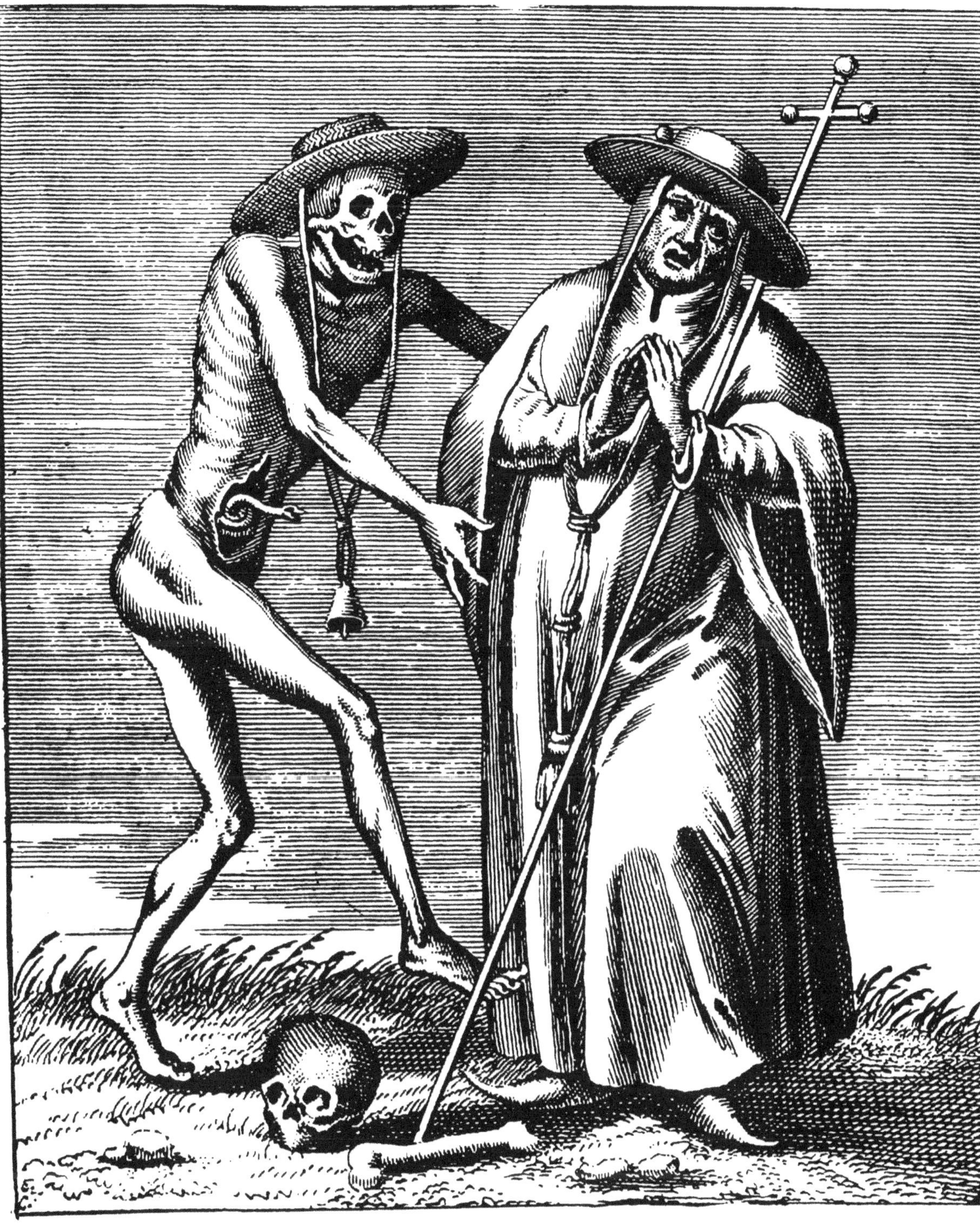

73. Death and the Cardinal, Matthäus Merian the
Elder. 1593–1650.

74

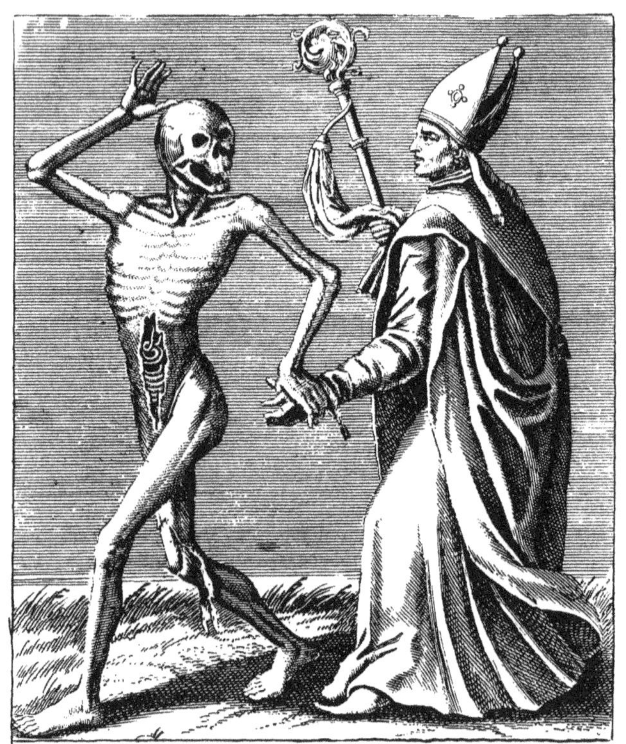

75

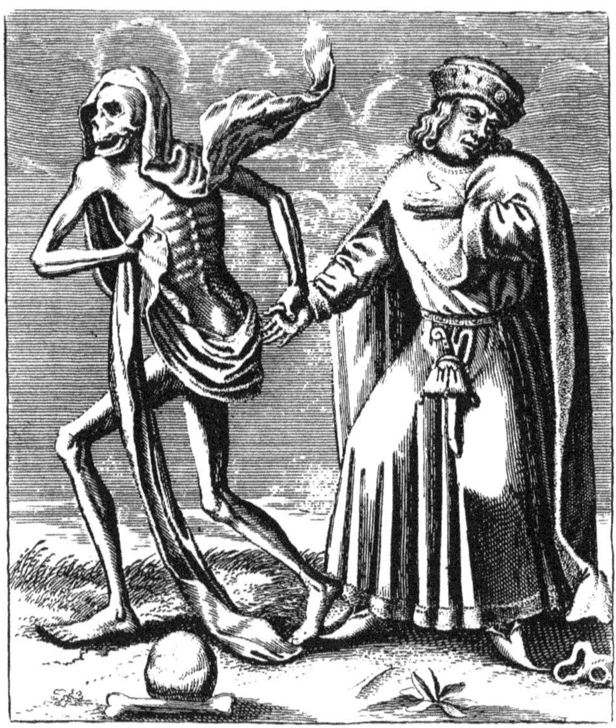

76

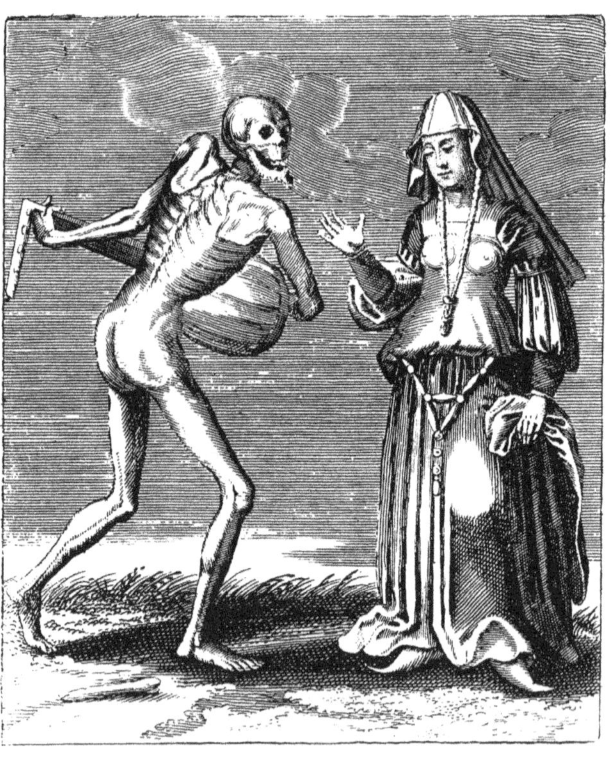

77

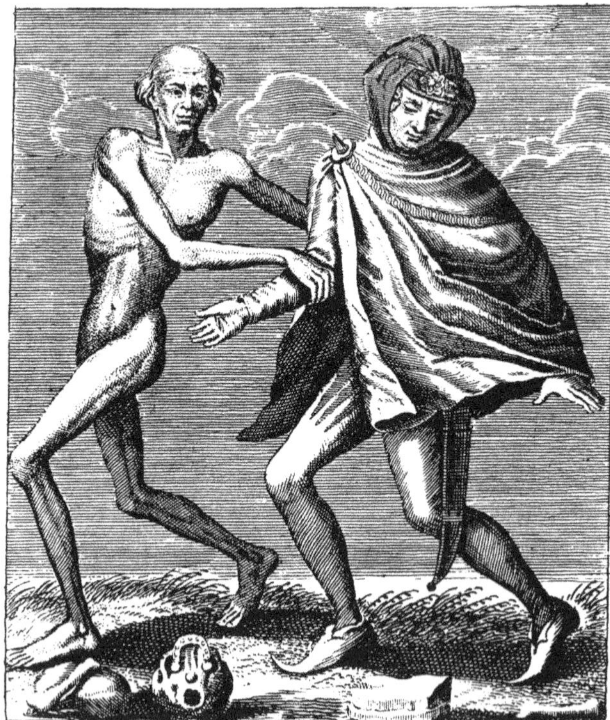

74. Death and the Bishop, Matthâus Merian the Elder. 1593–1650.

75. Death and the Duke, Matthâus Merian the Elder. 1593–1650.

76. Death and the Duchess, Matthâus Merian the Elder. 1593–1650.

77. Death and the Count, Matthâus Merian the Elder. 1593–1650.

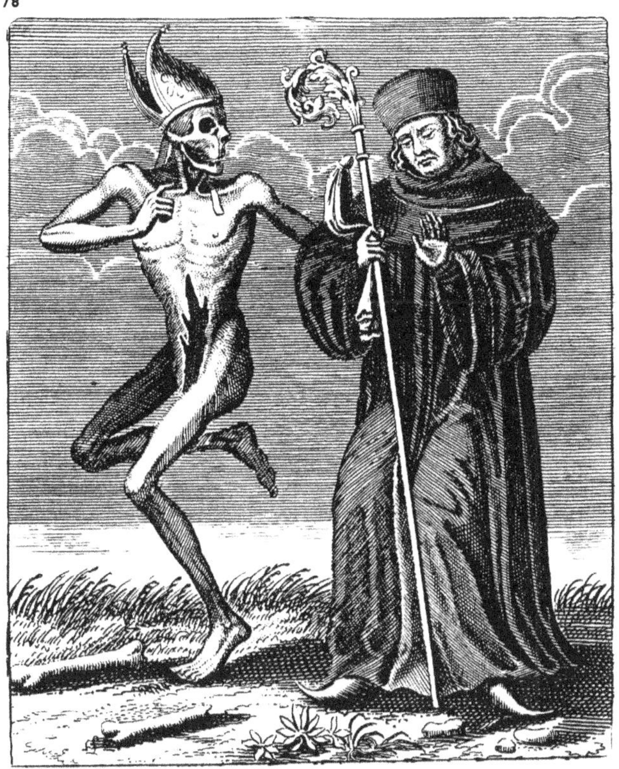

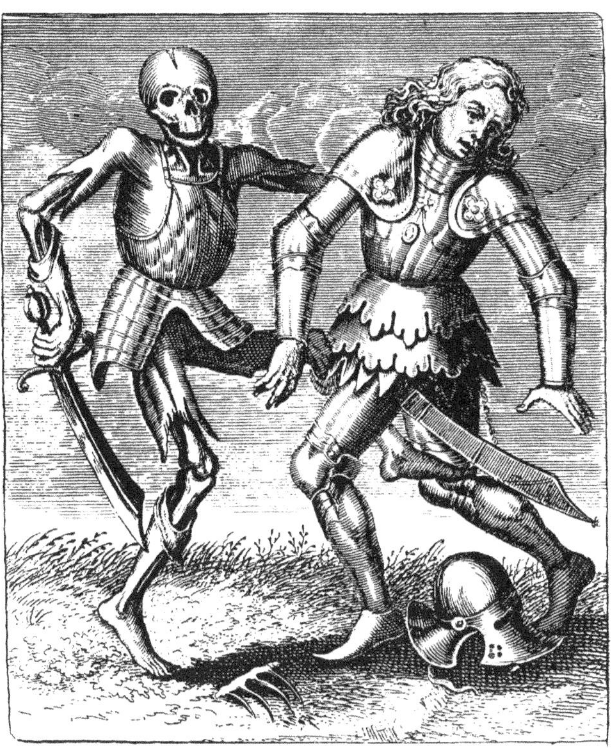

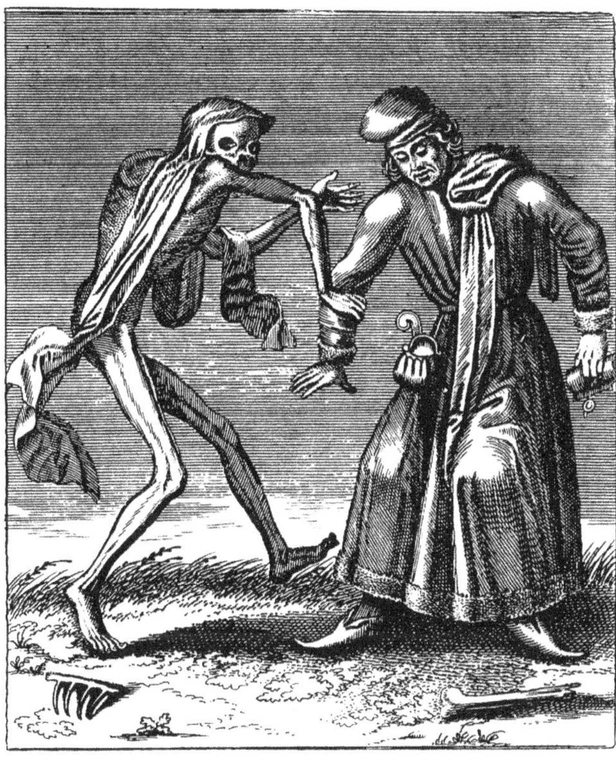

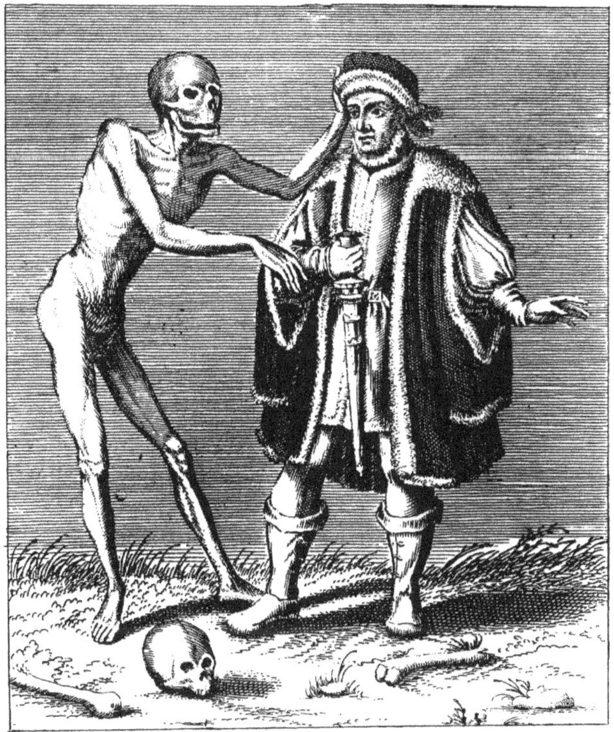

78. Death and the Abbot, Matthäus Merian the Elder. 1593–1650.

79. Death and the Knight, Matthäus Merian the Elder. 1593–1650.

80. Death and the Lawyer, Matthäus Merian the Elder. 1593–1650.

81. Death and the Councillor, Matthäus Merian the Elder. 1593–1650.

82

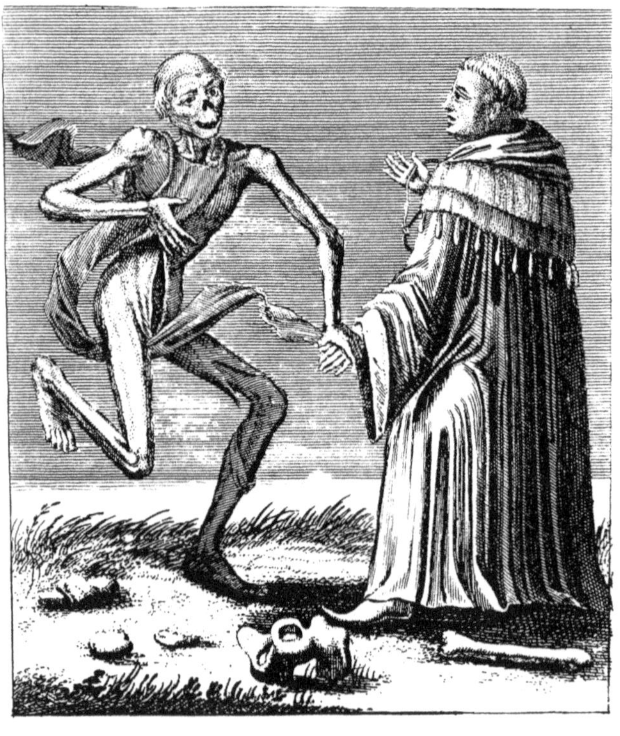

83

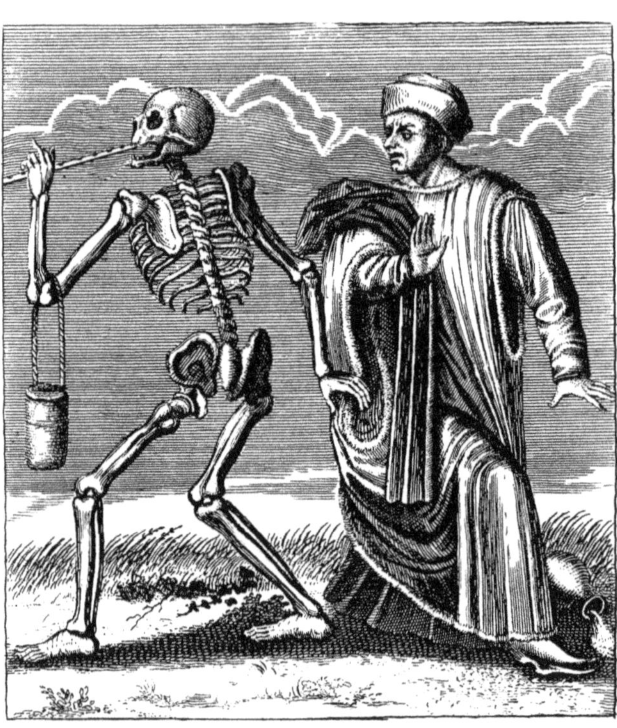

84

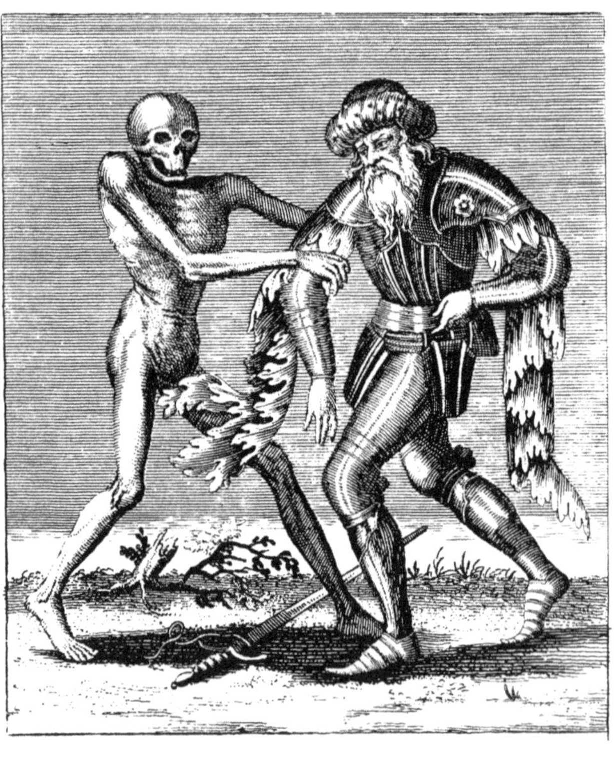

85

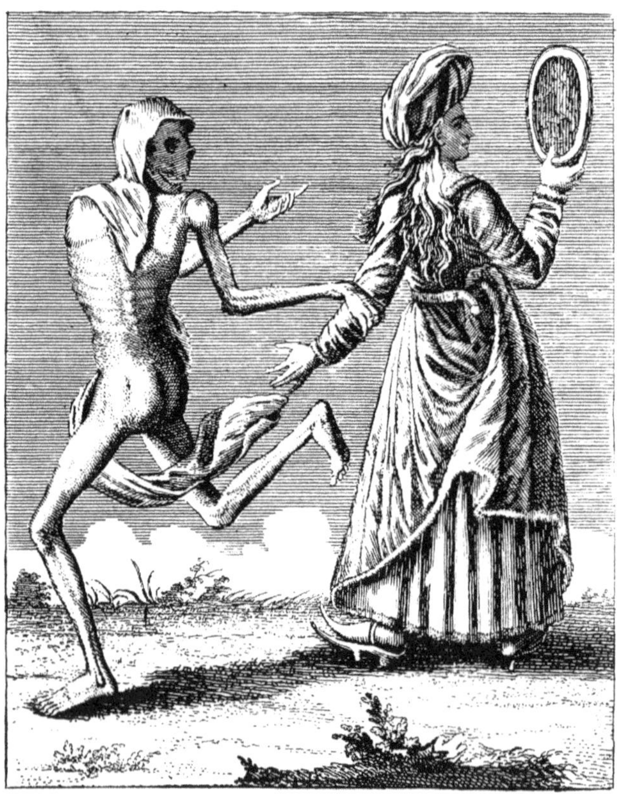

82. Death and the Canon, Matthäus Merian the Elder. 1593–1650.

83. Death and the Doctor, Matthäus Merian the Elder. 1593–1650.

84. Death and the Nobleman, Matthäus Merian the Elder. 1593–1650.

85. Death and the Noblewoman, Matthäus Merian the Elder. 1593–1650.

86

87

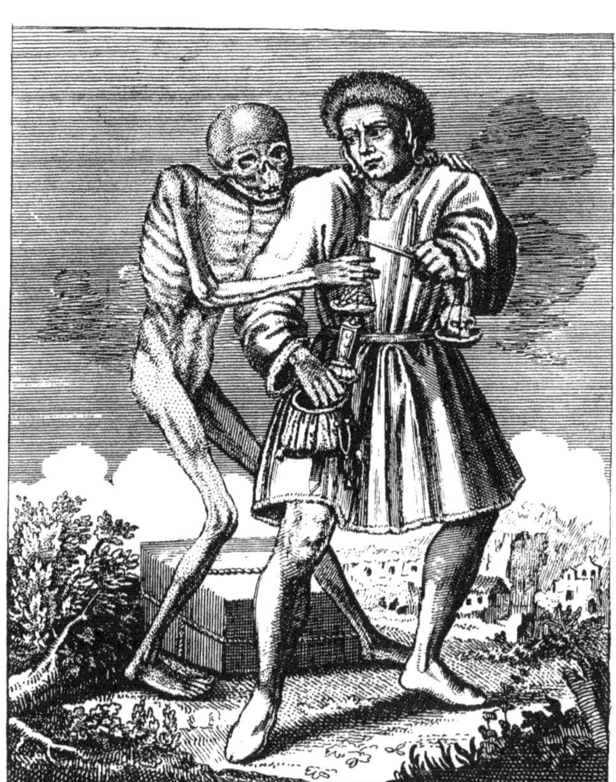

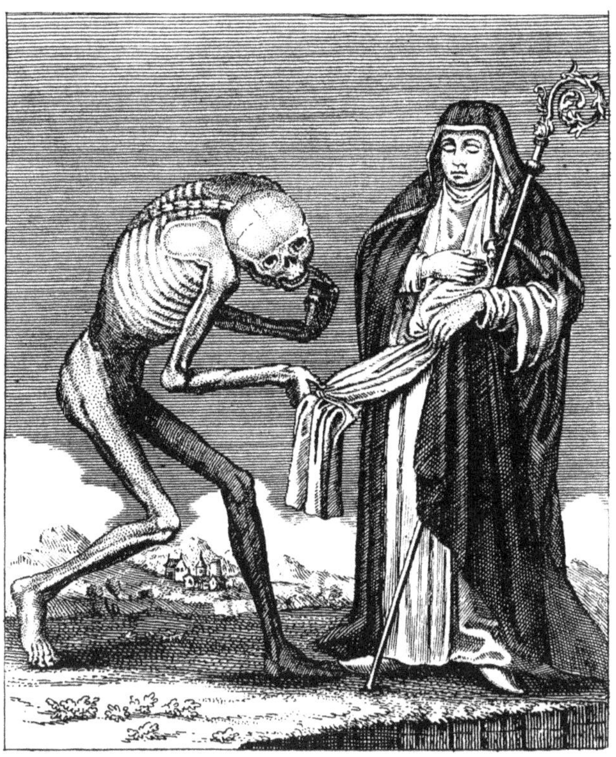

88

89

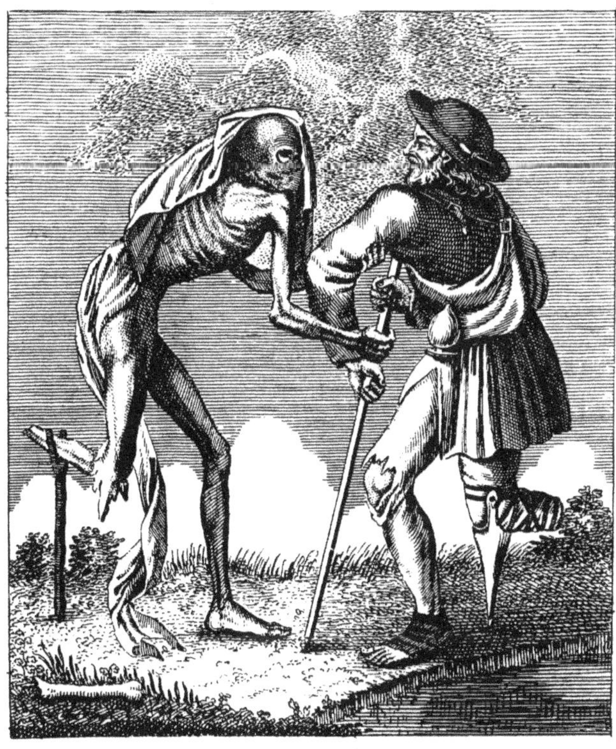

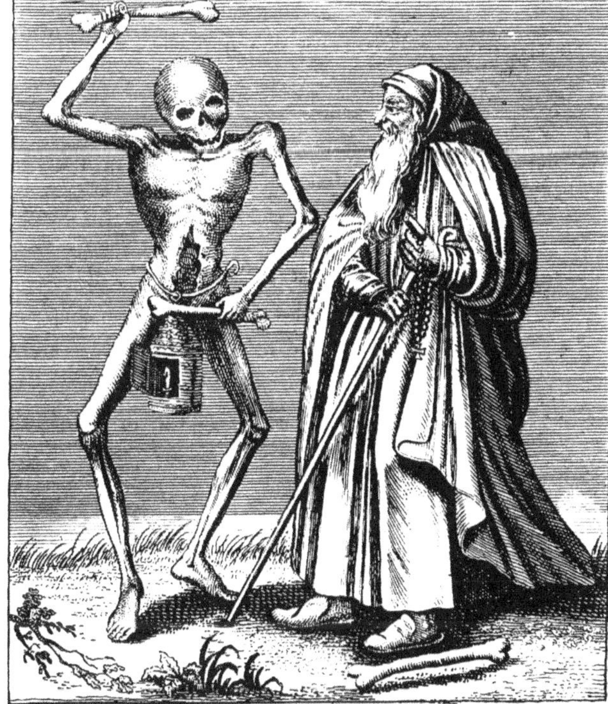

86. Death and the Merchant, Matthäus Merian the Elder. 1593–1650.

87. Death and the Abbess, Matthäus Merian the Elder. 1593–1650.

88. Death and the Disabled Man, Matthäus Merian the Elder. 1593–1650.

89. Death and the Hermit, Matthäus Merian the Elder. 1593–1650.

90

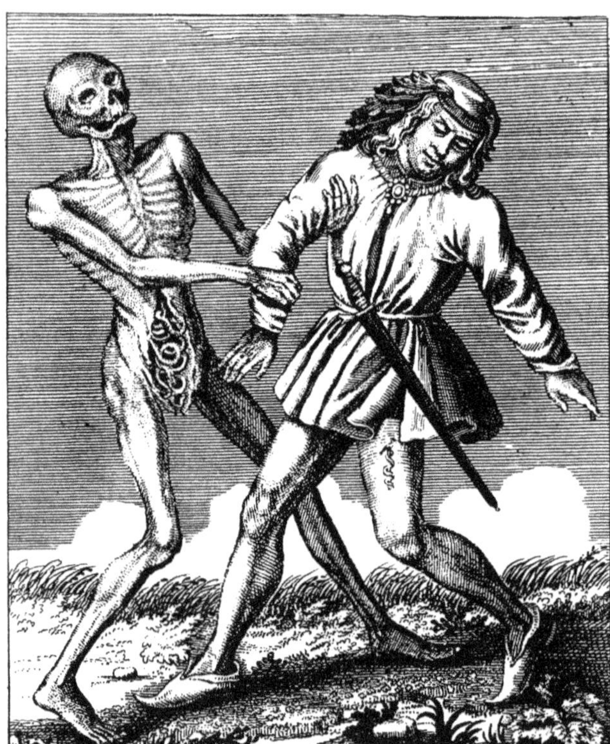

91

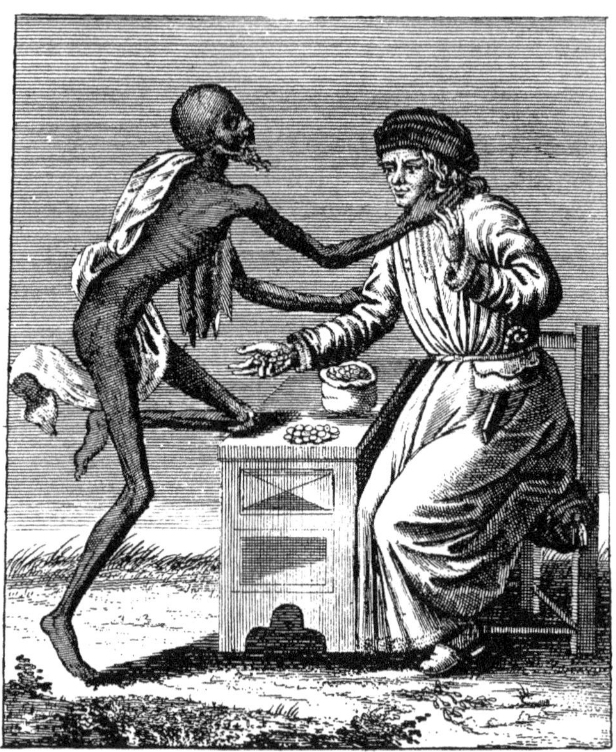

92

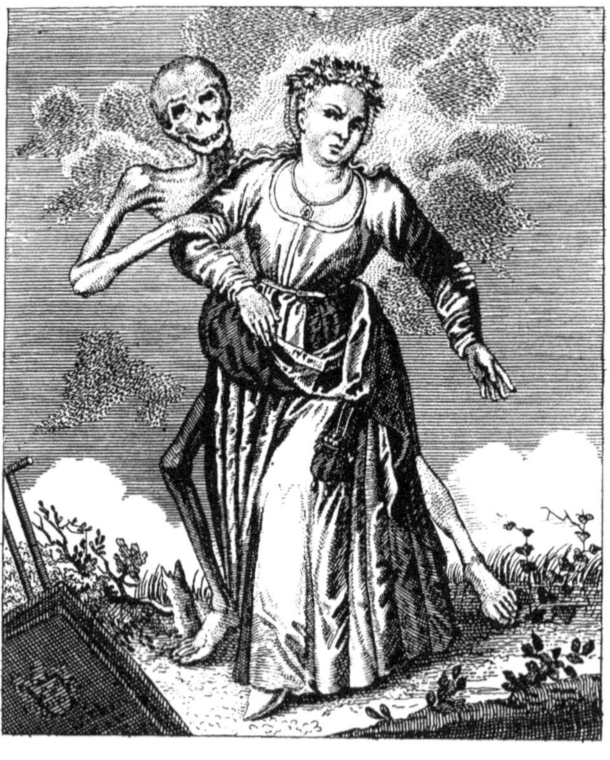

93

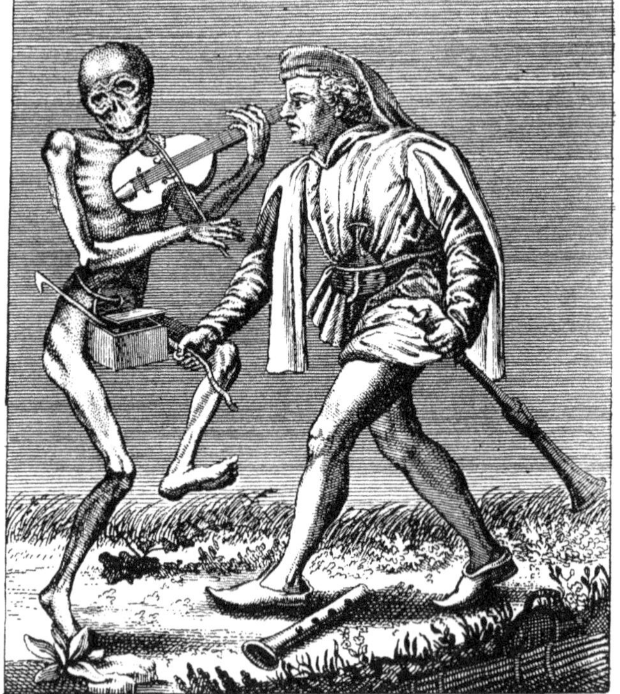

90. Death to the Young Man, Matthäus Merian the Elder. 1593–1650.

91. Death and the Usurer, Matthäus Merian the Elder. 1593–1650.

92. Death to the Young Woman, Matthäus Merian the Elder. 1593–1650.

93. Death and the Piper, Matthäus Merian the Elder. 1593–1650.

94

95

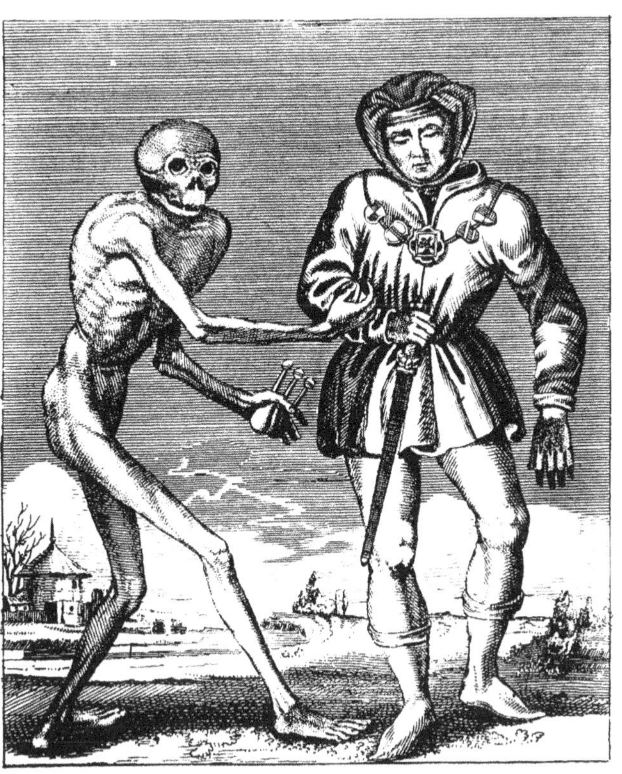

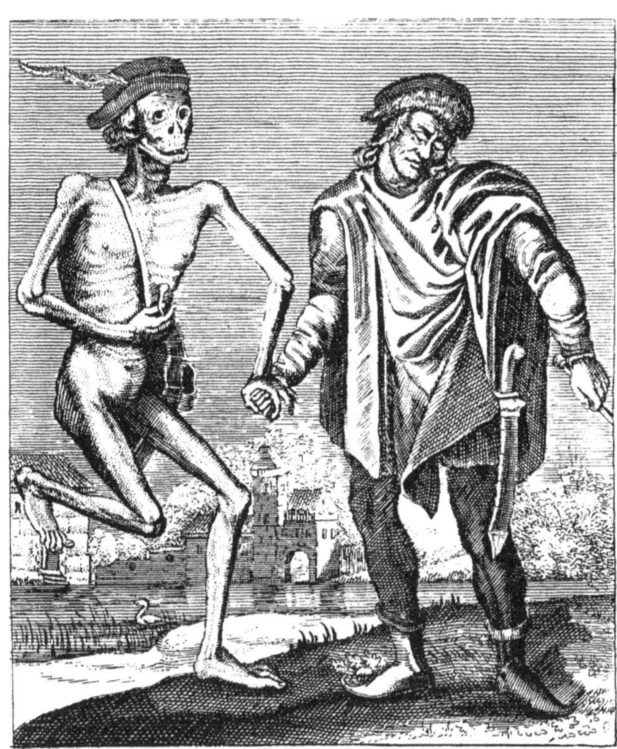

96

97

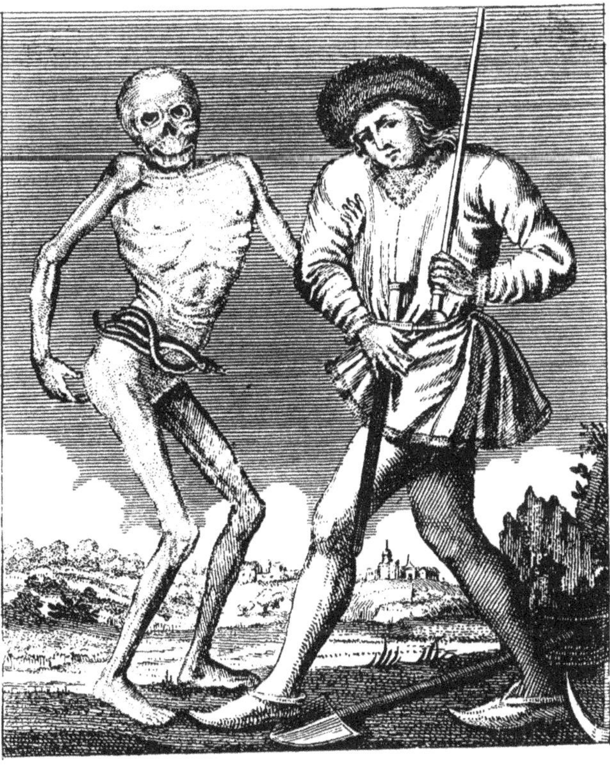

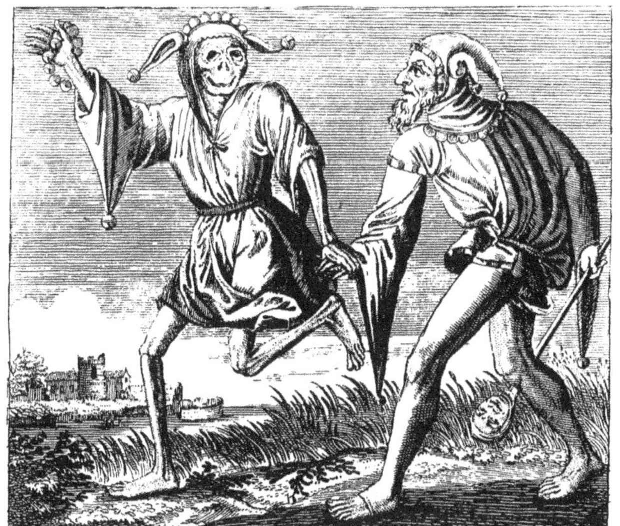

THE DANCE OF DEATH

94. Death and the Herald, Matthäus Merian the Elder. 1593–1650.

95. Death and the Mayor, Matthäus Merian the Elder. 1593–1650.

96. Death and the Baliff, Matthäus Merian the Elder. 1593–1650.

97. Death and the Jester, Matthäus Merian the Elder. 1593–1650.

98

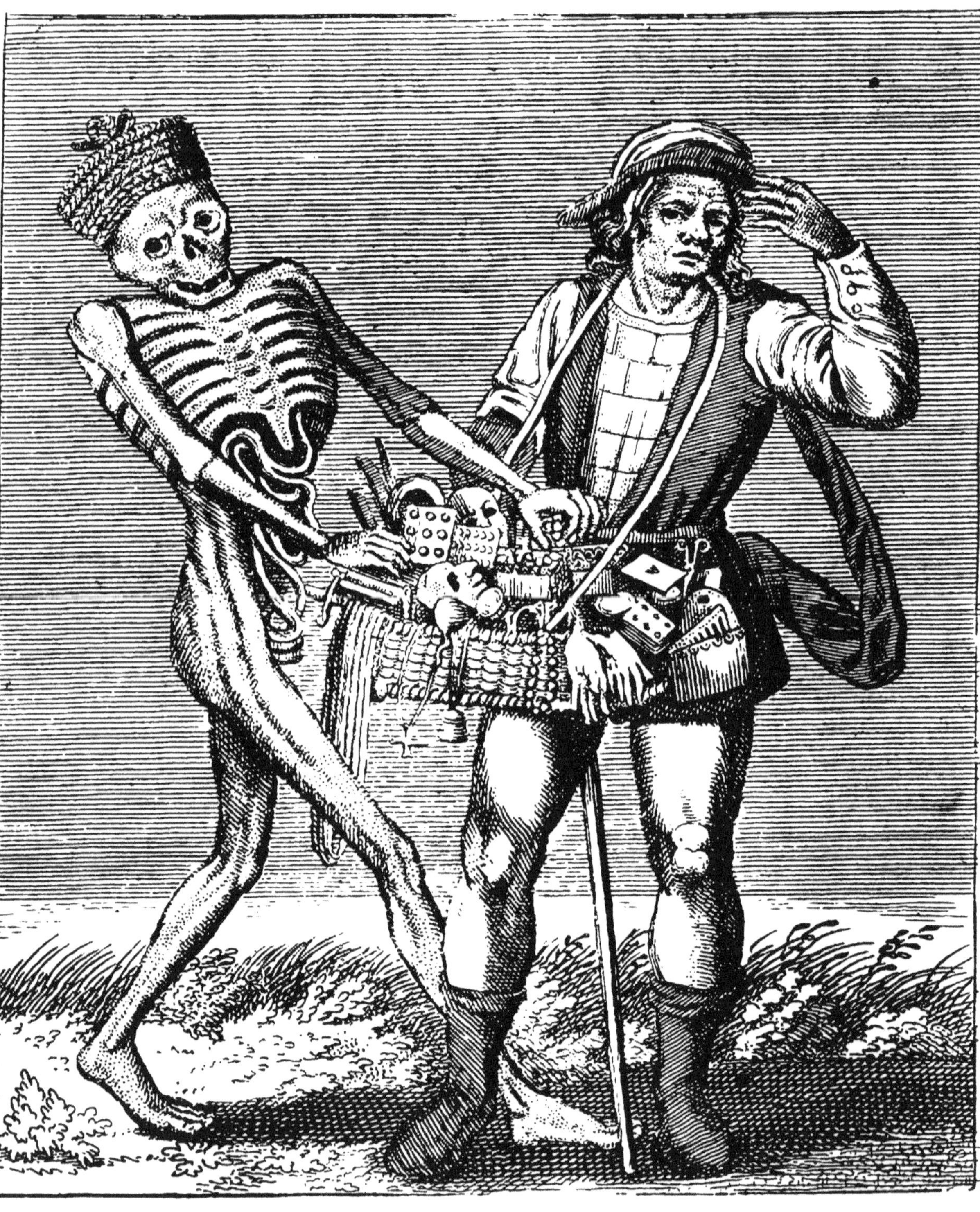

98. Death and the Shopkeeper, Matthäus Merian
the Elder. 1593–1650.

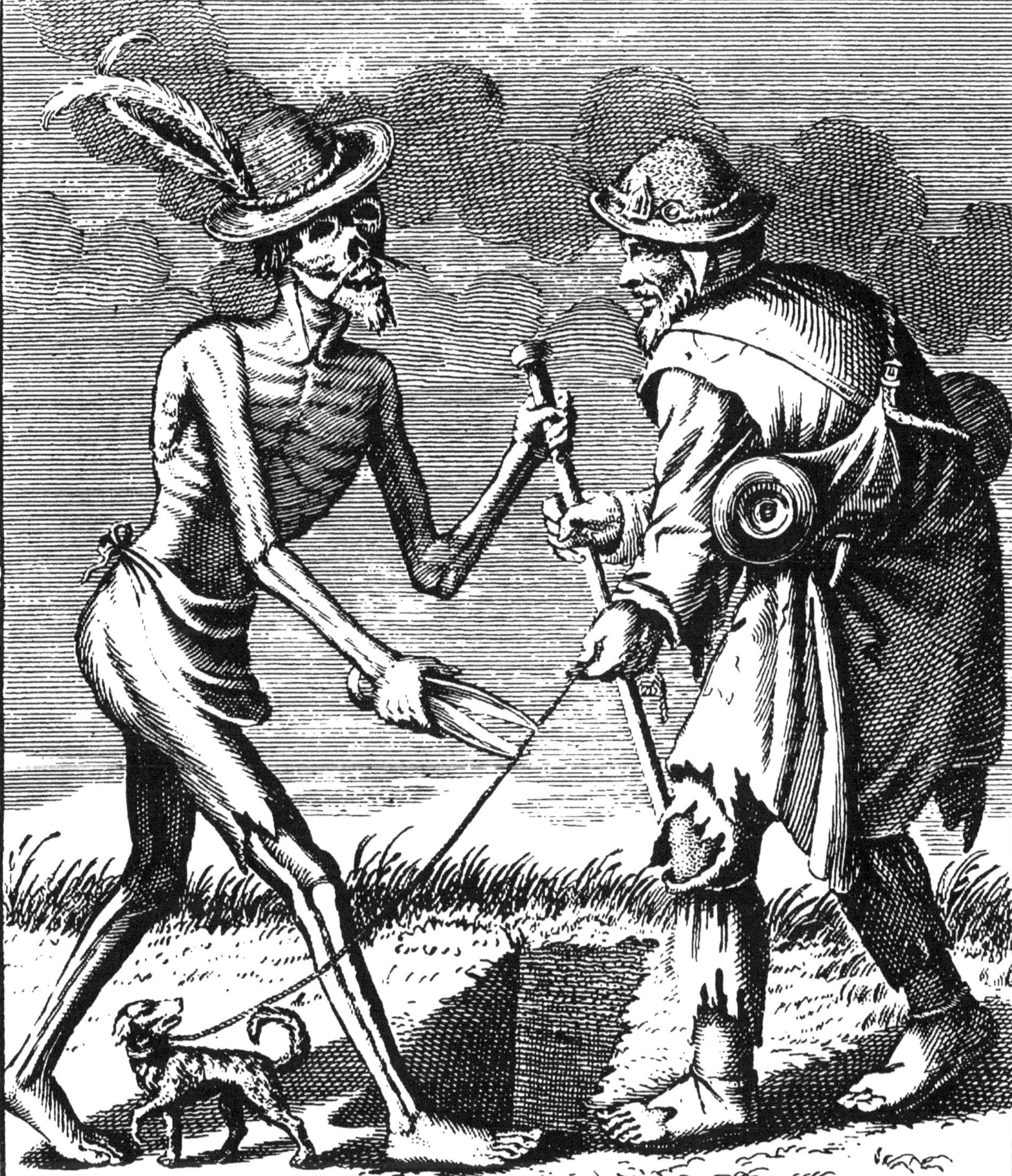

99. Death and the Blind Man, Matthäus Merian
the Elder. 1593–1650.

100

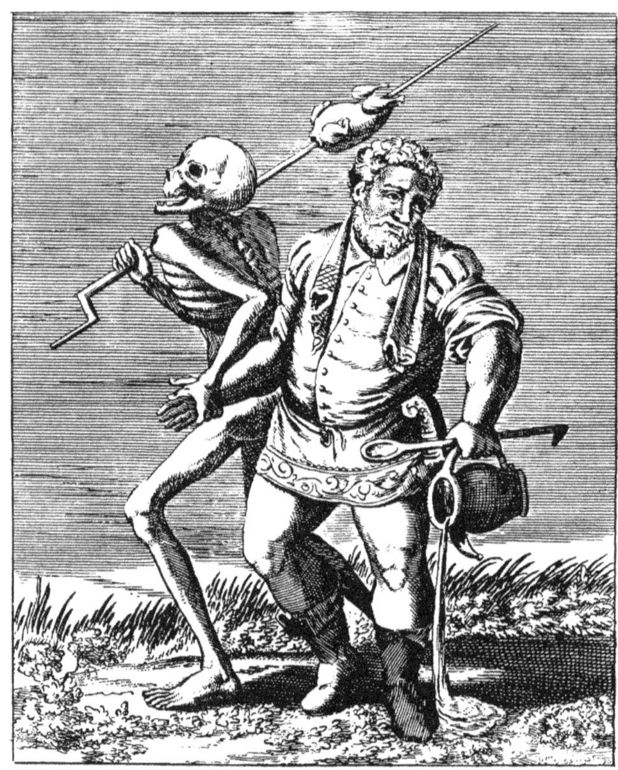

101

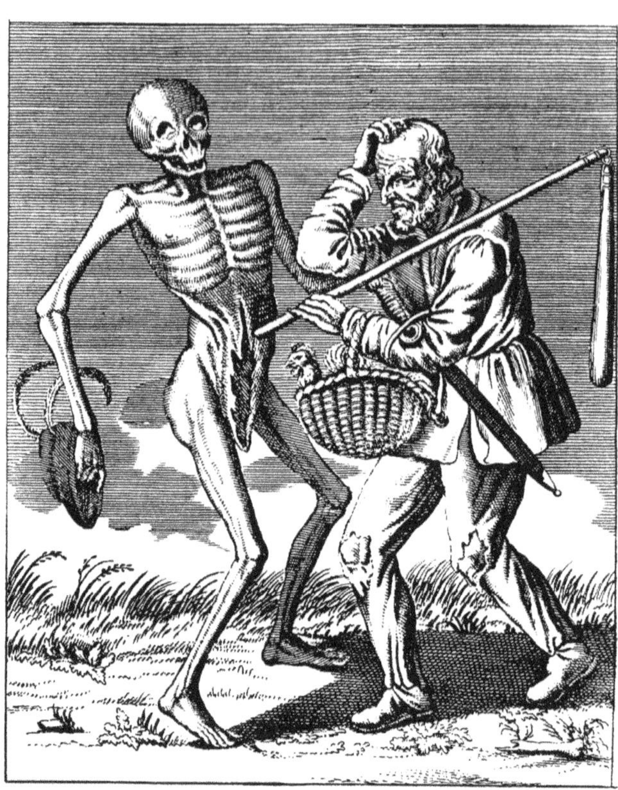

102

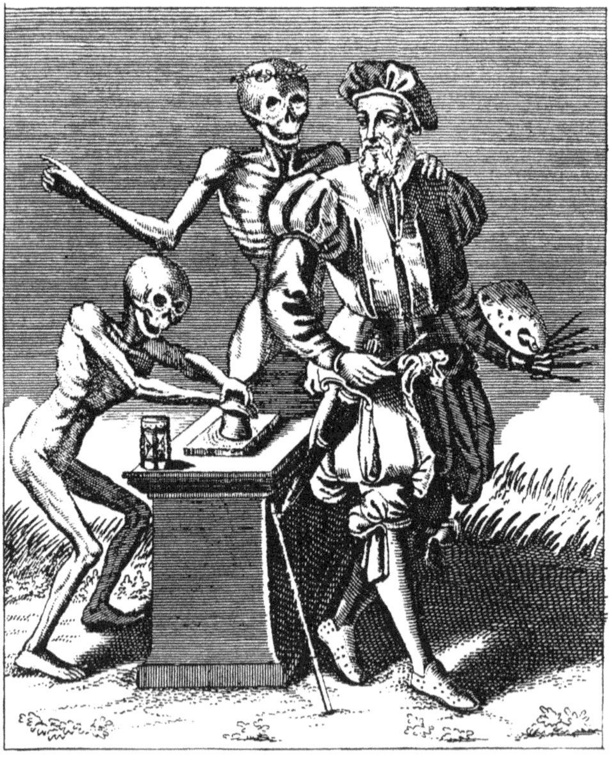

103

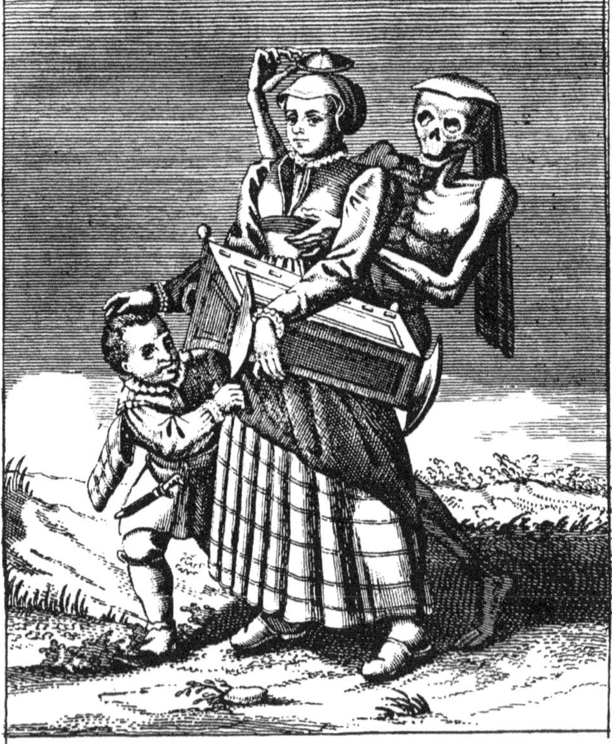

100. Death and the Cook, Matthäus Merian the Elder. 1593–1650.

101. Death and the Farmer, Matthäus Merian the Elder. 1593–1650.

102. Death and the Male Painter, Matthäus Merian the Elder. 1593–1650.

103. Death and the Female Painter Matthäus Merian the Elder. 1593–1650.

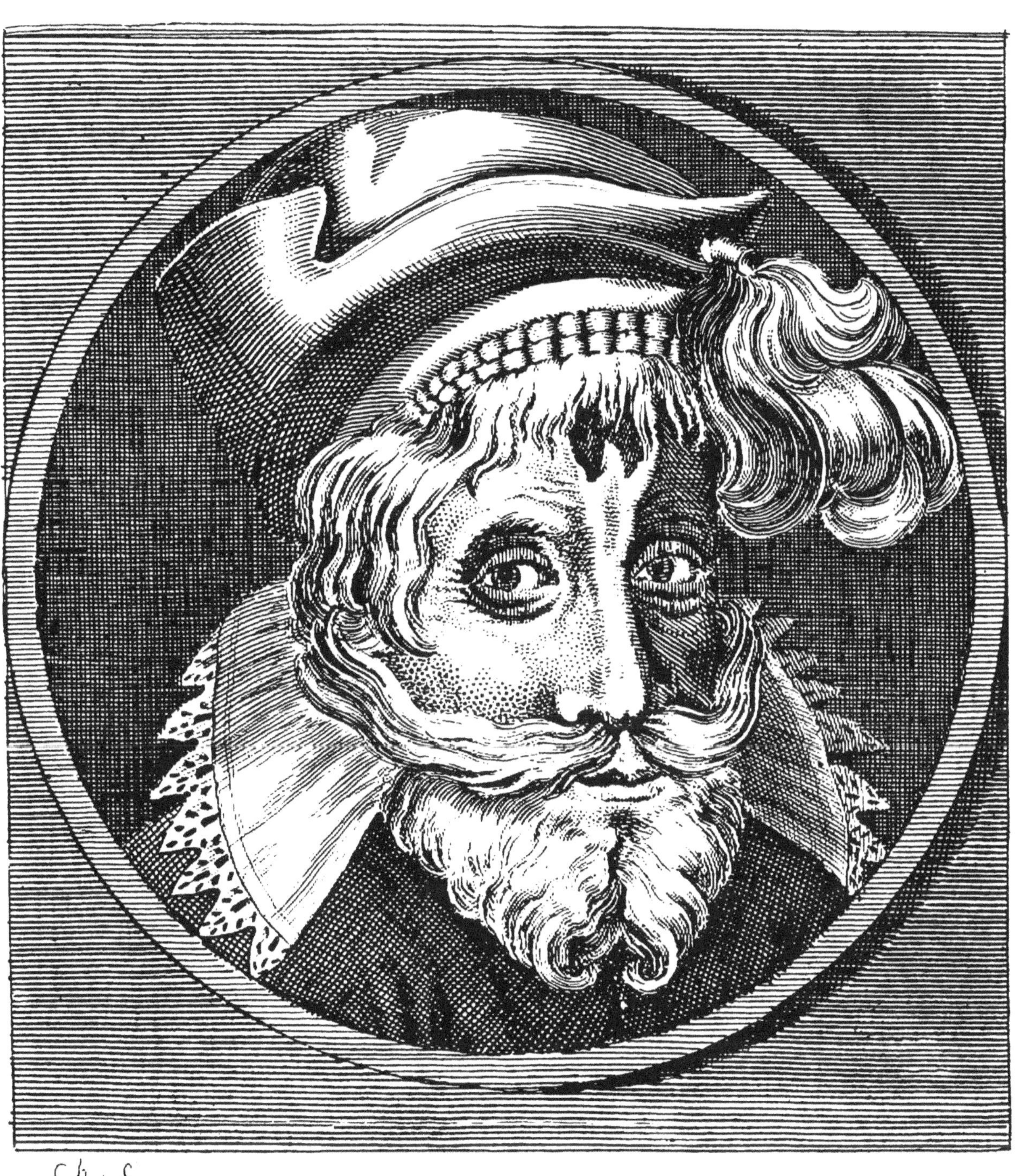

104. The Dance of the Dead, Matthäus Merian
the Elder. 1593–1650.

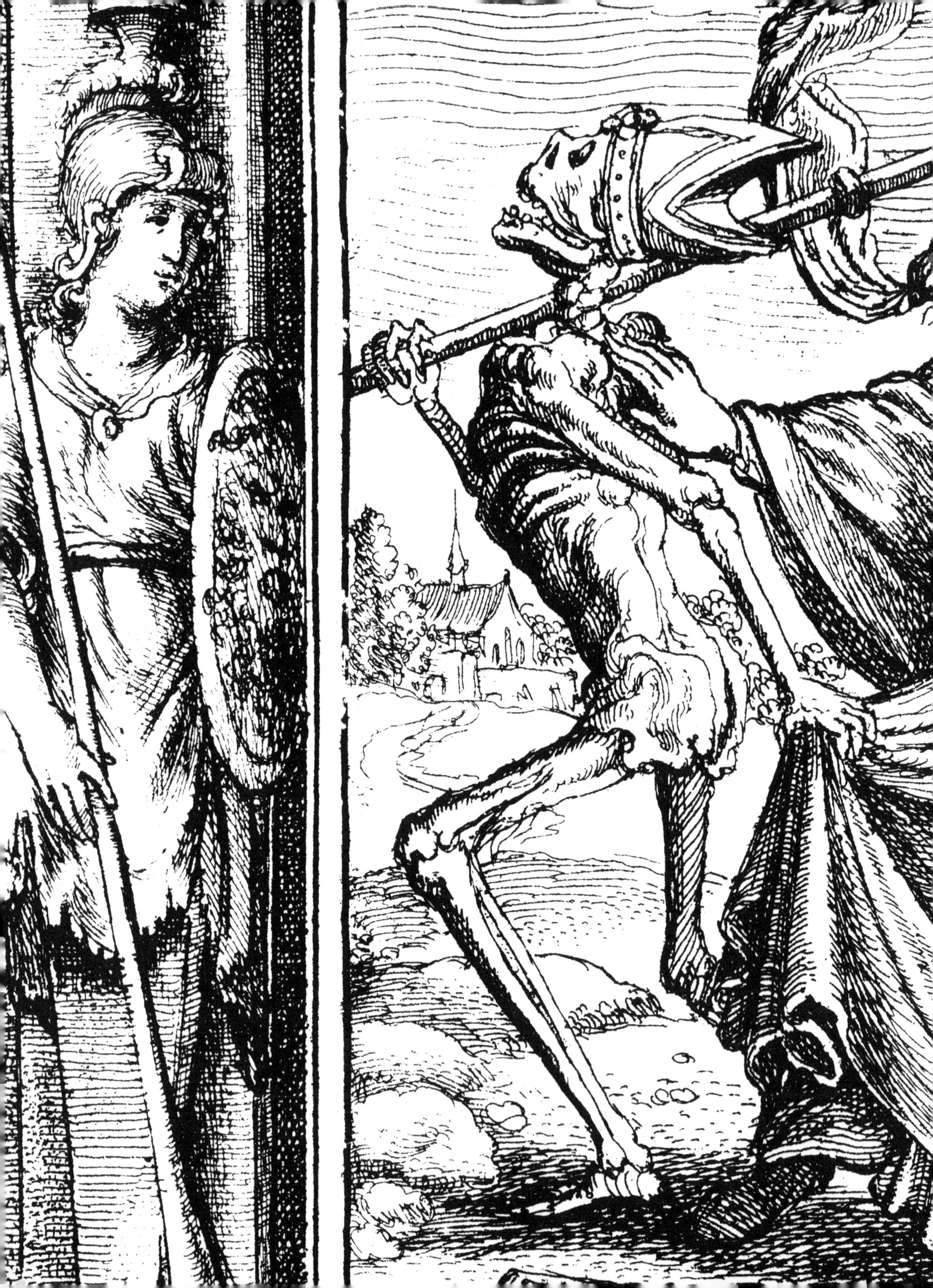

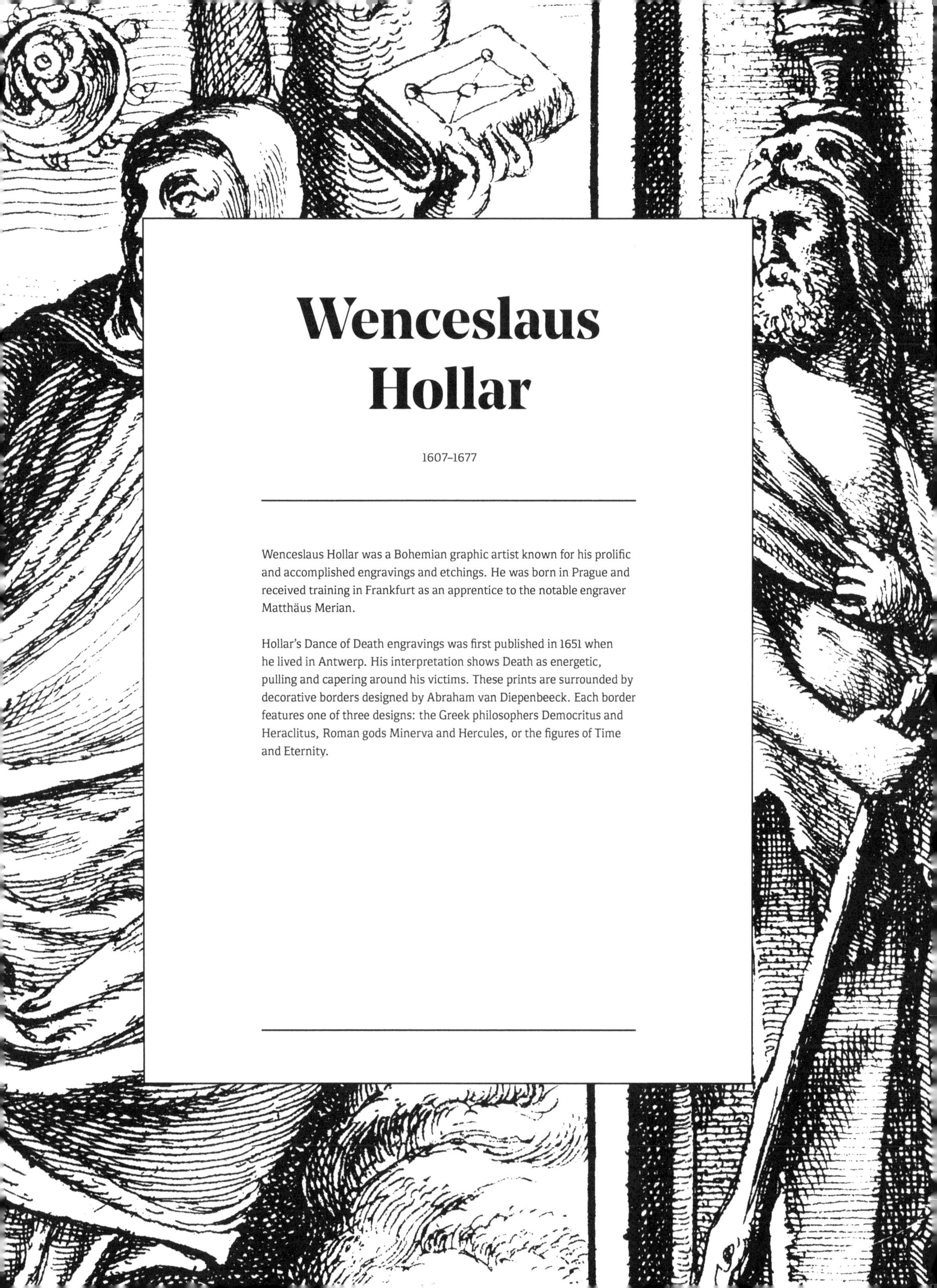

Wenceslaus Hollar

1607–1677

Wenceslaus Hollar was a Bohemian graphic artist known for his prolific and accomplished engravings and etchings. He was born in Prague and received training in Frankfurt as an apprentice to the notable engraver Matthäus Merian.

Hollar's Dance of Death engravings was first published in 1651 when he lived in Antwerp. His interpretation shows Death as energetic, pulling and capering around his victims. These prints are surrounded by decorative borders designed by Abraham van Diepenbeeck. Each border features one of three designs: the Greek philosophers Democritus and Heraclitus, Roman gods Minerva and Hercules, or the figures of Time and Eternity.

105

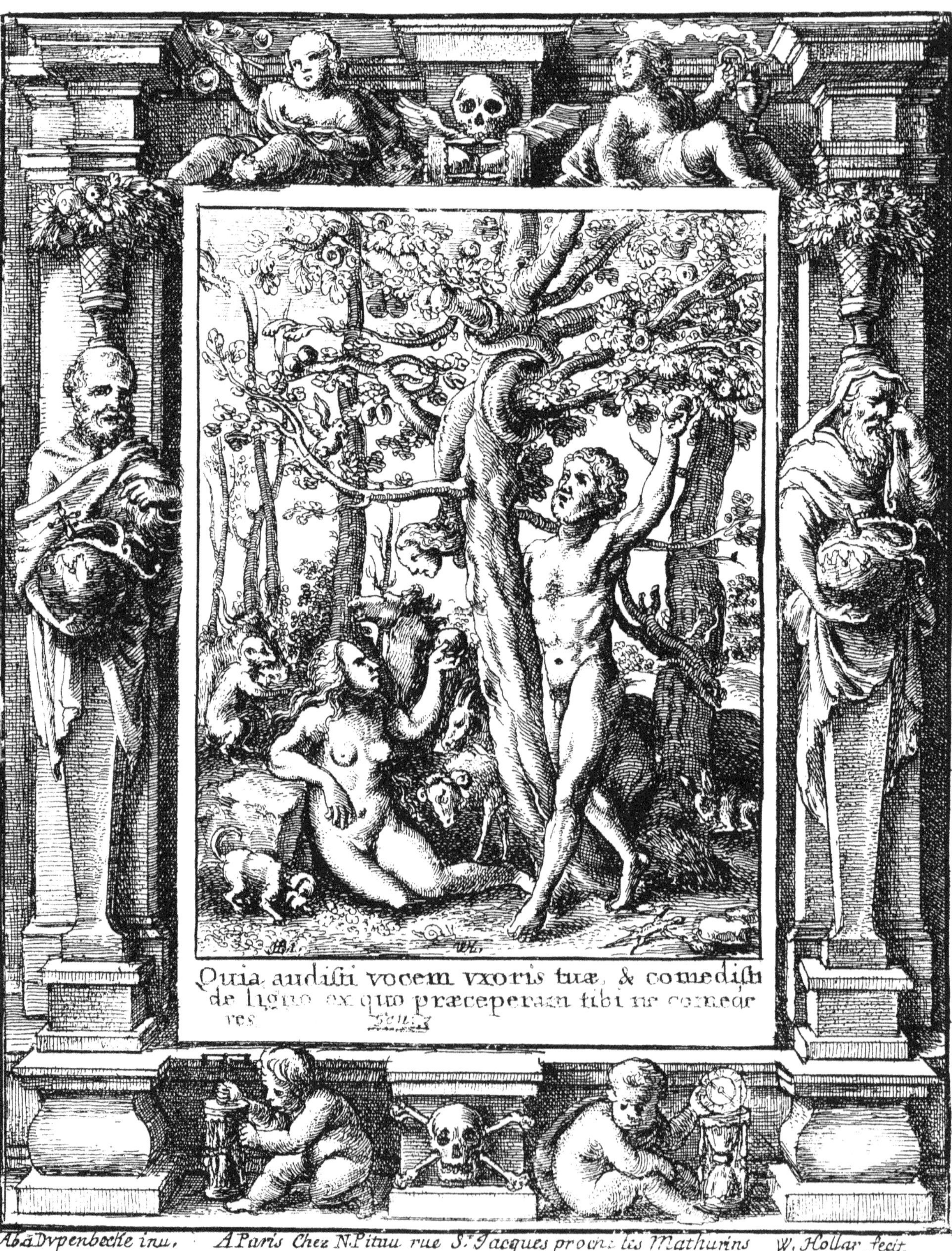

105. Adam and Eve Before the Fall, Wenceslaus
Hollar, after Abraham van Diepenbeeck, after
Hans Holbein (II), 1651.

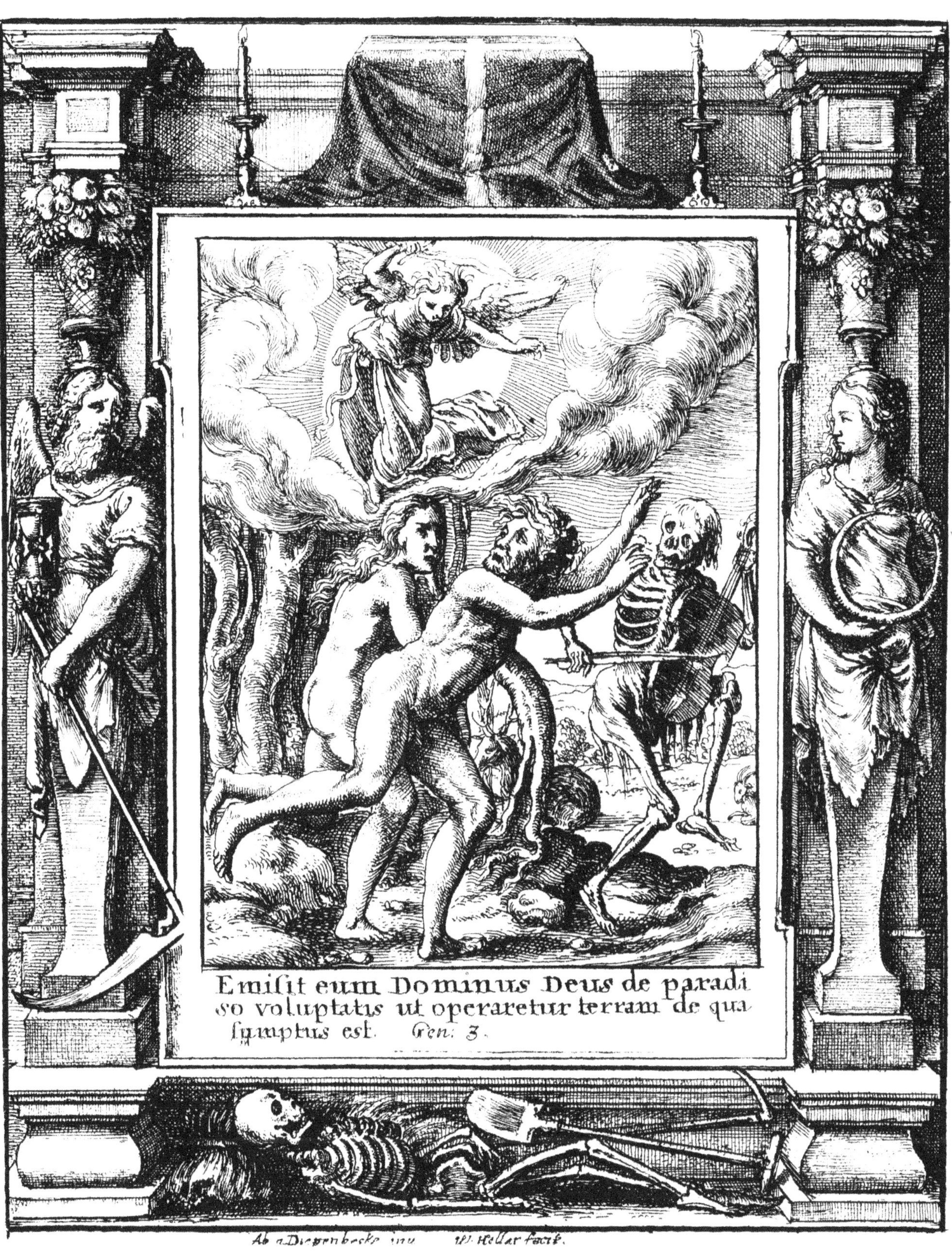

106. Expulsion from Paradise, Wenceslaus Hollar,
after Abraham van Diepenbeeck, after Hans
Holbein (II), 1651.

107

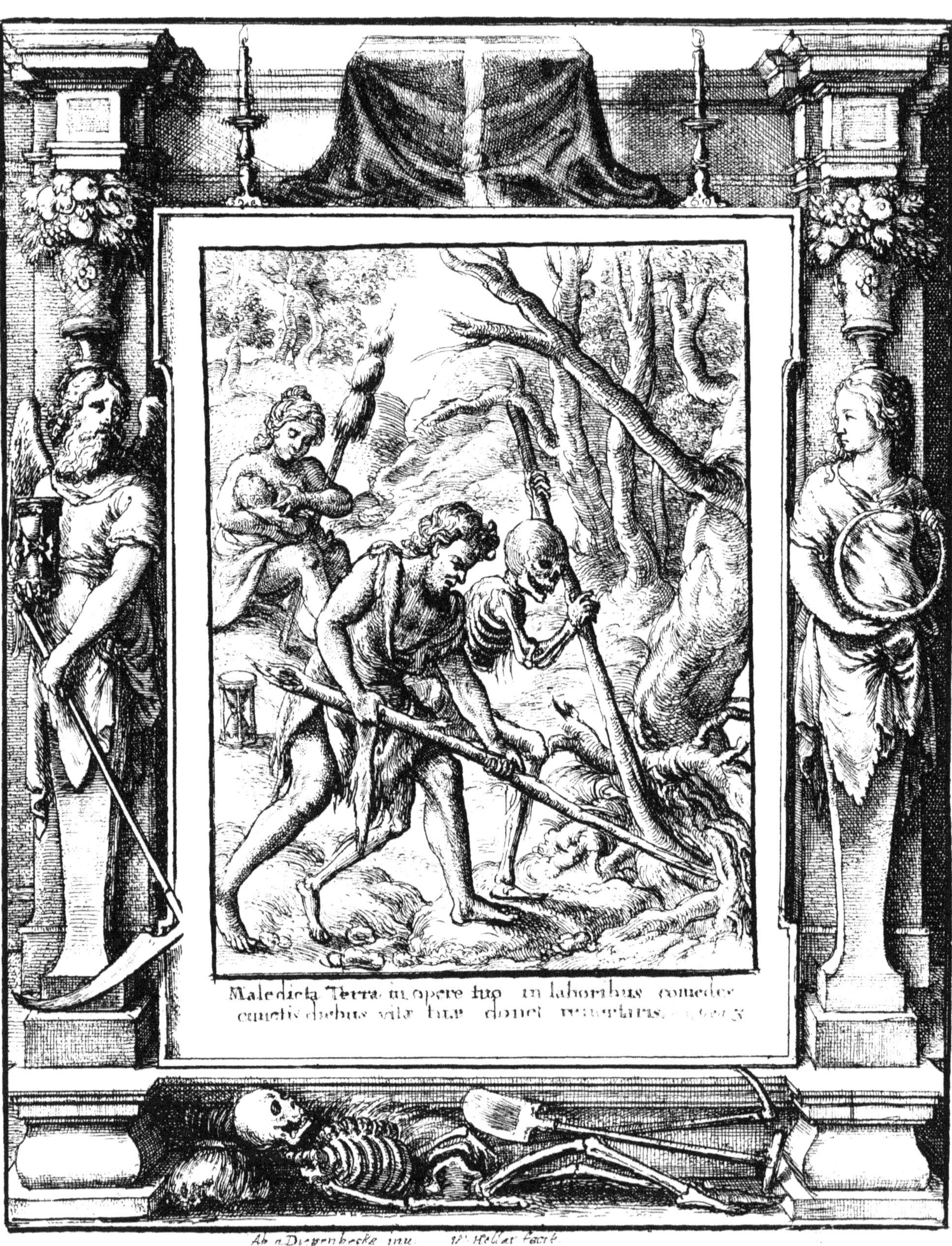

107. Adam and Eve after the Fall, Wenceslaus
Hollar, after Abraham van Diepenbeeck, after
Hans Holbein (II), 1651.

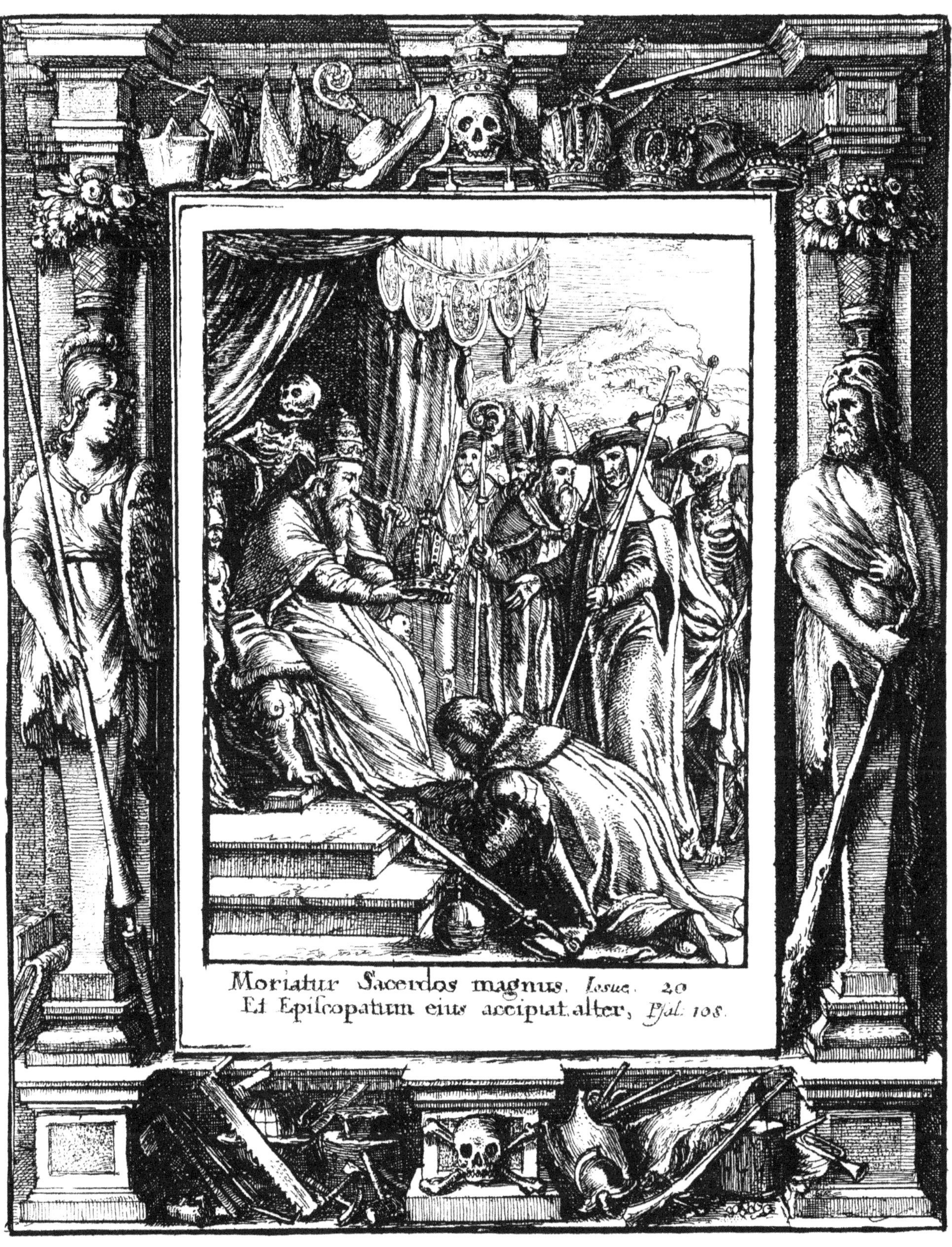

108. The Pope and Death, Wenceslaus Hollar,
after Abraham van Diepenbeeck, after Hans
Holbein (II), 1651.

109

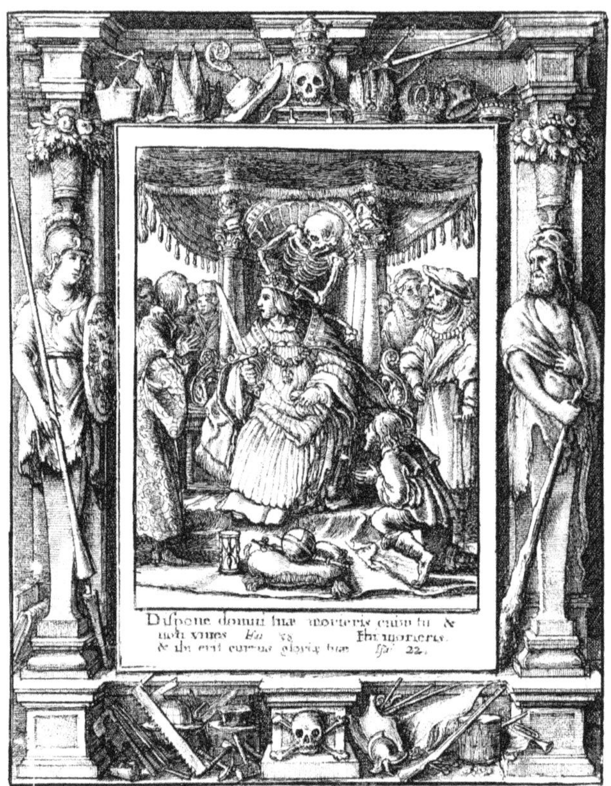

110

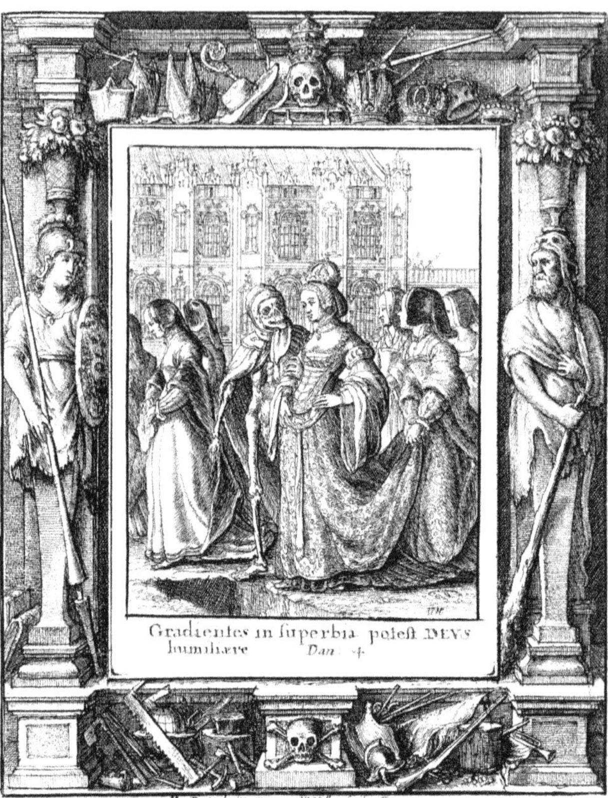

111

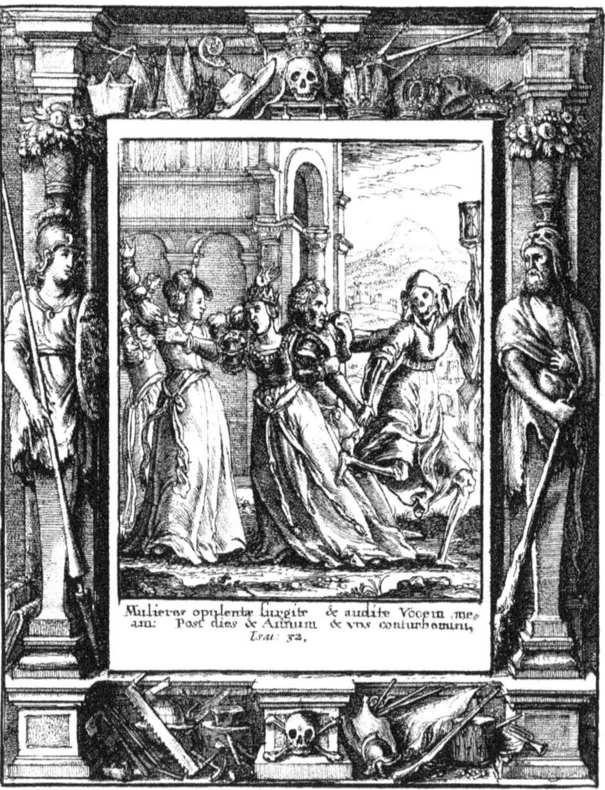

112

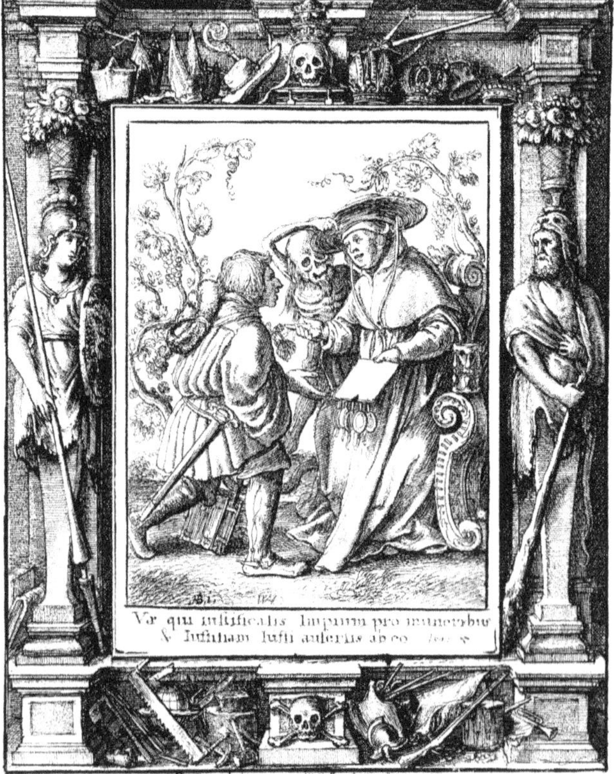

109. The Emperor and Death, Wenceslaus Hollar, after Abraham van Diepenbeeck, after Hans Holbein (II), 1651.

110. The Empress and Death, Wenceslaus Hollar, after Abraham van Diepenbeeck, after Hans Holbein (II), 1651.

111. The Queen and Death, Wenceslaus Hollar, after Abraham van Diepenbeeck, after Hans Holbein (II), 1651.

112. The Cardinal and Death, Wenceslaus Hollar, after Hans Holbein (II), ca. 1680.

113

114

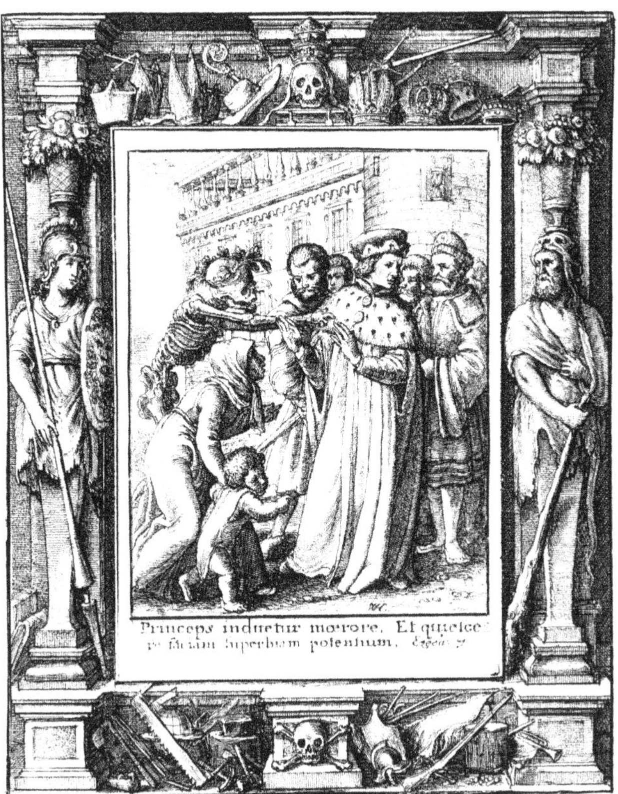

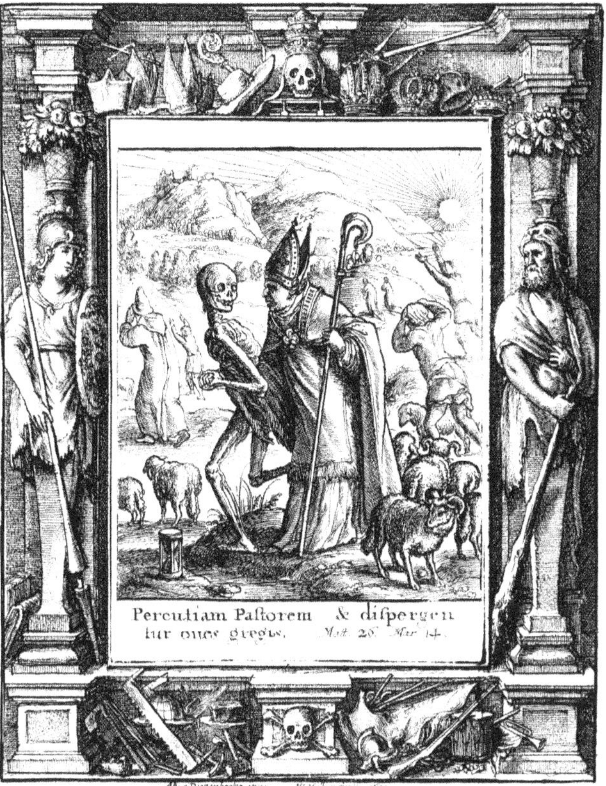

115

116

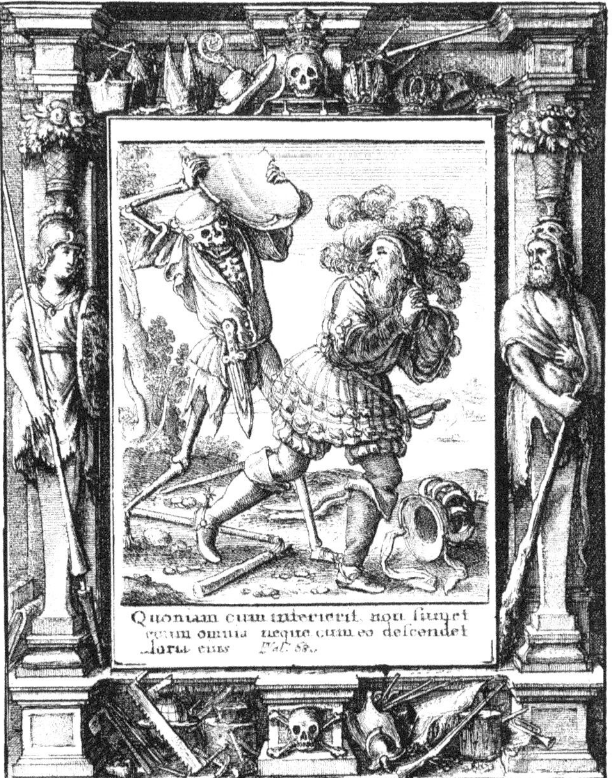

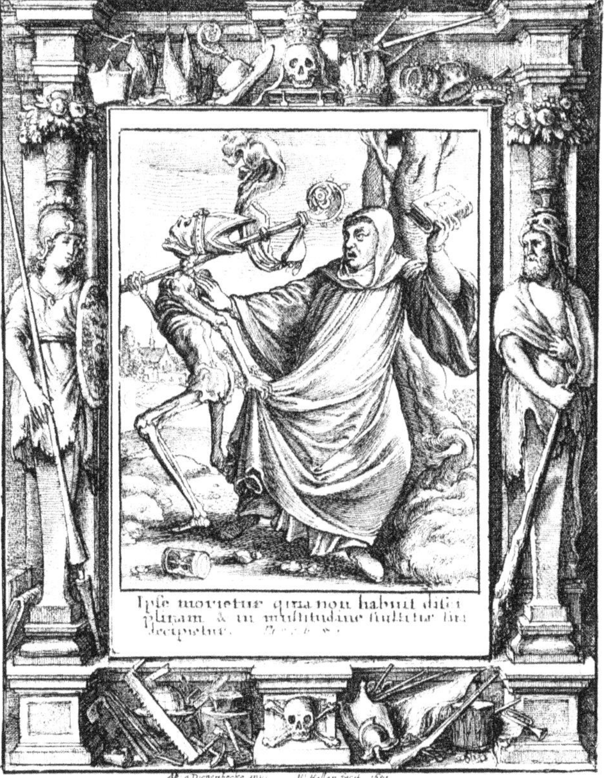

113. The Duke and Death, Wenceslaus Hollar, after Abraham van Diepenbeeck, after Hans Holbein (II), 1651.

114. The Bishop and Death, Wenceslaus Hollar, after Abraham van Diepenbeeck, after Hans Holbein (II), 1651.

115. The Count and Death, Wenceslaus Hollar, after Abraham van Diepenbeeck, after Hans Holbein (II), 1651.

116. The Abbot and Death, Wenceslaus Hollar, after Abraham van Diepenbeeck, after Hans Holbein (II), 1651.

117

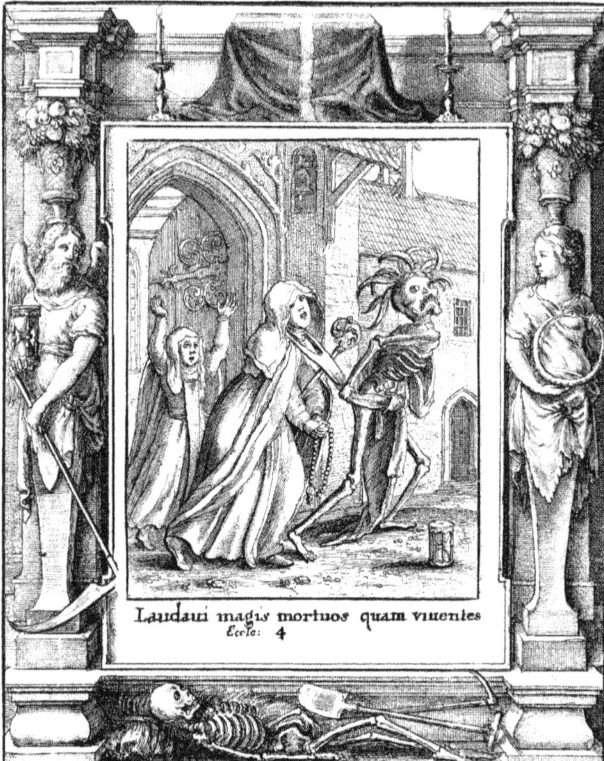

118

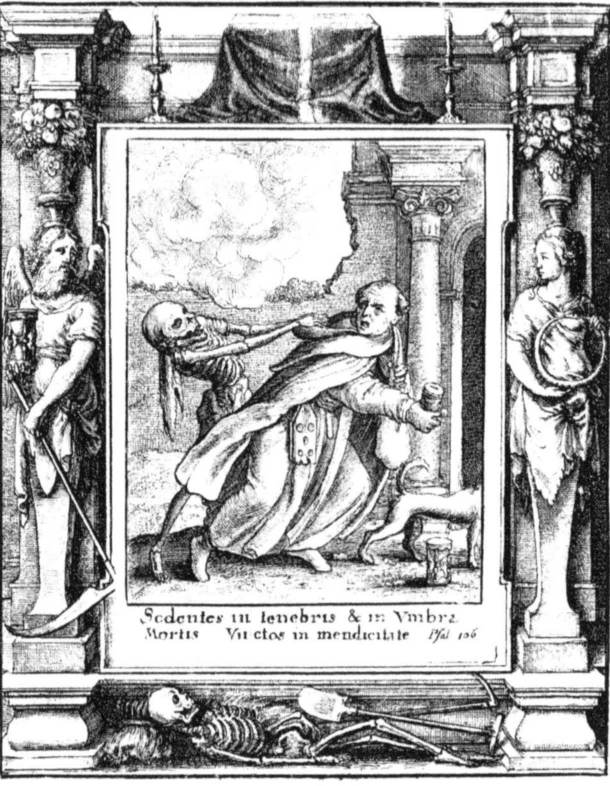

119

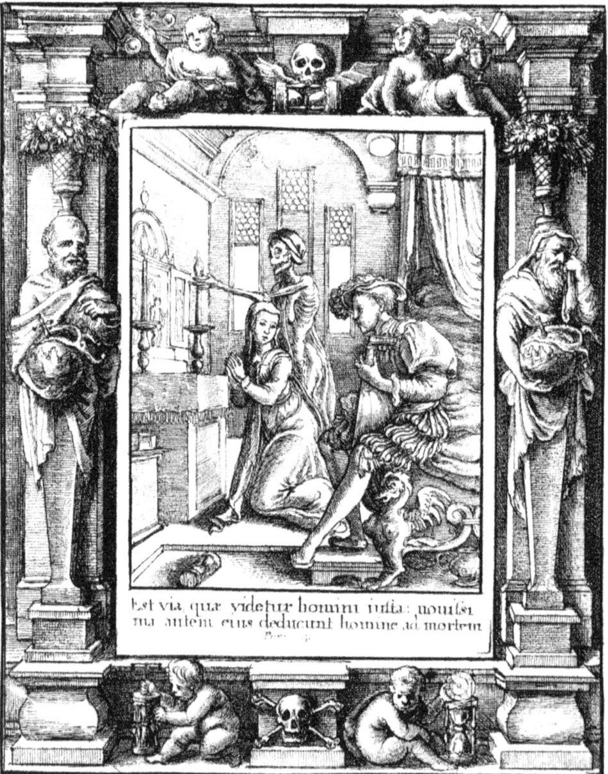

120

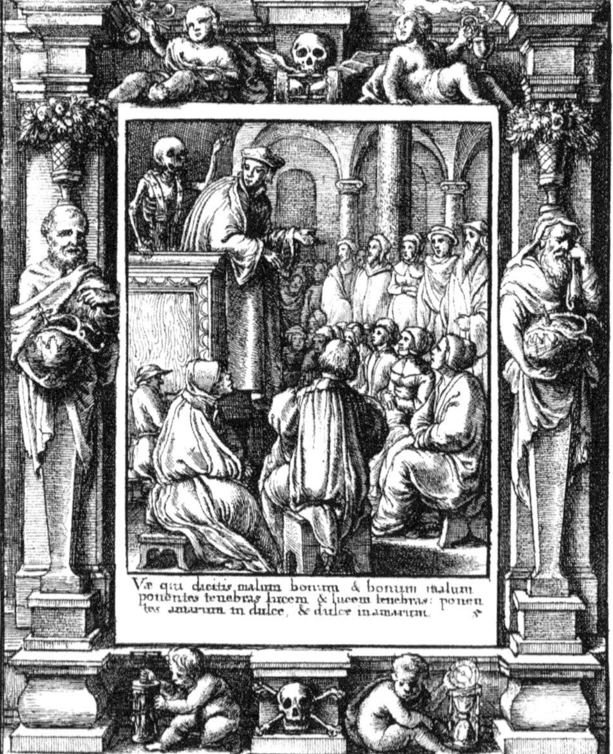

117. The Abbess and Death, Wenceslaus Hollar, after Abraham van Diepenbeeck, after Hans Holbein (II), 1651.

118. The Monk and Death, Wenceslaus Hollar, after Abraham van Diepenbeeck, after Hans Holbein (II), 1651.

119. The Nun and Death, Wenceslaus Hollar, after Abraham van Diepenbeeck, after Hans Holbein (II), 1651.

120. The Preacher and Death, Wenceslaus Hollar, after Abraham van Diepenbeeck, after Hans Holbein (II), 1651.

121

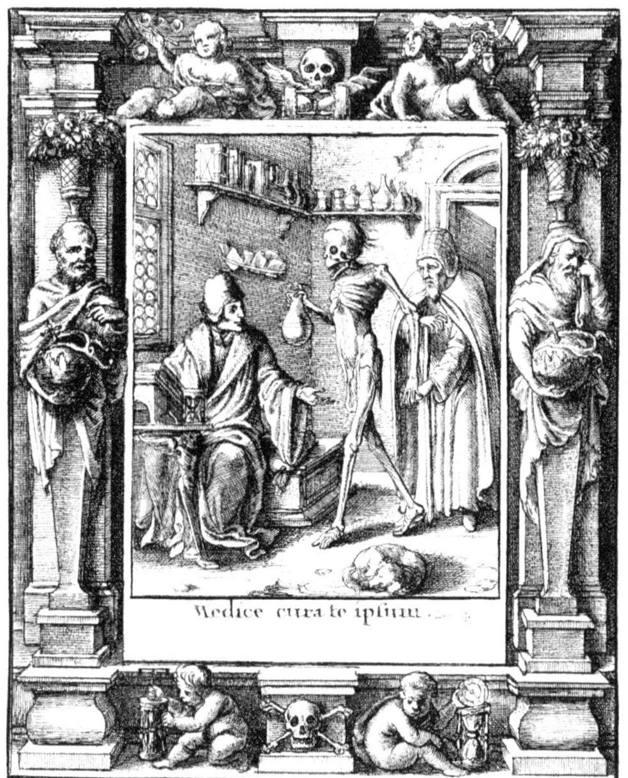

122

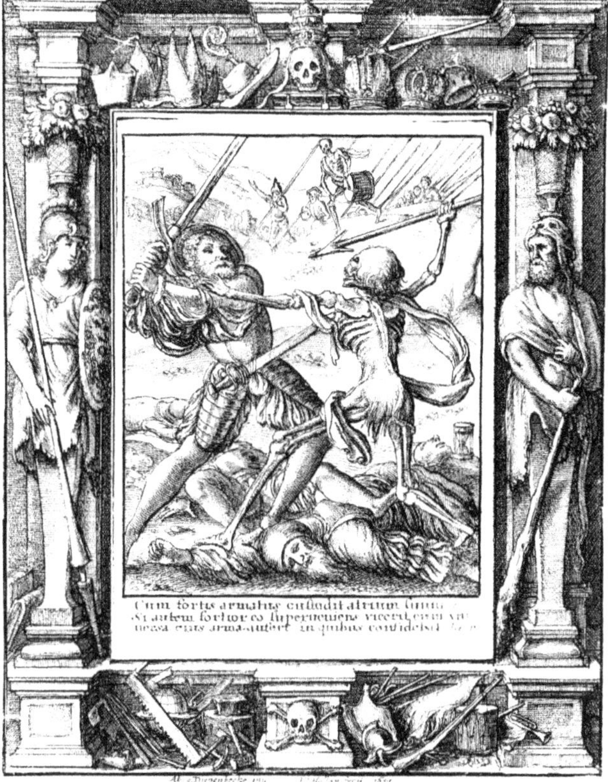

123

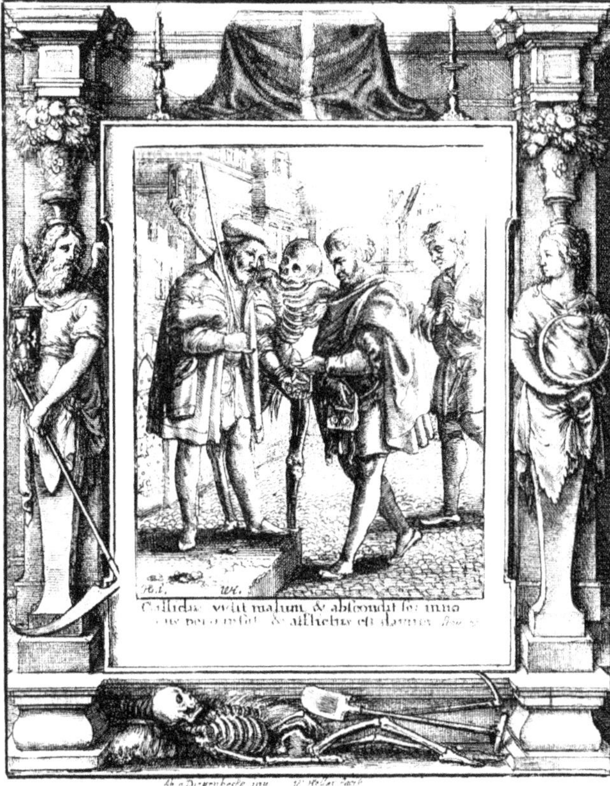

124

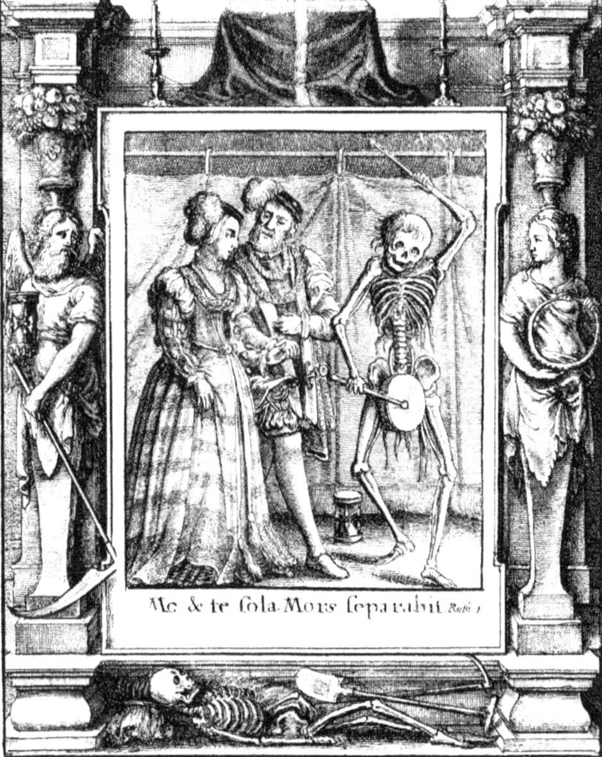

121. The Doctor and Death, Wenceslaus Hollar, after Abraham van Diepenbeeck, after Hans Holbein (II), 1651.

122. The Knight and Death, Wenceslaus Hollar, after Abraham van Diepenbeeck, after Hans Holbein (II), 1651.

123. The Lawyer and Death, Wenceslaus Hollar, after Hans Holbein (II), ca. 1680.

124. The Bridal Couple and Death, Wenceslaus Hollar, after Abraham van Diepenbeeck, after Hans Holbein (II), 1651.

125

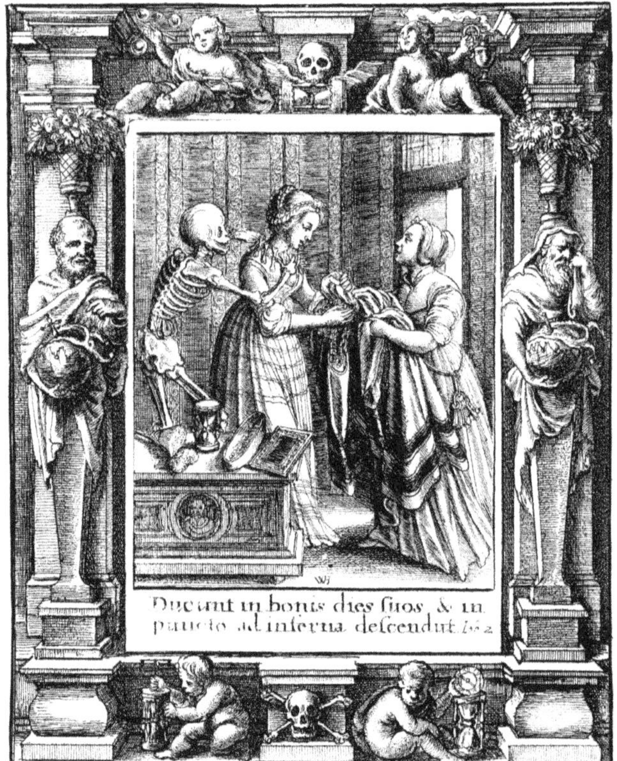

126

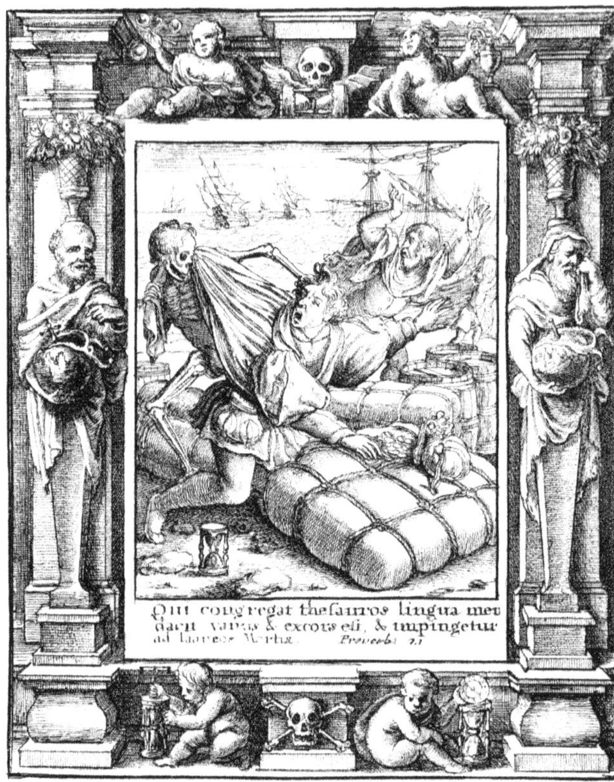

127

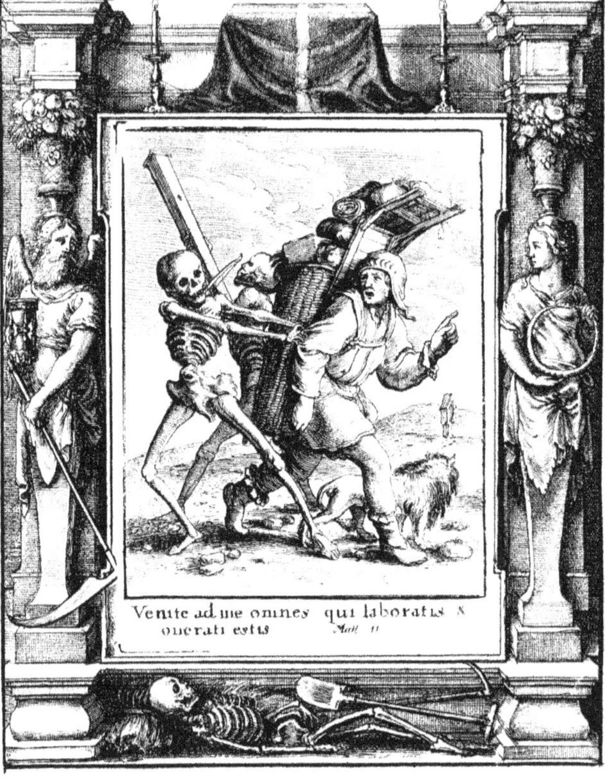

128

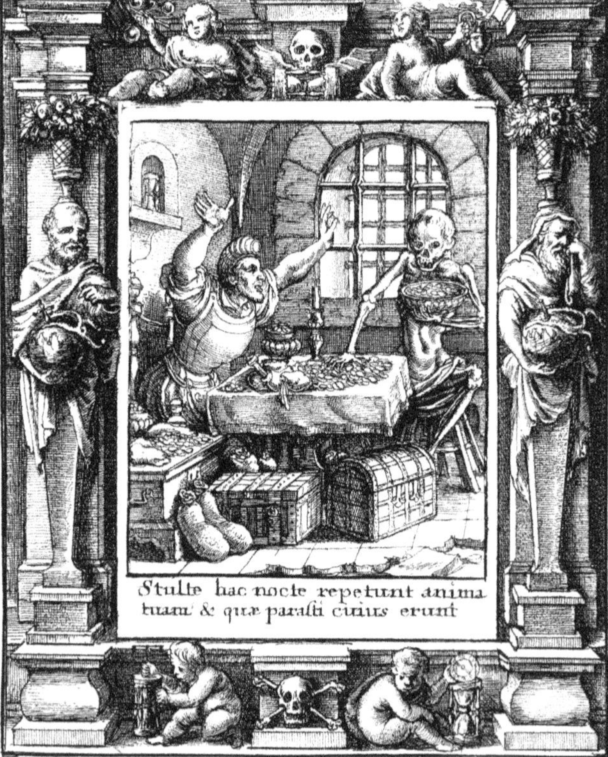

125. The Bride and Death, Wenceslaus Hollar, after Abraham van Diepenbeeck, after Hans Holbein (II), 1651.

126. The Merchant and Death, Wenceslaus Hollar, after Abraham van Diepenbeeck, after Hans Holbein (II), 1651.

127. The Pedlar and Death, Wenceslaus Hollar, after Abraham van Diepenbeeck, after Hans Holbein (II), 1651.

128. The Rich Man and Death, Wenceslaus Hollar, after Abraham van Diepenbeeck, after Hans Holbein (II), 1651.

129

130

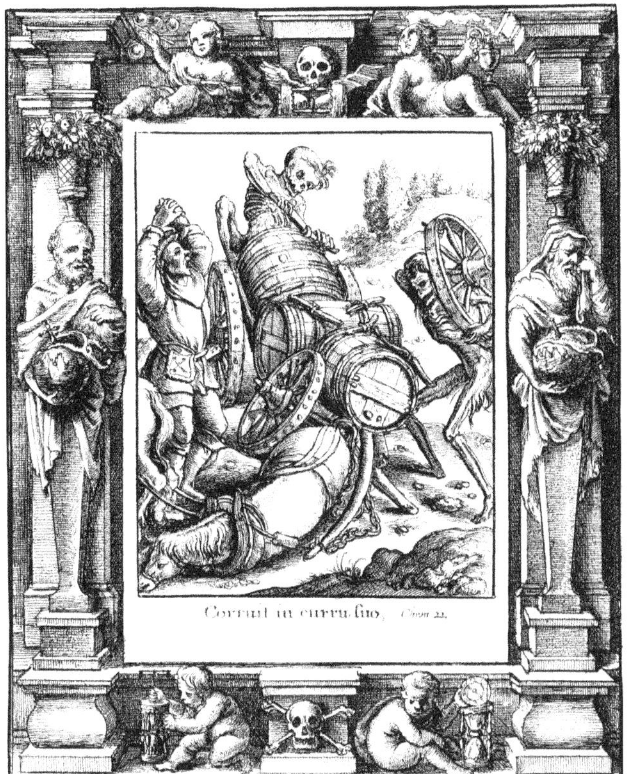

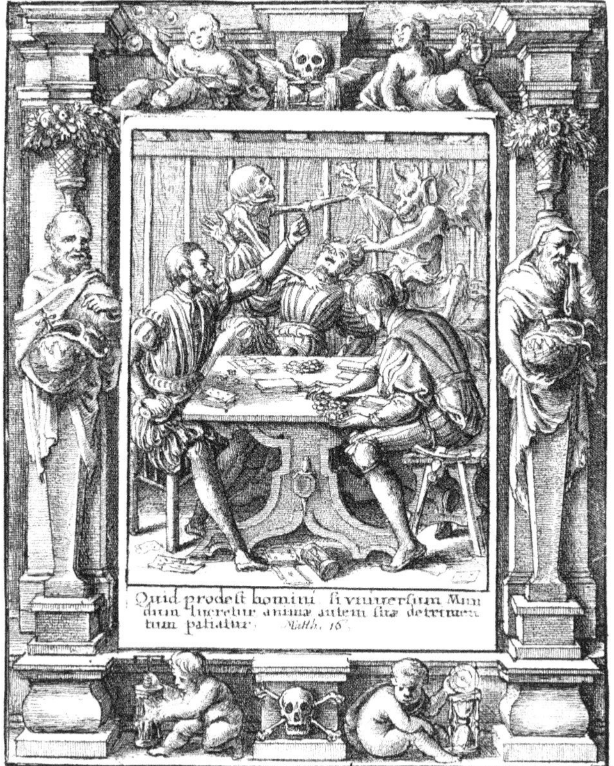

131

132

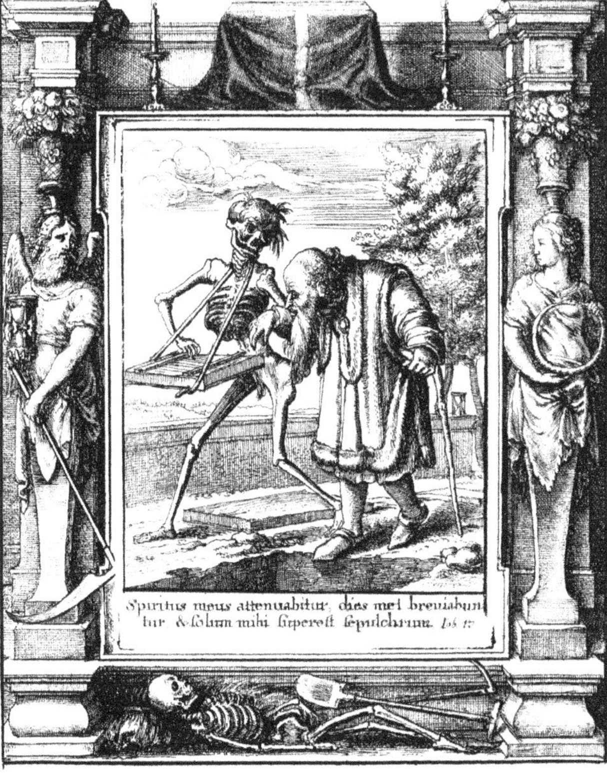

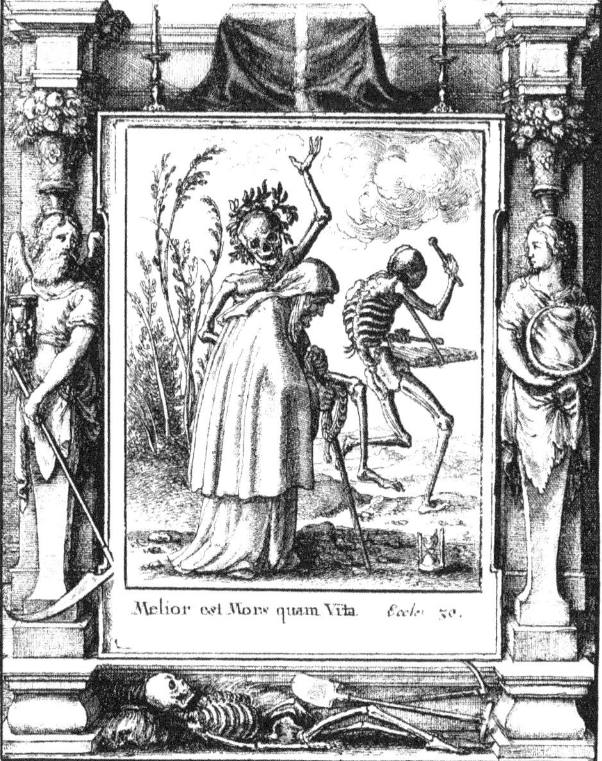

129. The Driver and Death, Wenceslaus Hollar, after Abraham van Diepenbeeck, after Hans Holbein (II), 1651.

130. The Gamesters and Death, Wenceslaus Hollar, after Abraham van Diepenbeeck, after Hans Holbein (II), 1651.

131. The Old Man and Death, Wenceslaus Hollar, after Abraham van Diepenbeeck, after Hans Holbein (II), 1651.

132. The Old Woman and Death, Wenceslaus Hollar, after Abraham van Diepenbeeck, after Hans Holbein (II), 1651.

133

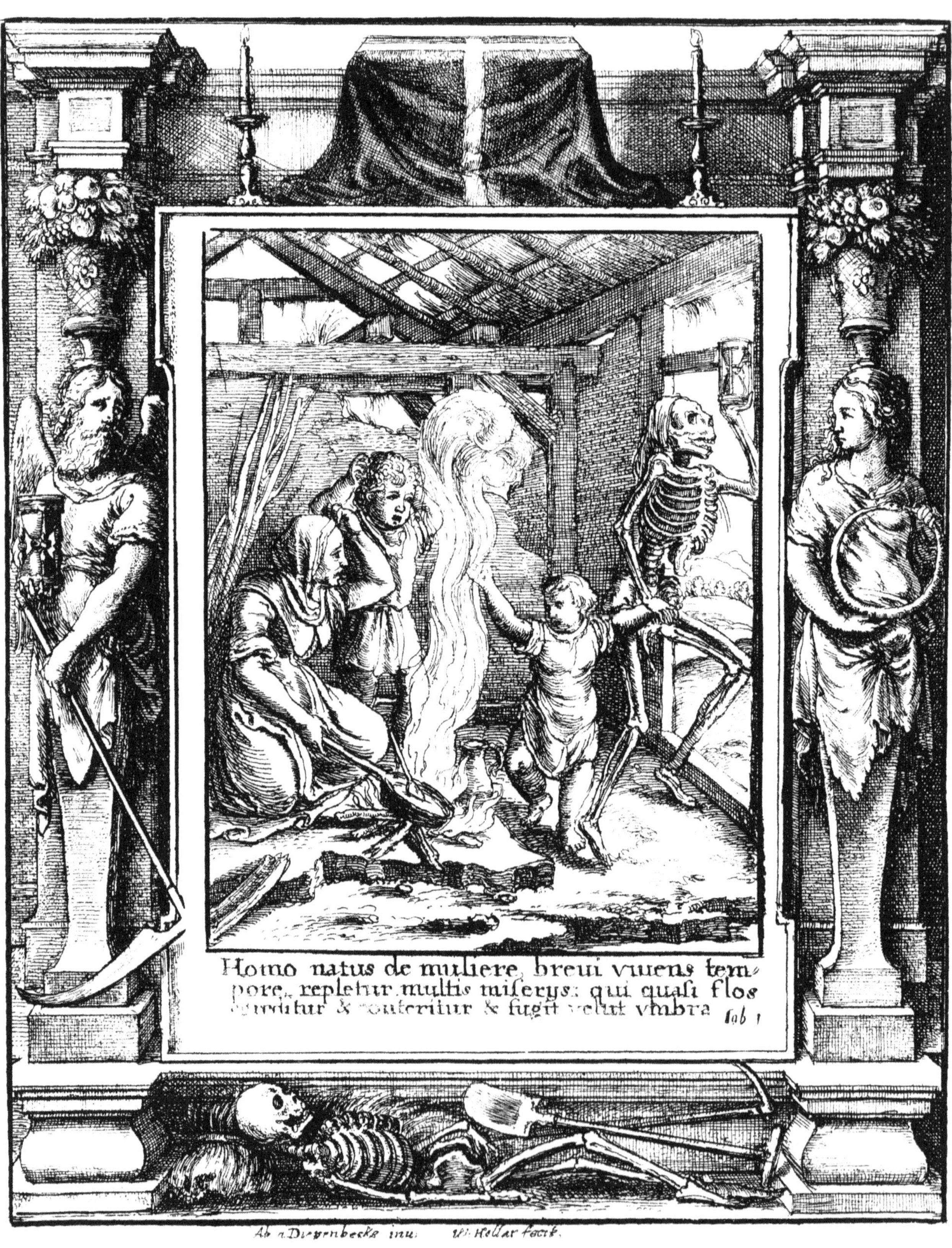

133. The Child and Death, Wenceslaus Hollar,
after Abraham van Diepenbeeck, after Hans
Holbein (II), 1651.

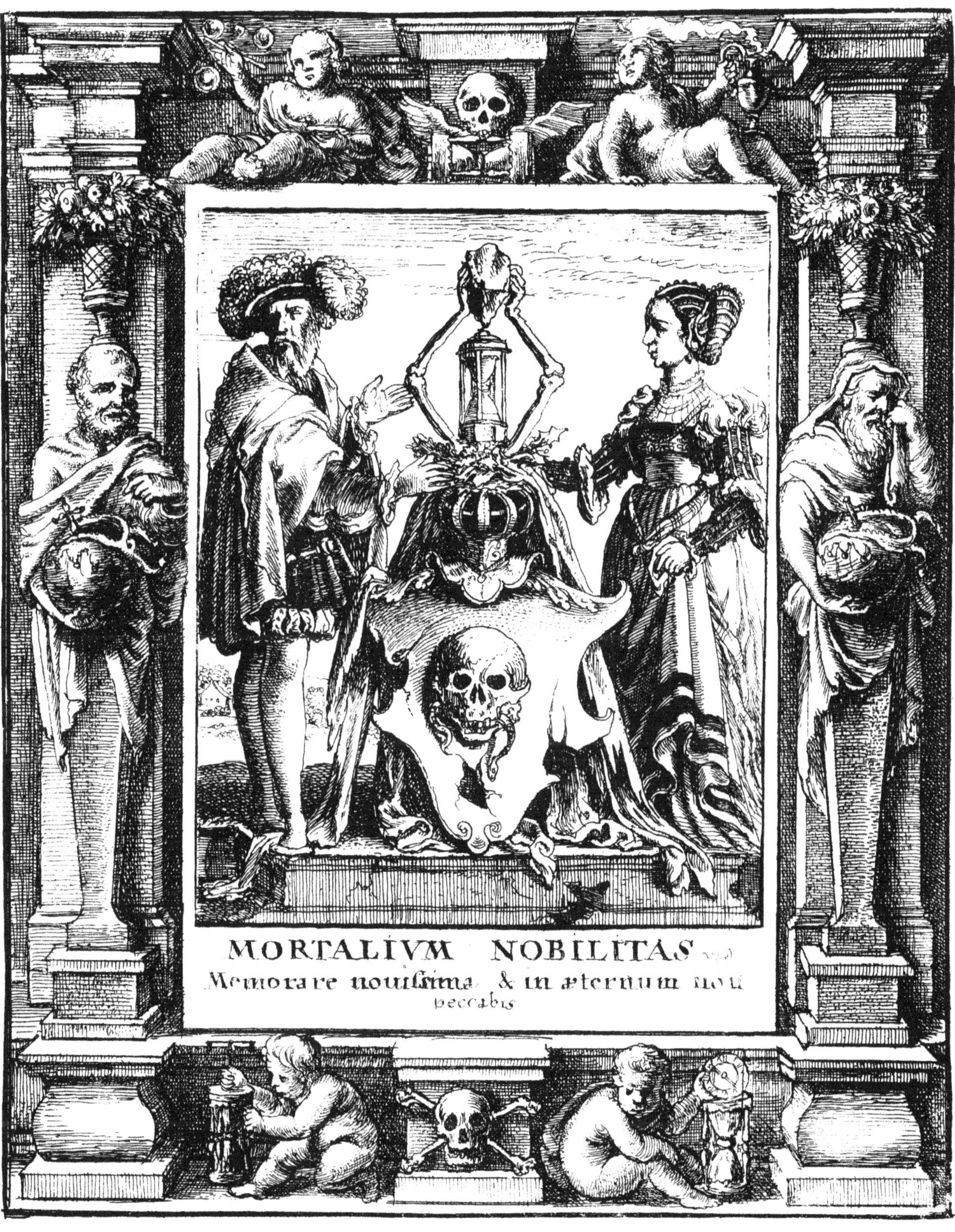

134. The Arms of Death, Wenceslaus Hollar, after
Abraham van Diepenbeeck, after Hans Holbein
(II), 1651.

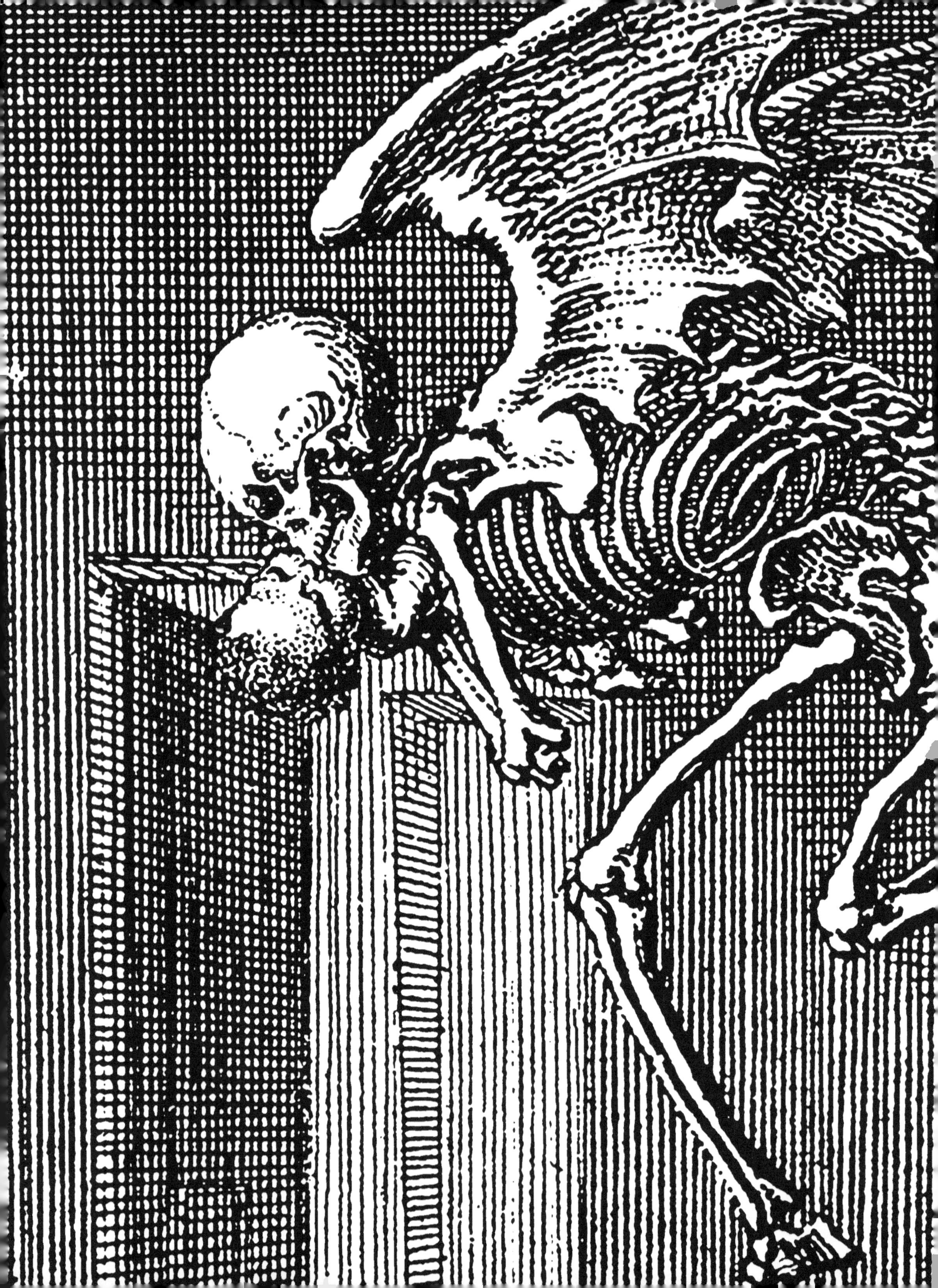

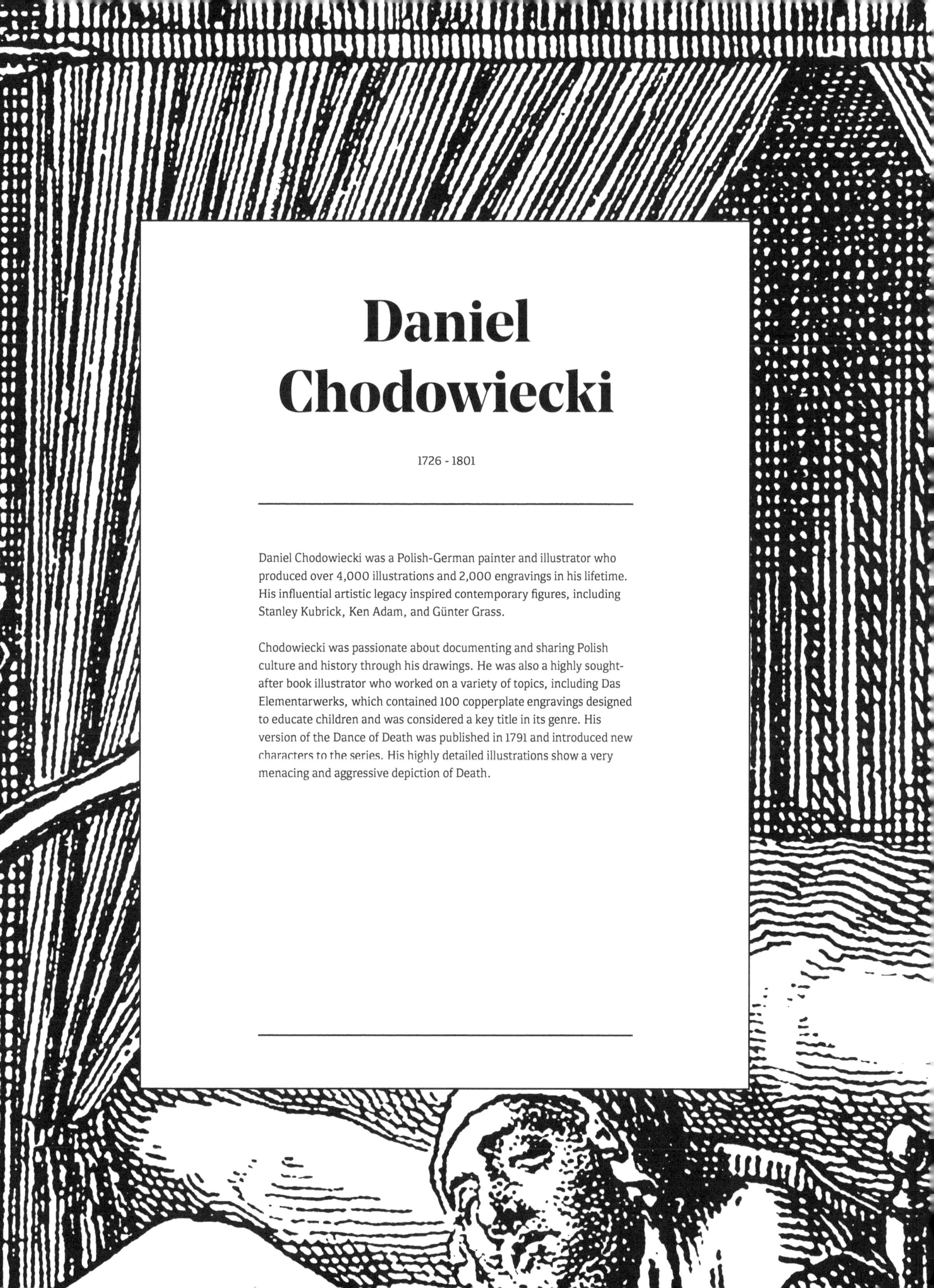

Daniel Chodowiecki

1726 - 1801

Daniel Chodowiecki was a Polish-German painter and illustrator who produced over 4,000 illustrations and 2,000 engravings in his lifetime. His influential artistic legacy inspired contemporary figures, including Stanley Kubrick, Ken Adam, and Günter Grass.

Chodowiecki was passionate about documenting and sharing Polish culture and history through his drawings. He was also a highly sought-after book illustrator who worked on a variety of topics, including Das Elementarwerks, which contained 100 copperplate engravings designed to educate children and was considered a key title in its genre. His version of the Dance of Death was published in 1791 and introduced new characters to the series. His highly detailed illustrations show a very menacing and aggressive depiction of Death.

135

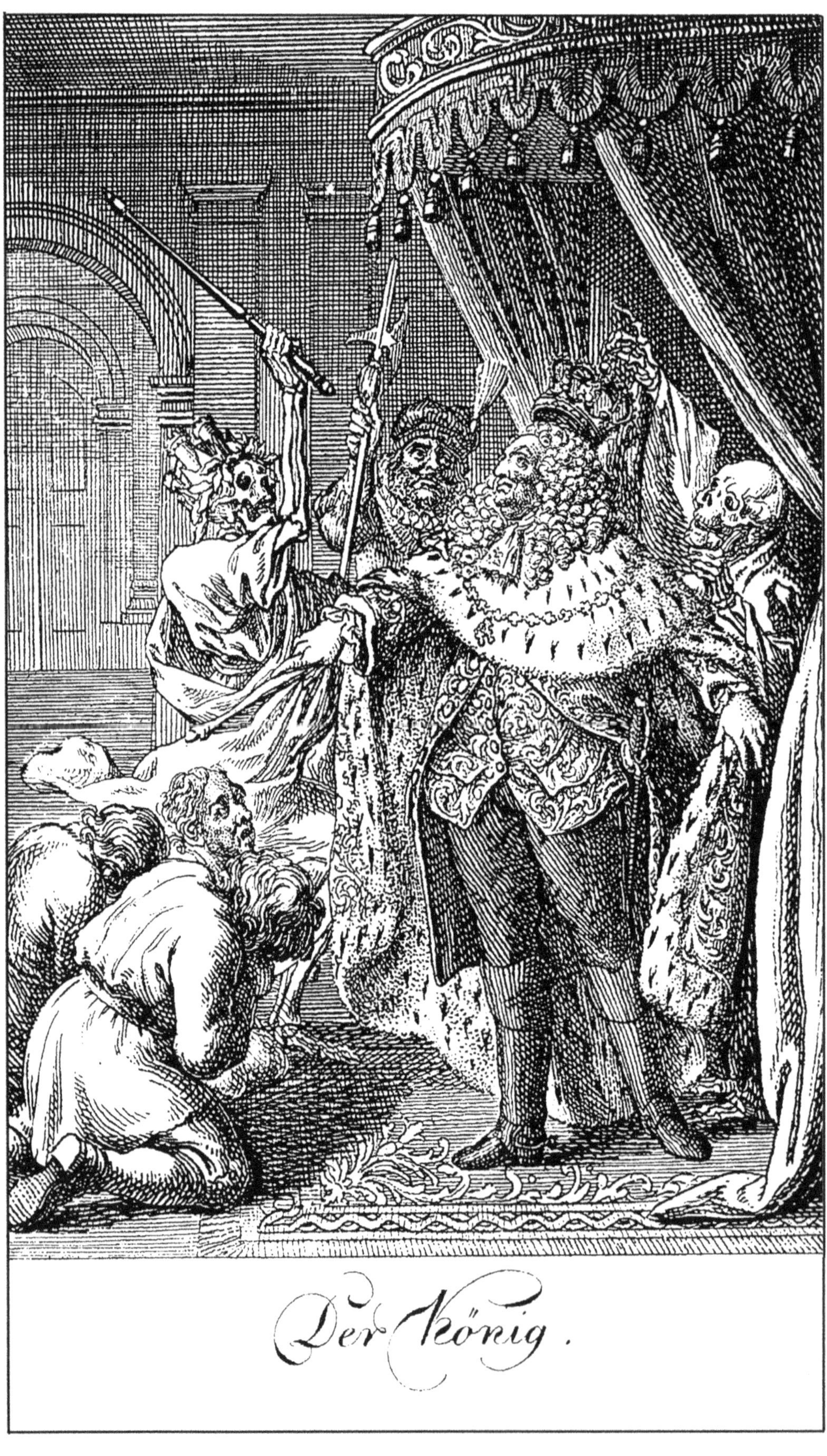

135. The dance of death– the king. Etching by
D.–N. Chodowiecki, 1791, after himself.

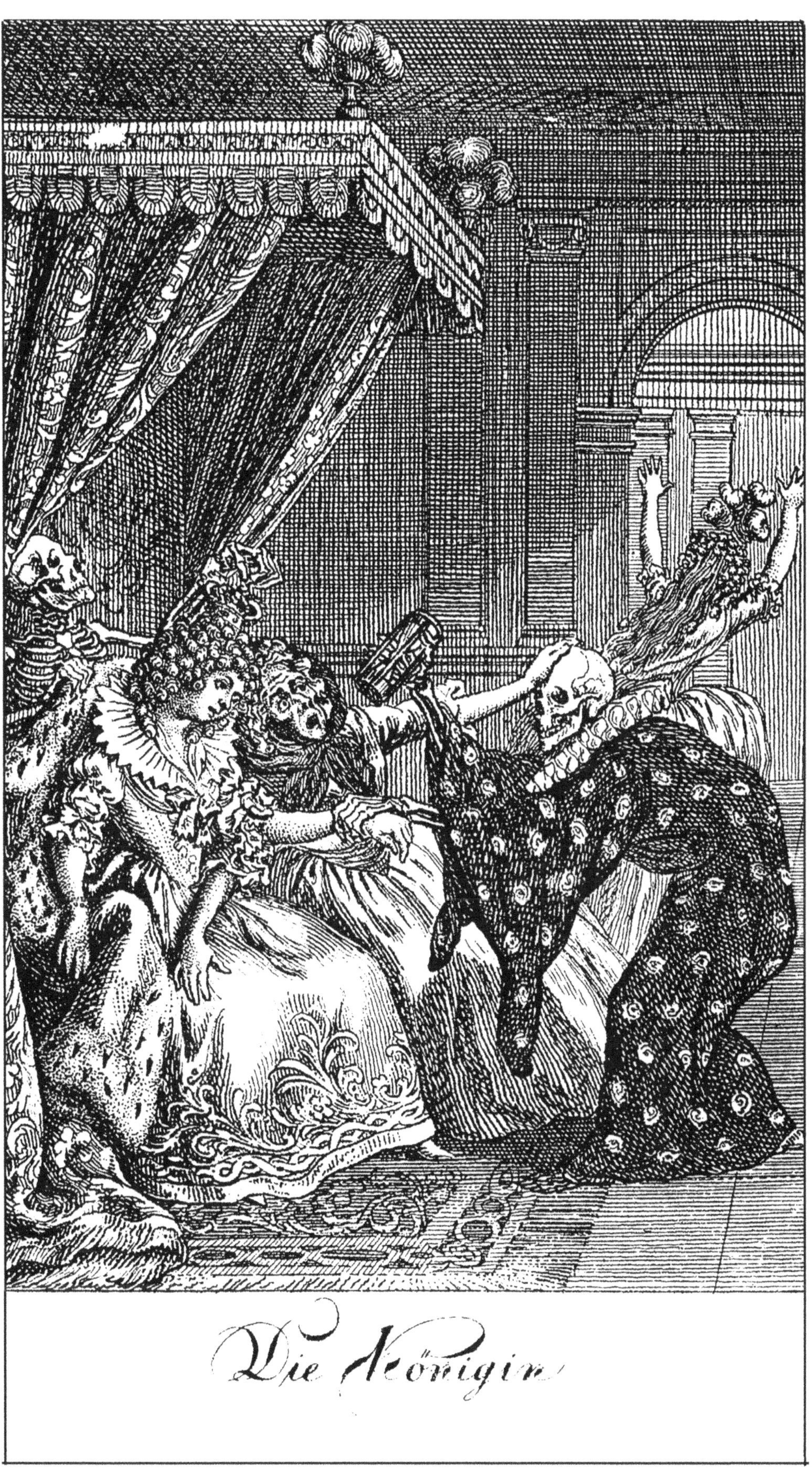

136. The dance of death– the queen. Etching by
D.–N. Chodowiecki, 1791, after himself.

137

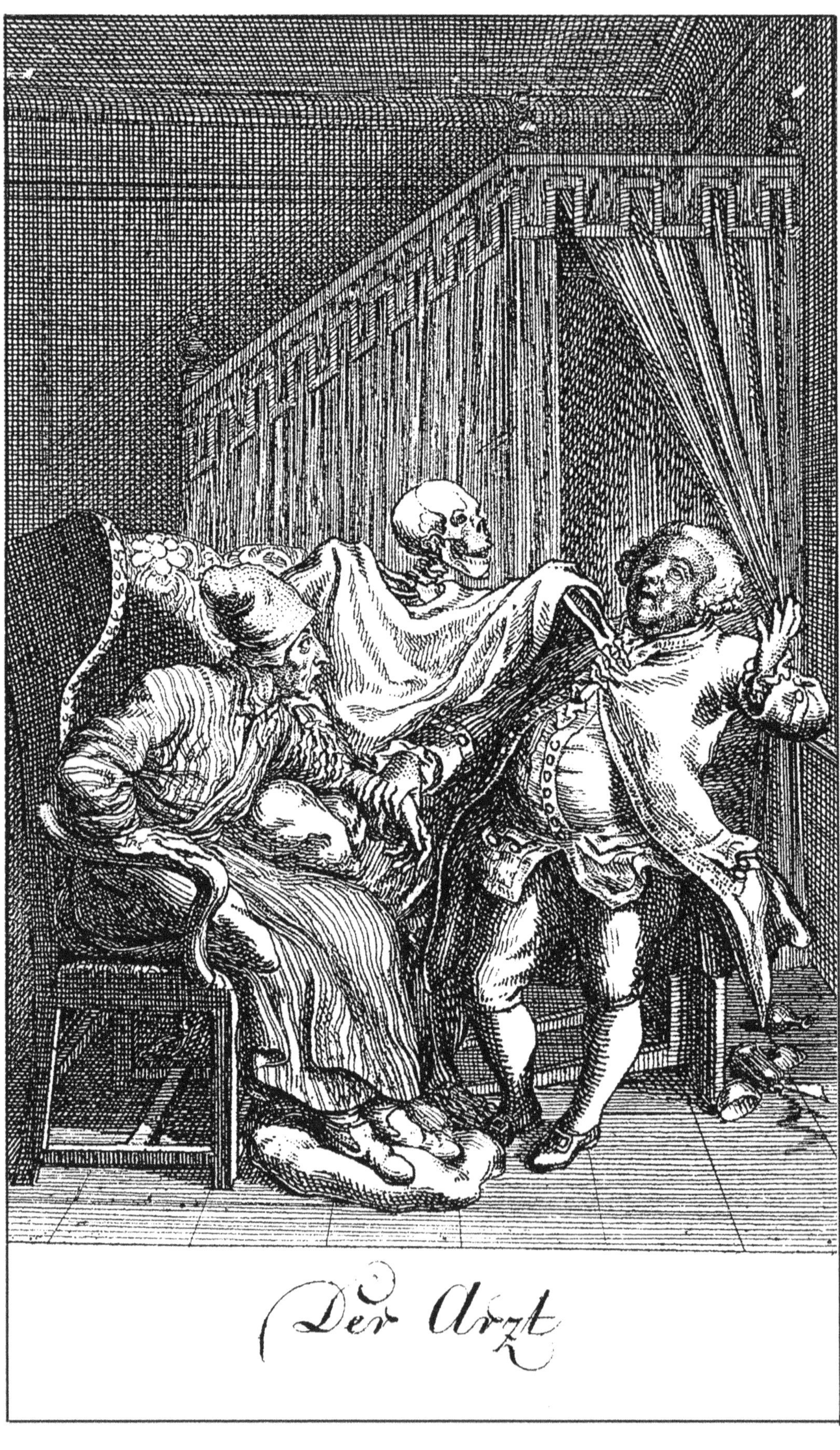

137. The Dance of Deat and the Doctor. Etching
by D.–N. Chodowiecki, 1791, after himself.

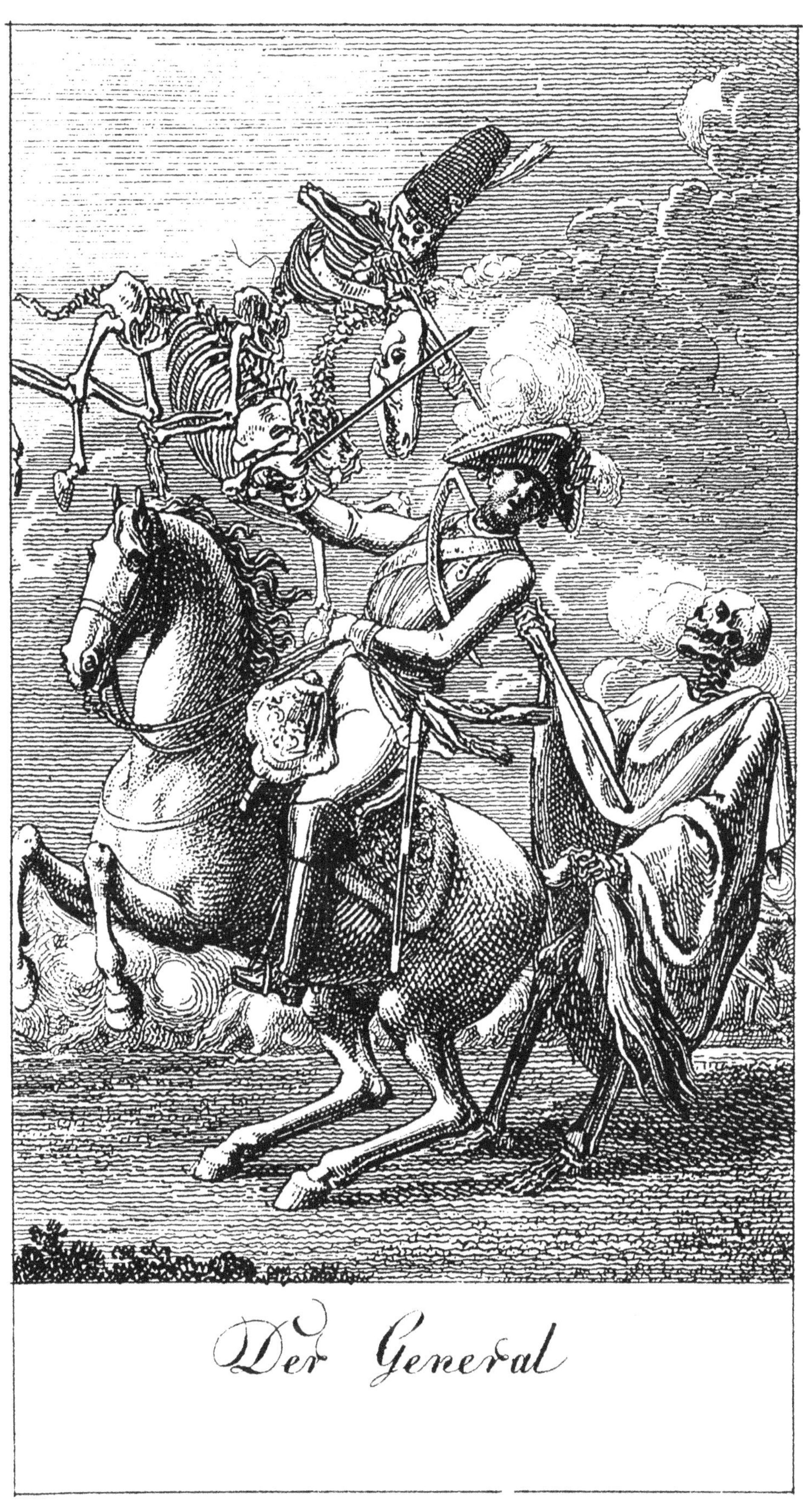

138. The dance of death– the general. Etching
by D.–N. Chodowiecki, 1791, after himself.

139

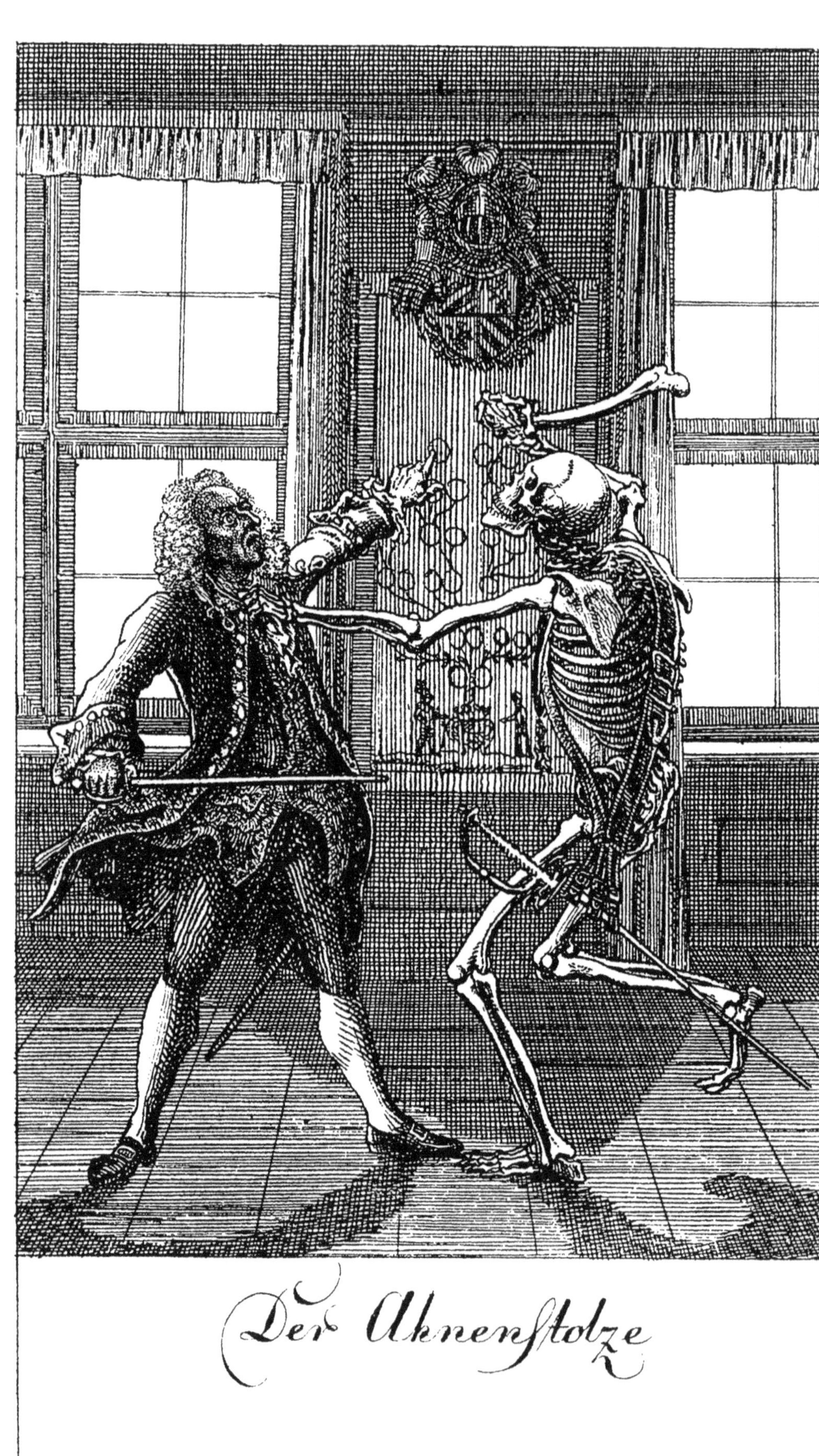

139. The dance of death– death and the man
who prides himself on his ancestry. Etching by
D.–N. Chodowiecki, 1791, after himself.

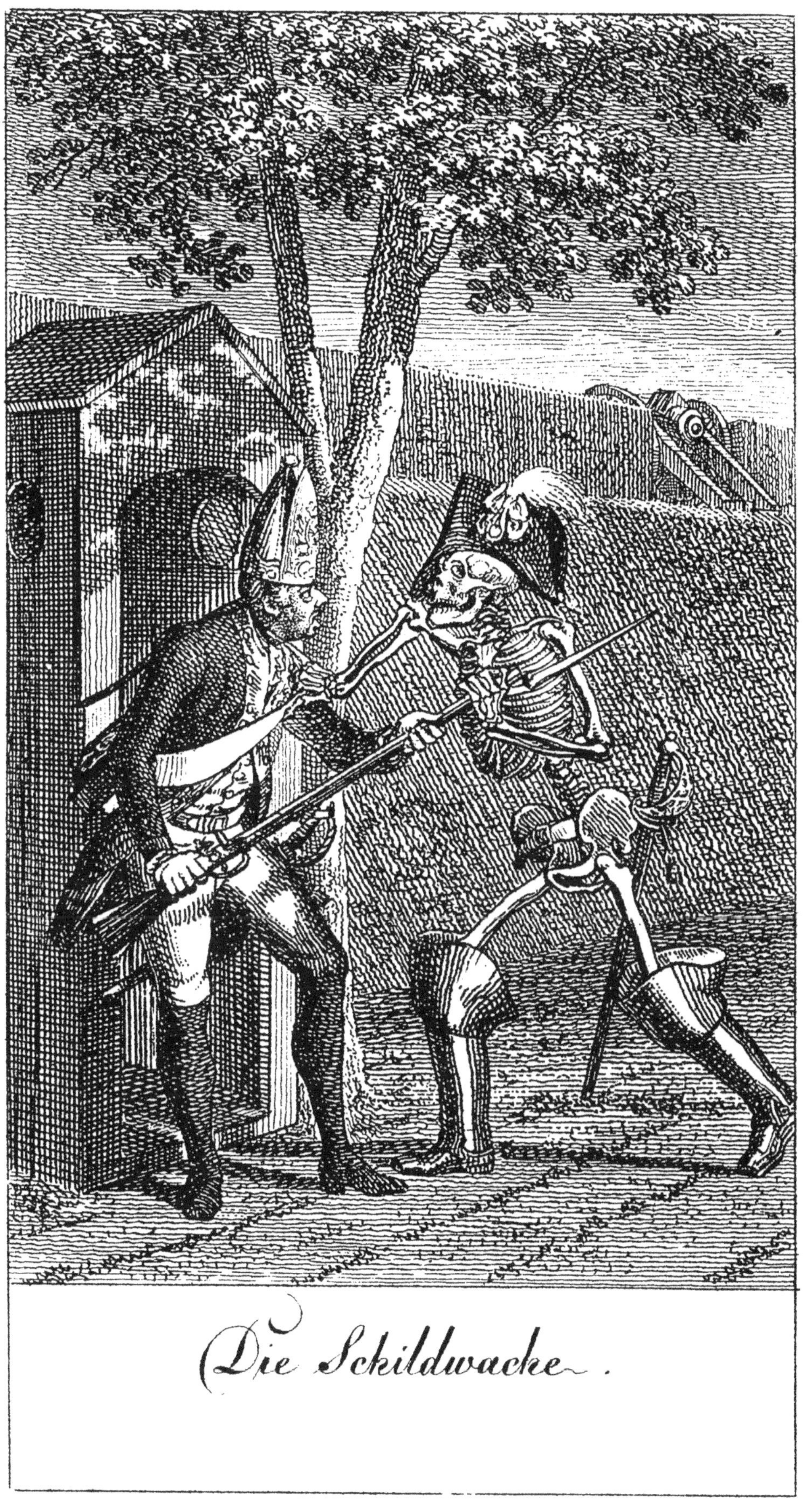

140. The dance of death– the sentinel. Etching
by D.–N. Chodowiecki, 1791, after himself.

141

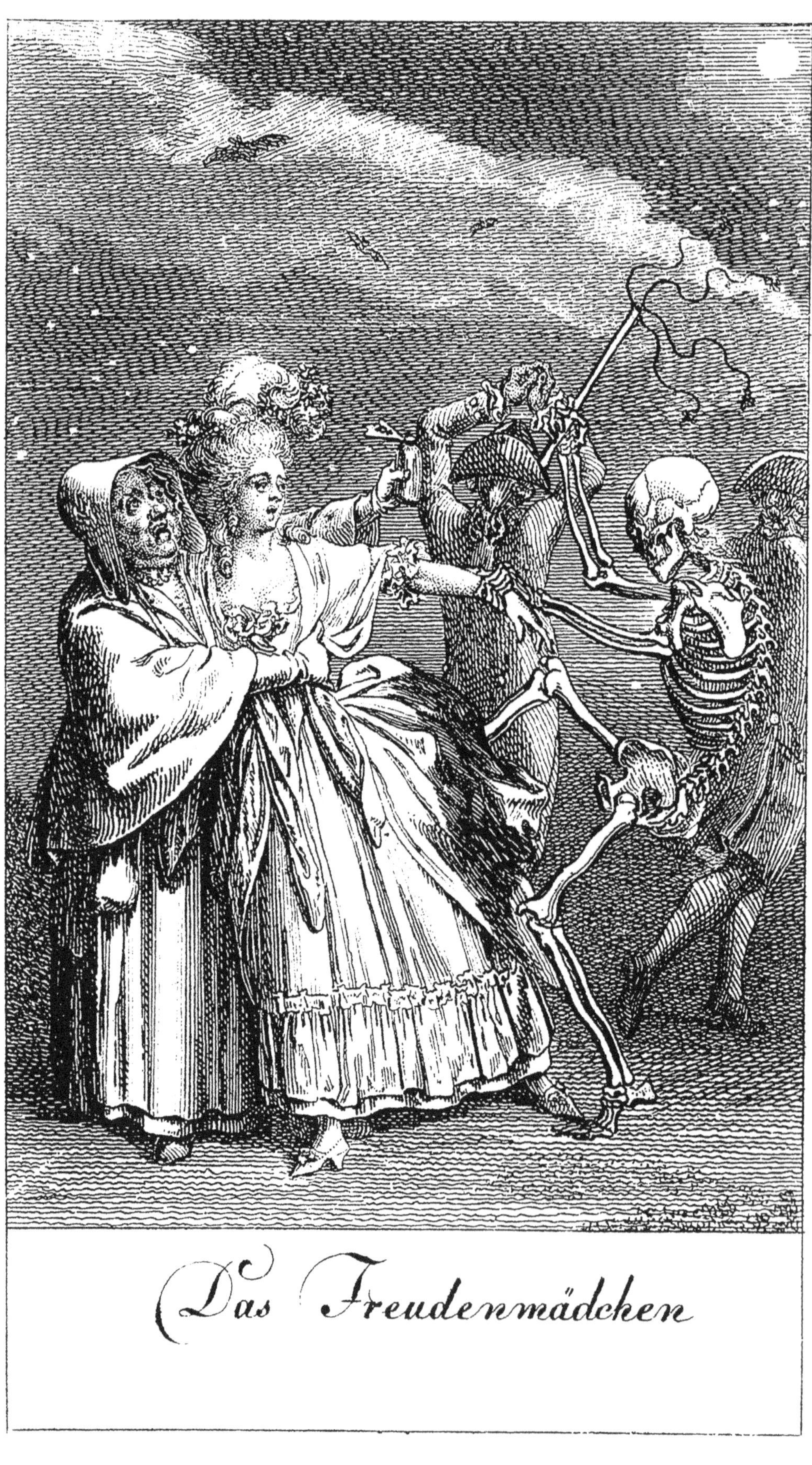

141. The dance of death— death and the
prostitute. Etching by D.–N. Chodowiecki, 1791,
after himself.

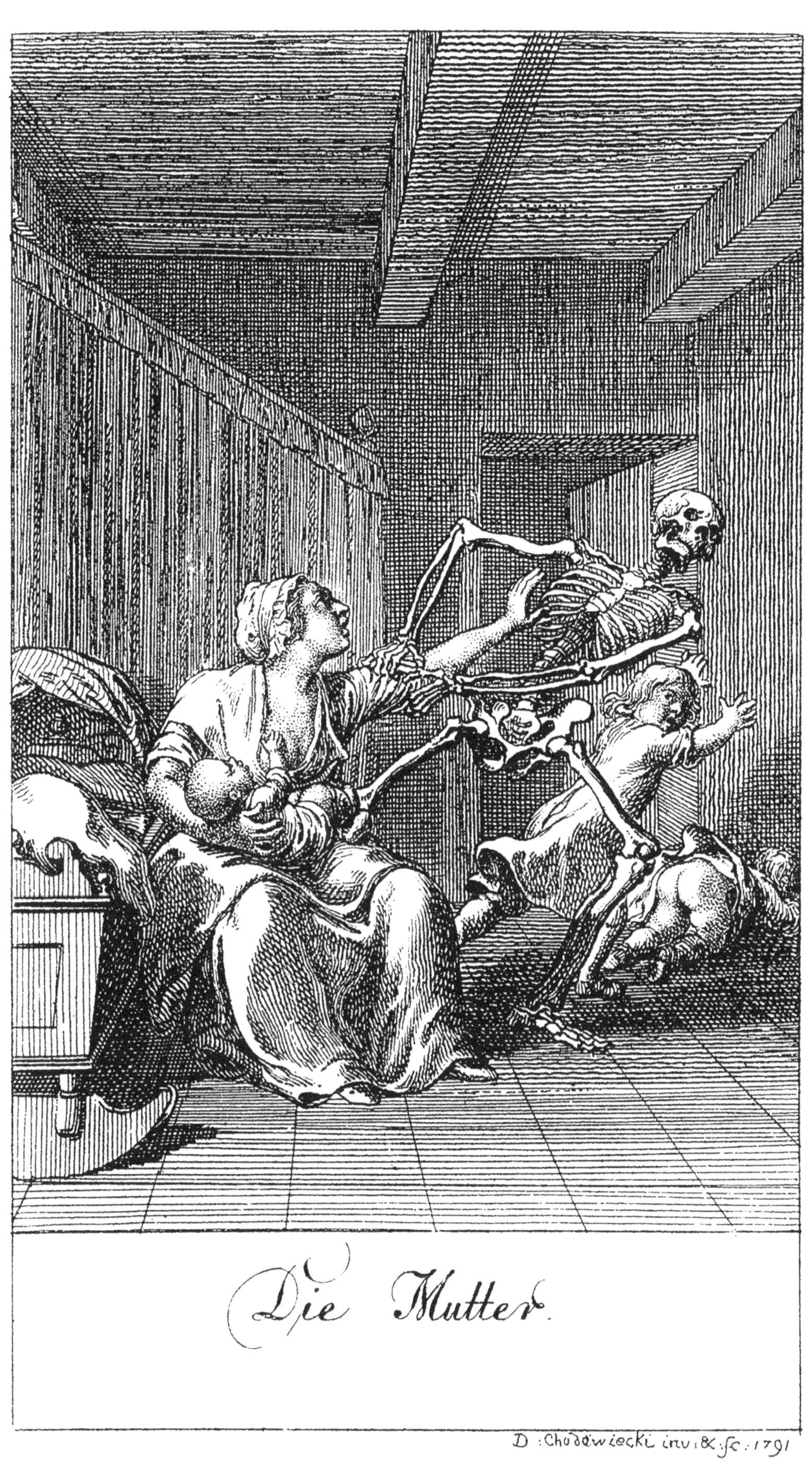

142. The dance of death– death and the mother.
Etching by D.–N. Chodowiecki, 1791, after
himself.

143

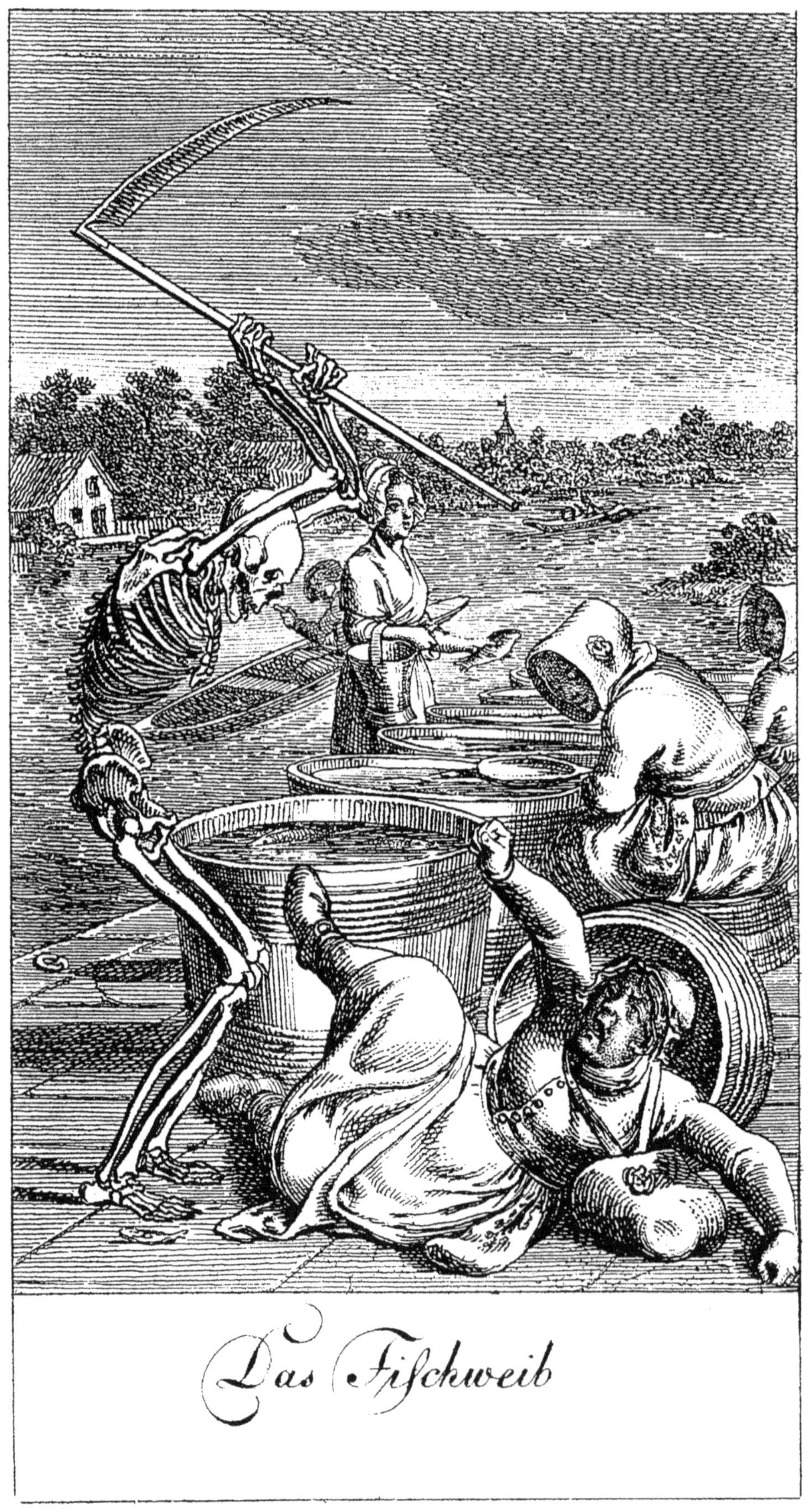

143. The dance of death– death and the
fishwife. Etching by D.–N. Chodowiecki, 1791,
after himself.

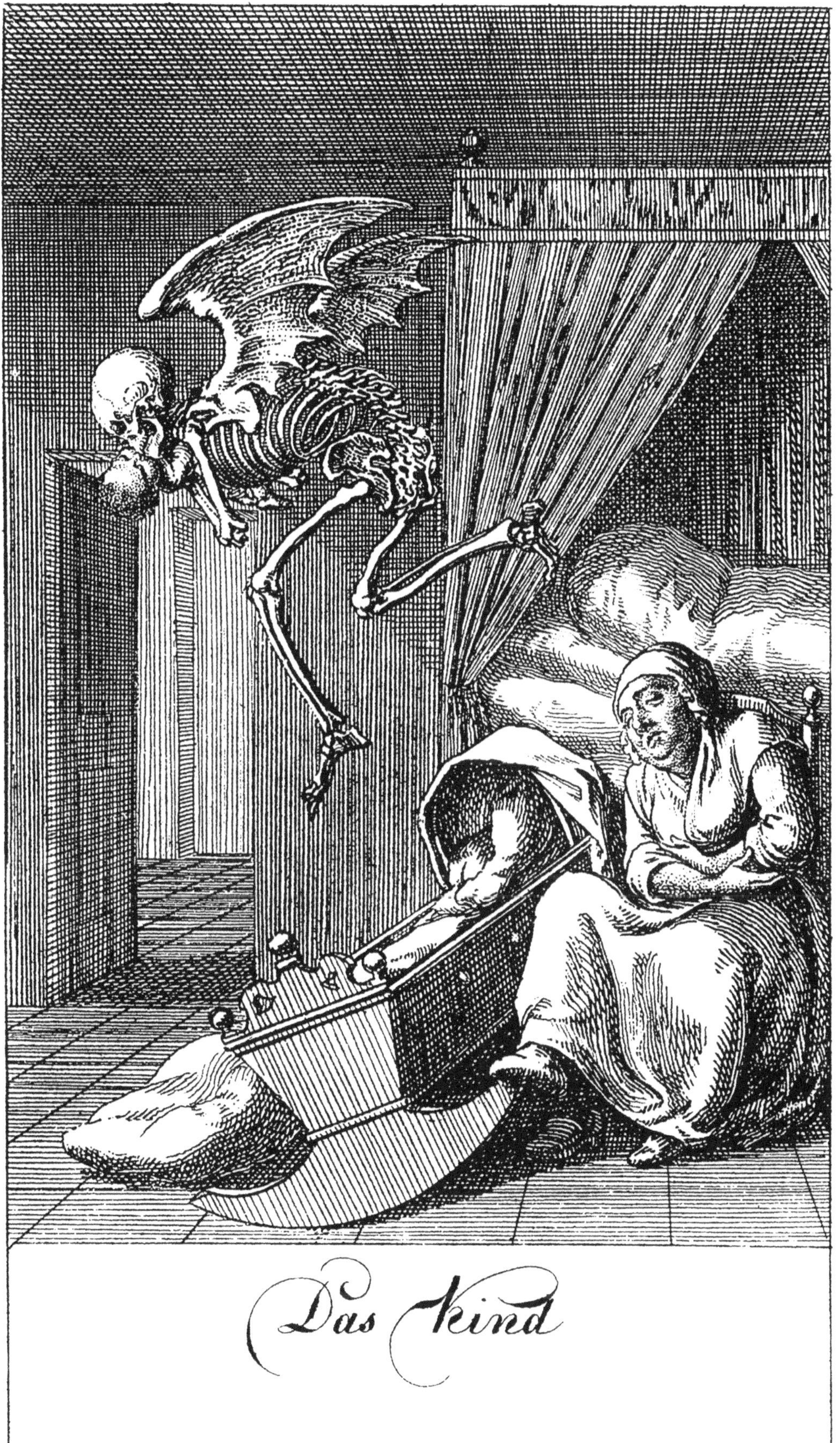

144. The dance of death– death and the child.
Etching by D.–N. Chodowiecki, 1791.

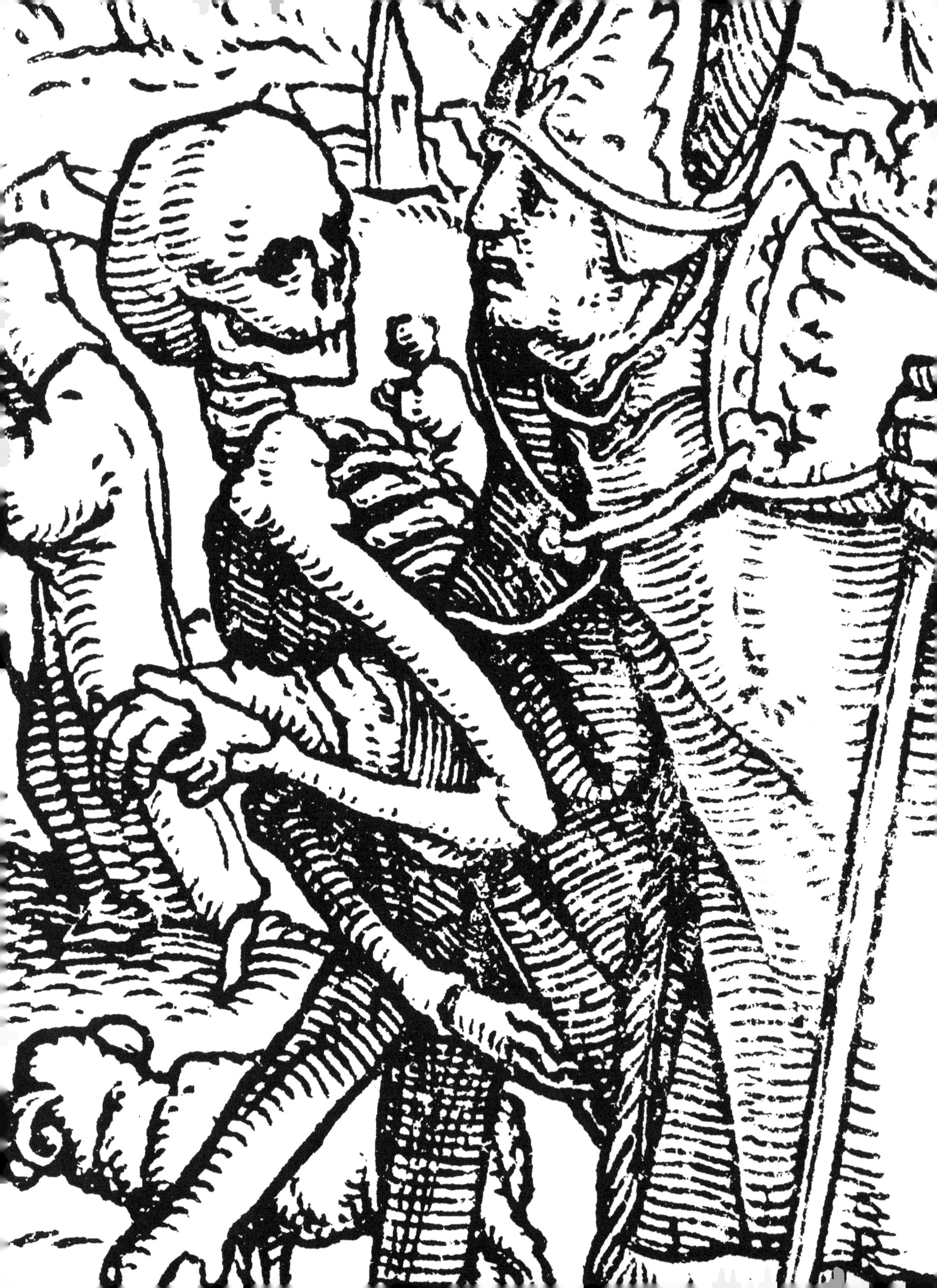

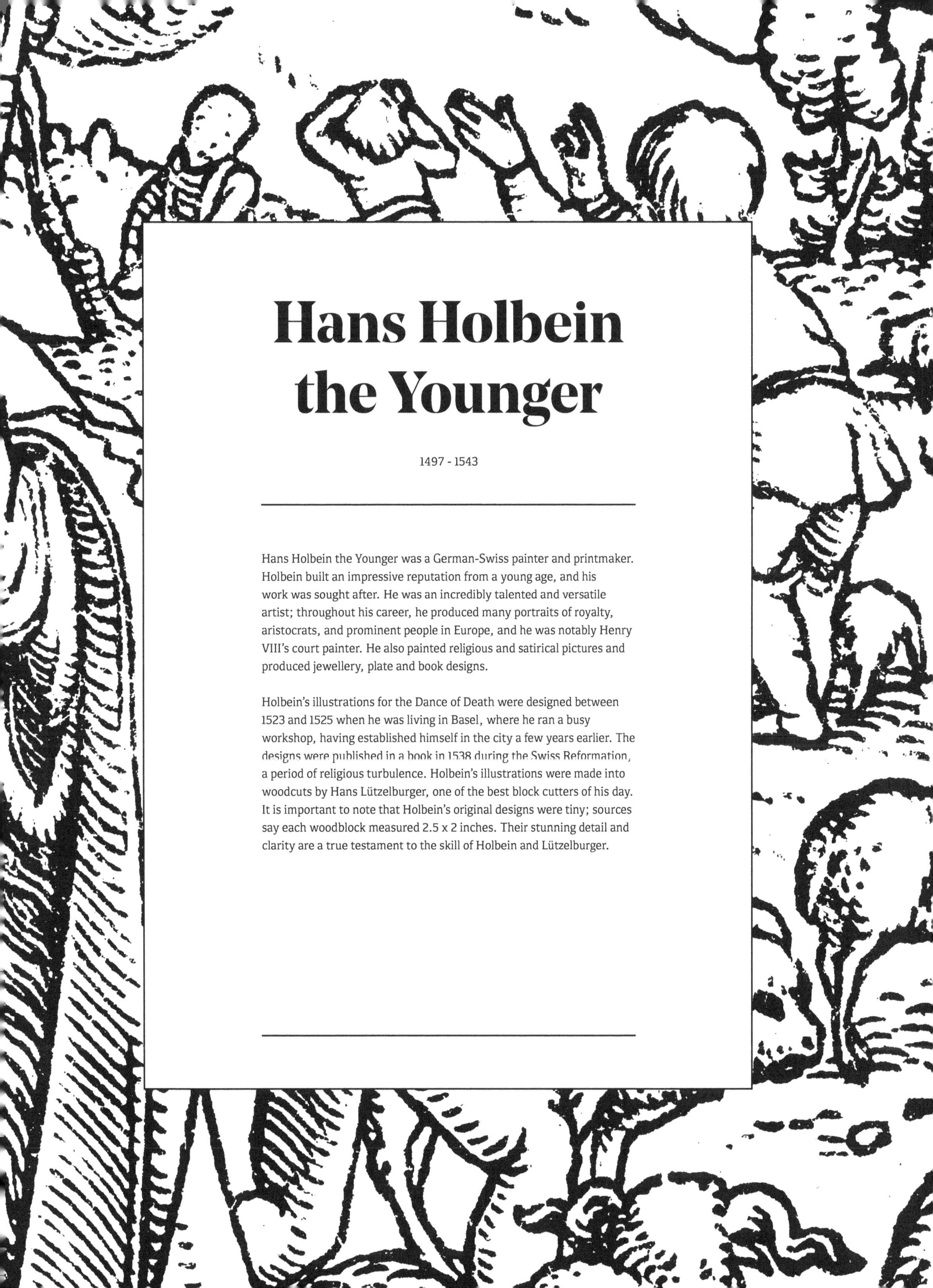

Hans Holbein the Younger

1497 - 1543

Hans Holbein the Younger was a German-Swiss painter and printmaker. Holbein built an impressive reputation from a young age, and his work was sought after. He was an incredibly talented and versatile artist; throughout his career, he produced many portraits of royalty, aristocrats, and prominent people in Europe, and he was notably Henry VIII's court painter. He also painted religious and satirical pictures and produced jewellery, plate and book designs.

Holbein's illustrations for the Dance of Death were designed between 1523 and 1525 when he was living in Basel, where he ran a busy workshop, having established himself in the city a few years earlier. The designs were published in a book in 1538 during the Swiss Reformation, a period of religious turbulence. Holbein's illustrations were made into woodcuts by Hans Lützelburger, one of the best block cutters of his day. It is important to note that Holbein's original designs were tiny; sources say each woodblock measured 2.5 x 2 inches. Their stunning detail and clarity are a true testament to the skill of Holbein and Lützelburger.

145

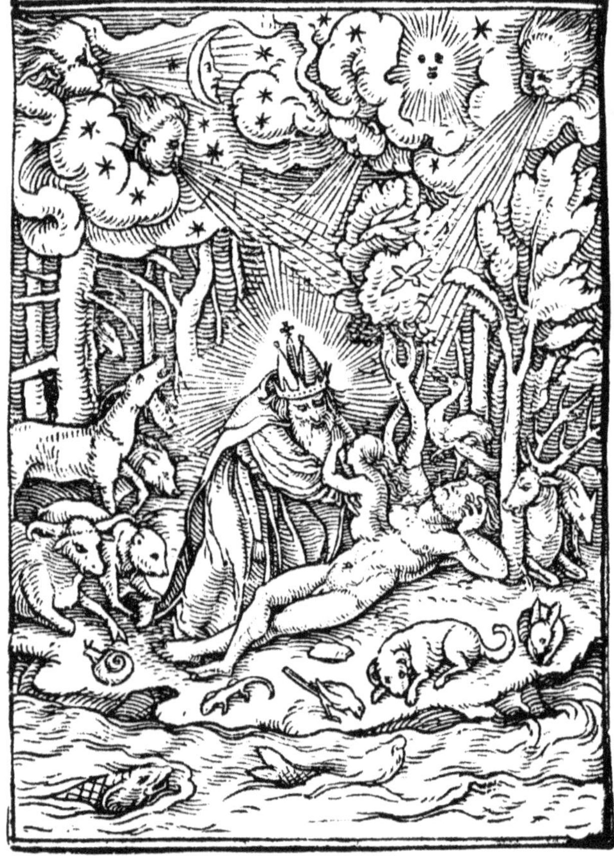

146

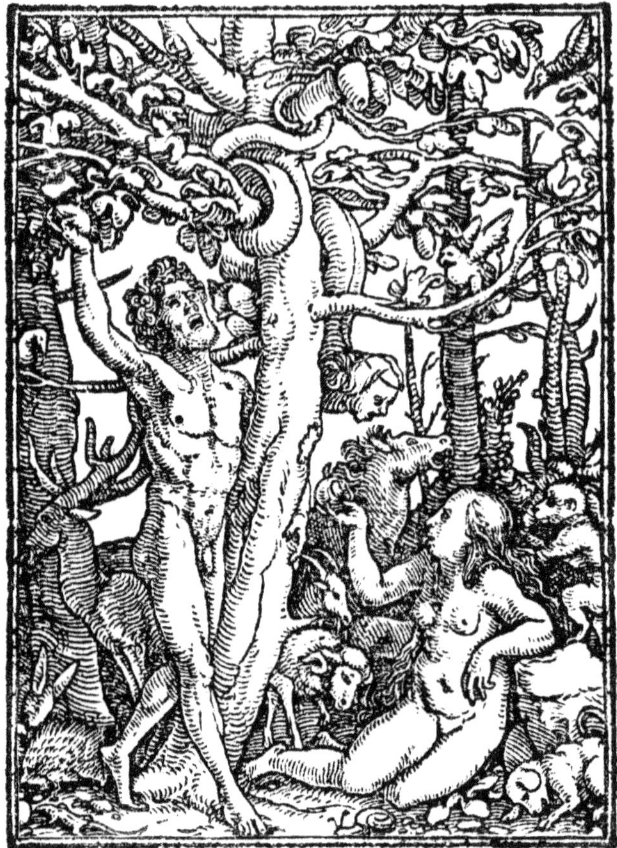

147

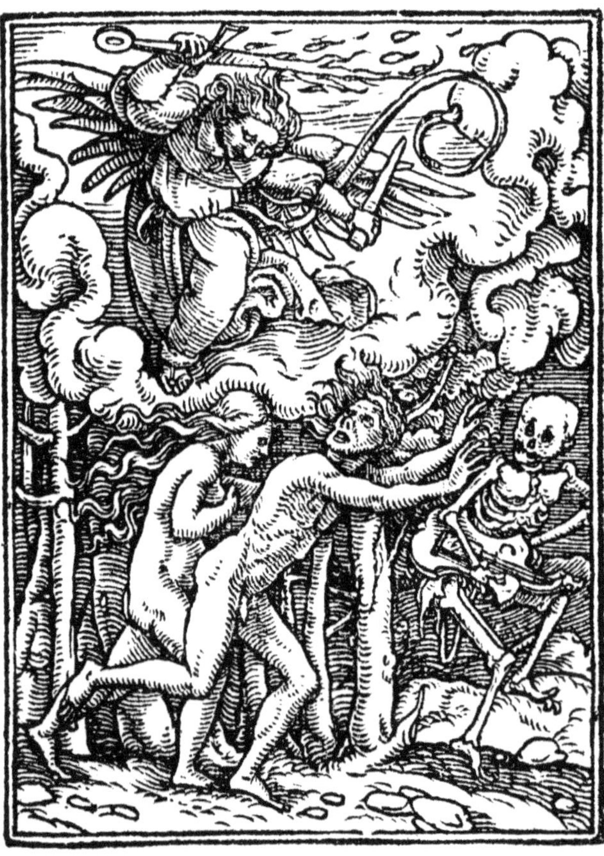

148

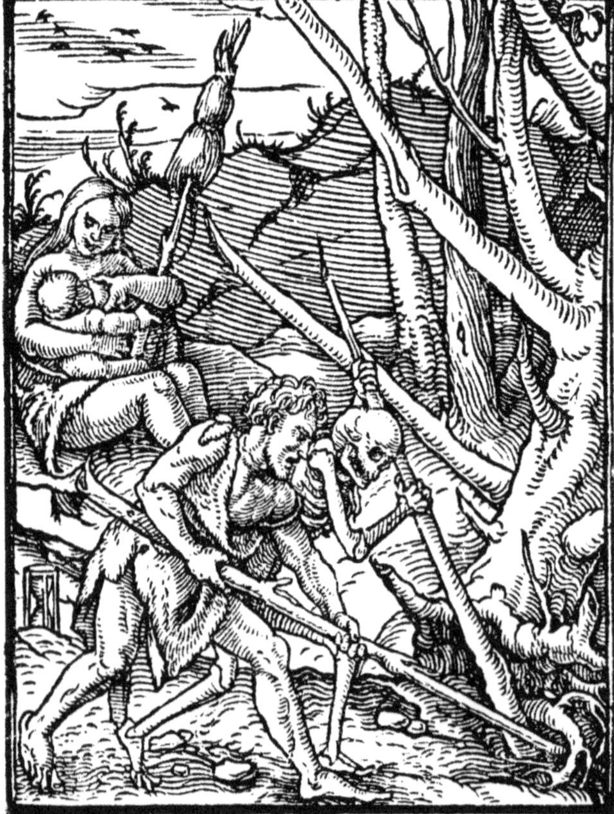

145. Death and the Creation, Hans Holbein the Younger.

146. The Garden of Eden, Hans Holbein (II), 1538.

147. Expulsion from Paradise, Hans Holbein (II), 1538.

148. Death and Adam and Eve, Adam Tilling the Earth, Hans Holbein the Younger.

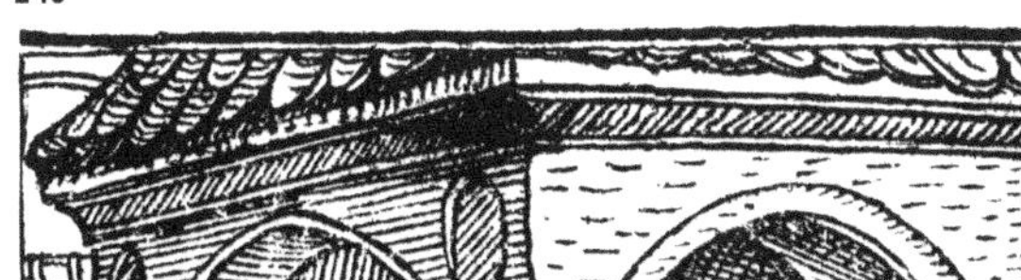

149

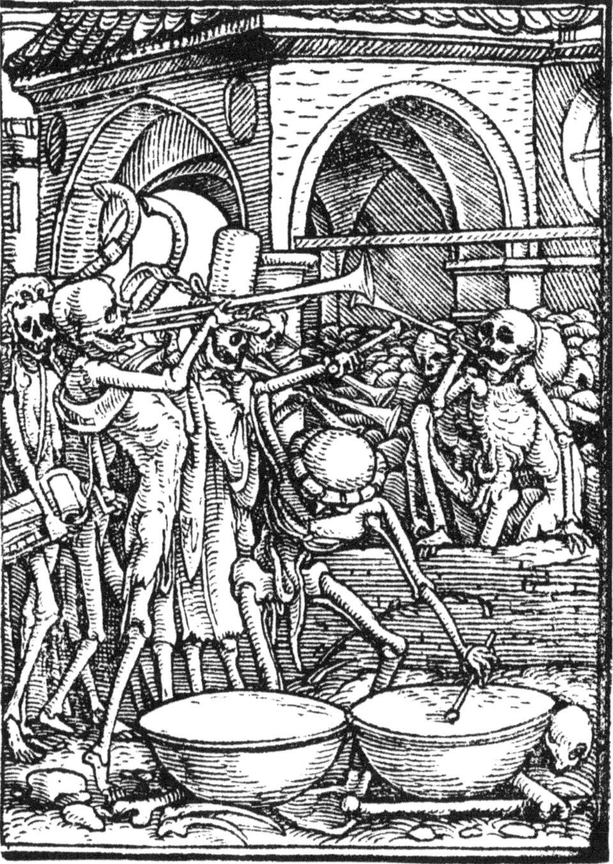

150

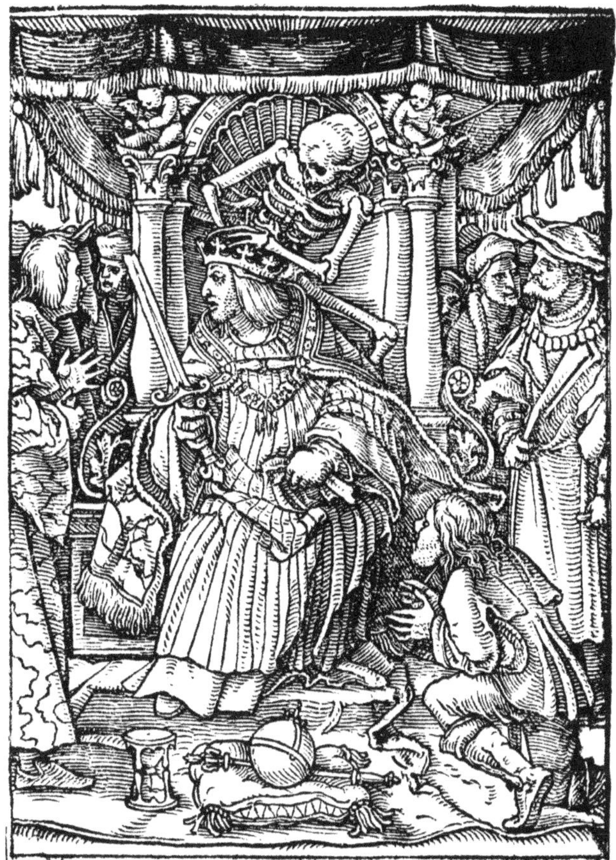

151

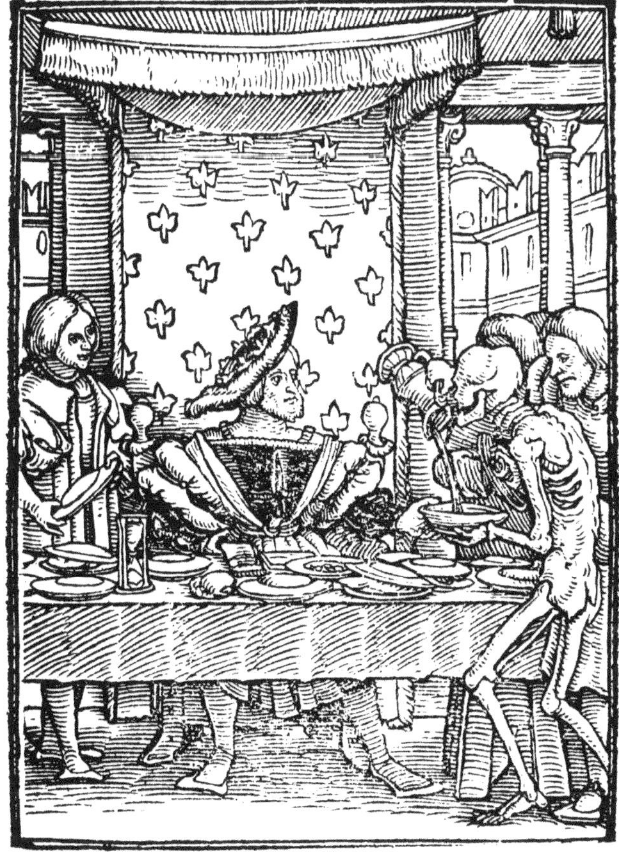

152

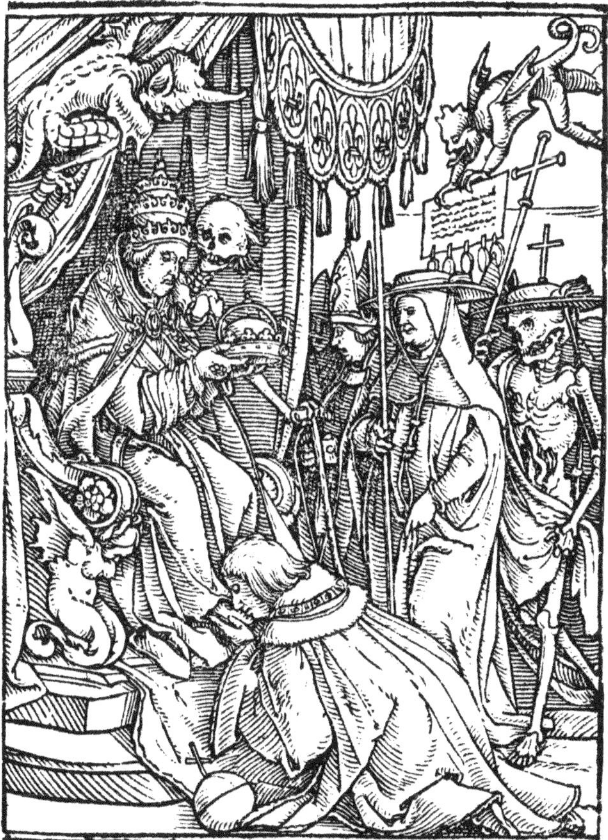

149. The Trumpeters of Death, Hans Holbein the Younger.

150. Death and the Emperor, Hans Holbein the Younger.

151. King and Death, Hans Holbein (II), 1538.

152. Death and the Pope, Hans Holbein the Younger.

153

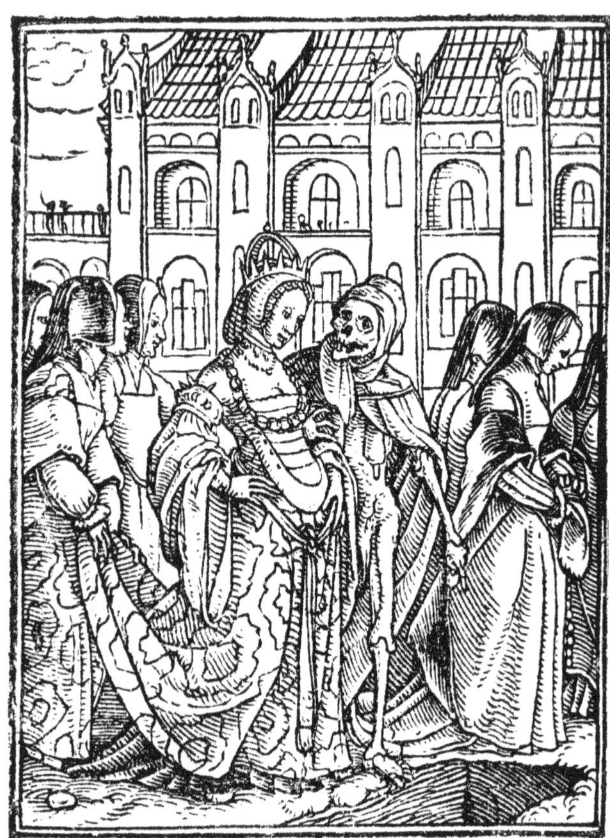

154

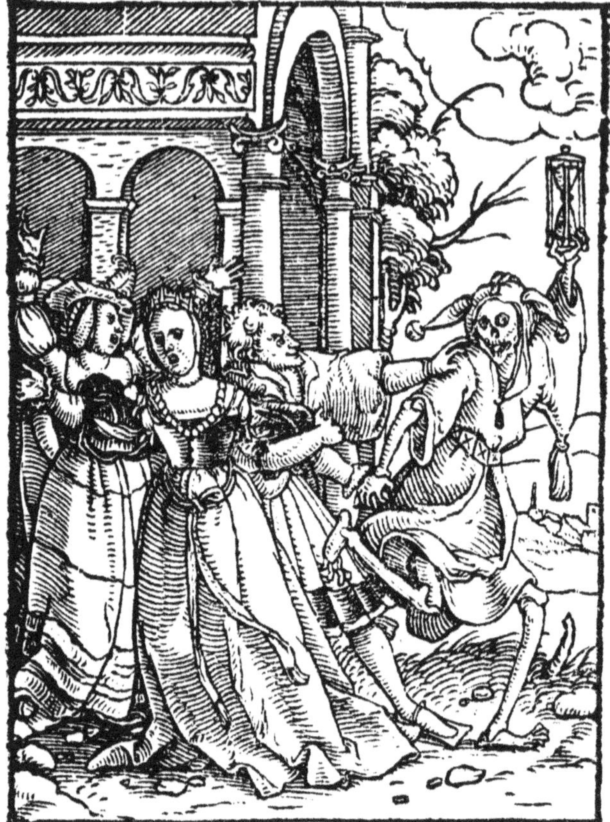

155

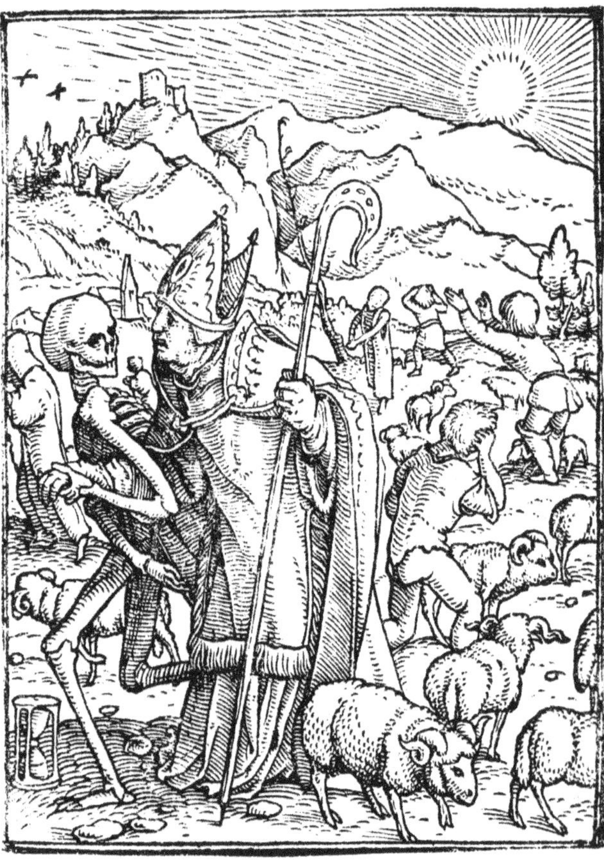

156

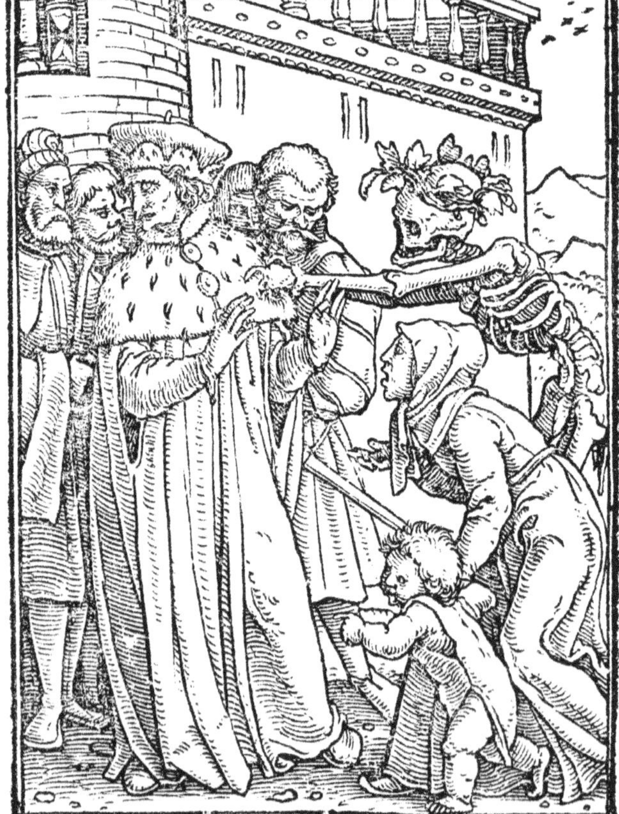

153. Death and the Empress, Hans Holbein the Younger.

154. Queen and Death as Jesta, Hans Holbein (II), 1538.

155. Death and the Bishop, Hans Holbein the Younger.

156. Duke and Death, Hans Holbein (II), 1538.

157

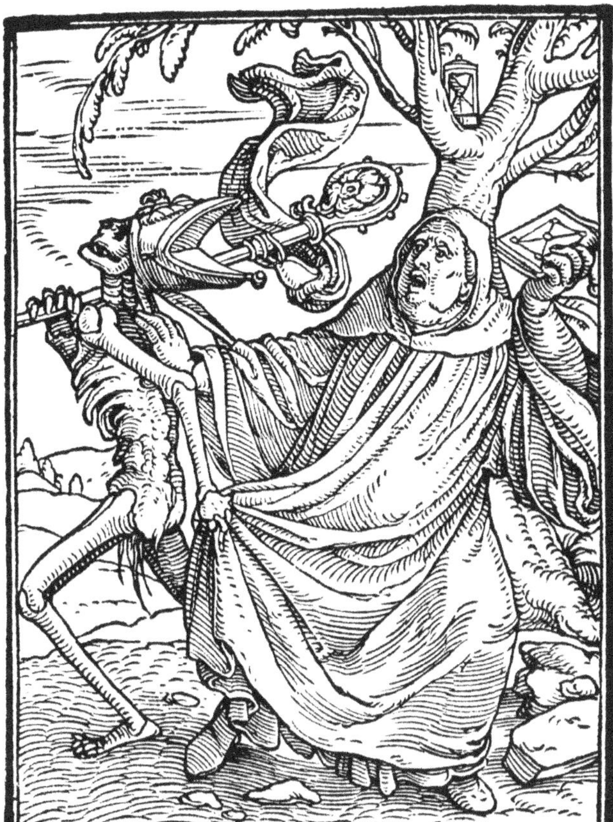

158

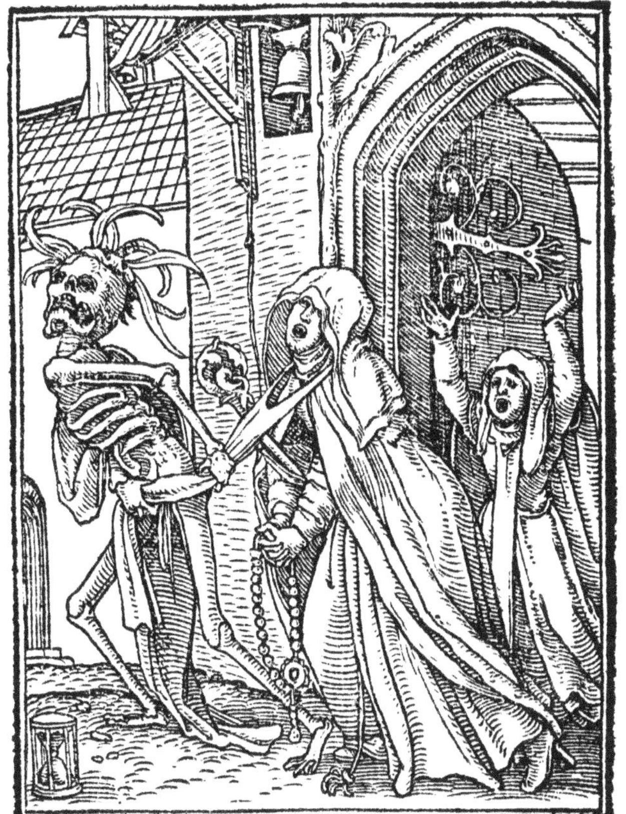

159

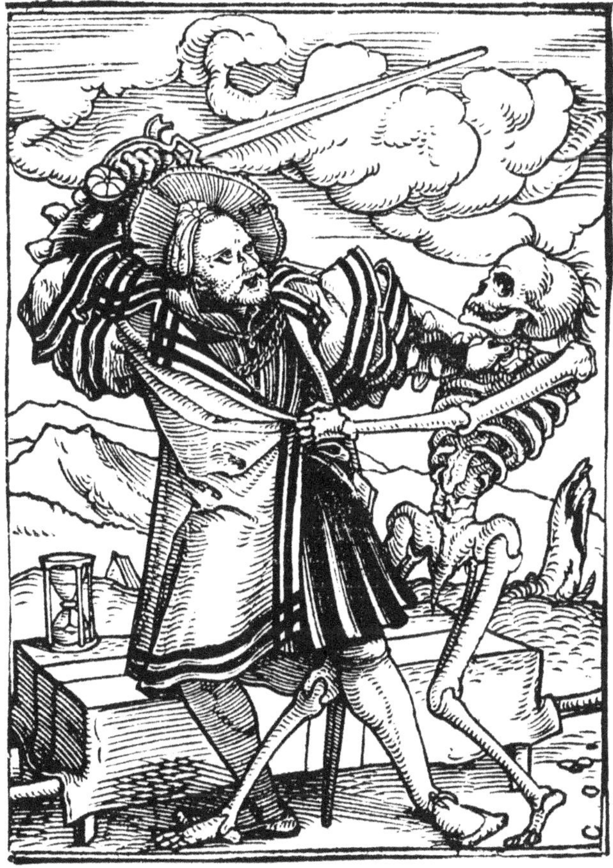

160

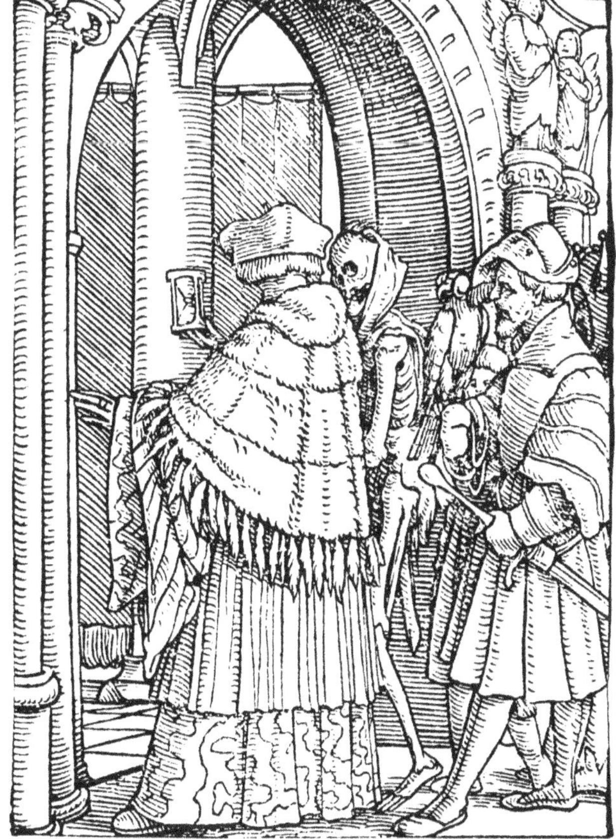

157. Death and the Abbot, Hans Holbein the Younger.

158. Abbess and Death, Hans Holbein (II), 1538.

159. Death and the Nobleman, Hans Holbein the Younger.

160. Death and the Canon, Hans Holbein the Younger.

161

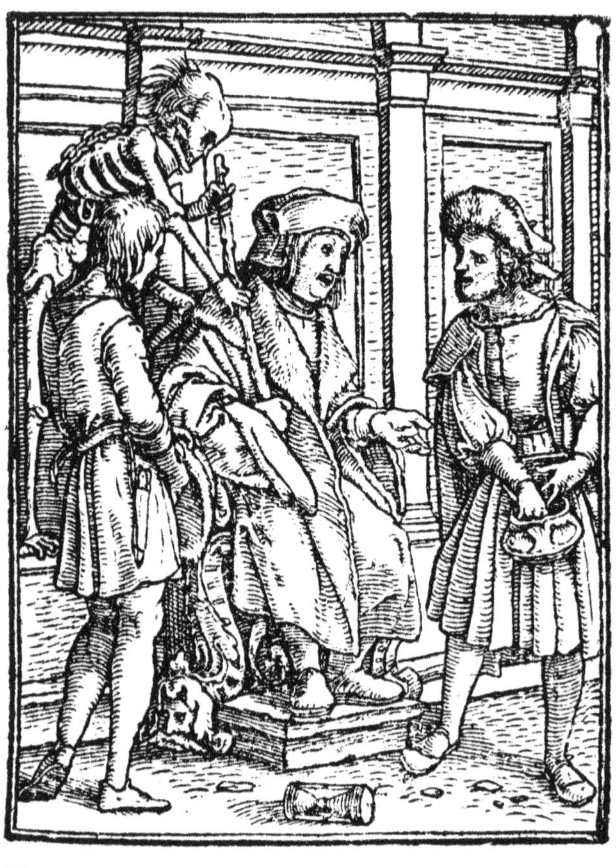

162

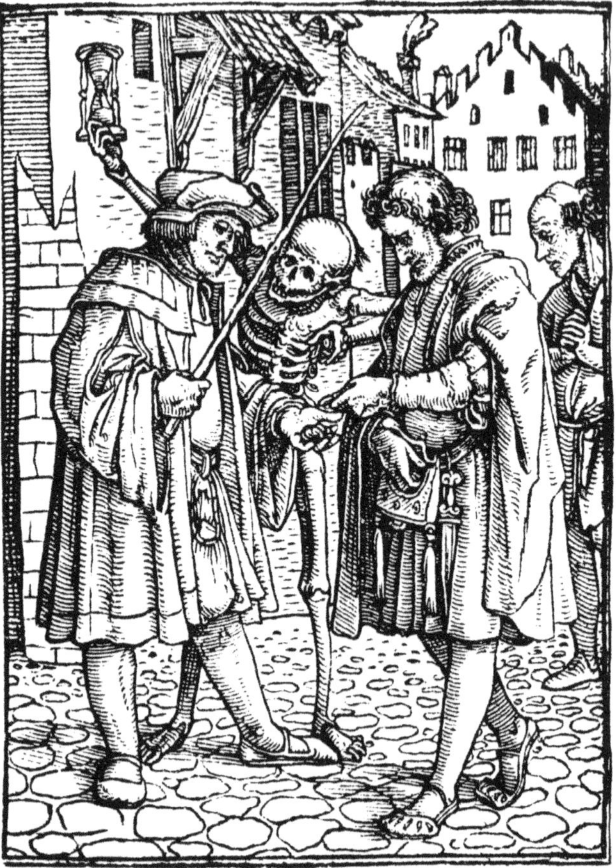

163

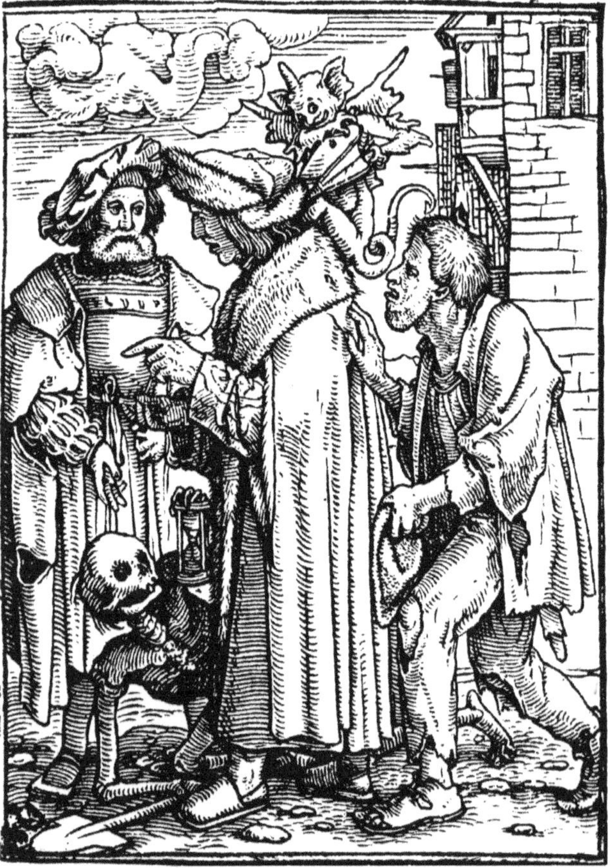

164

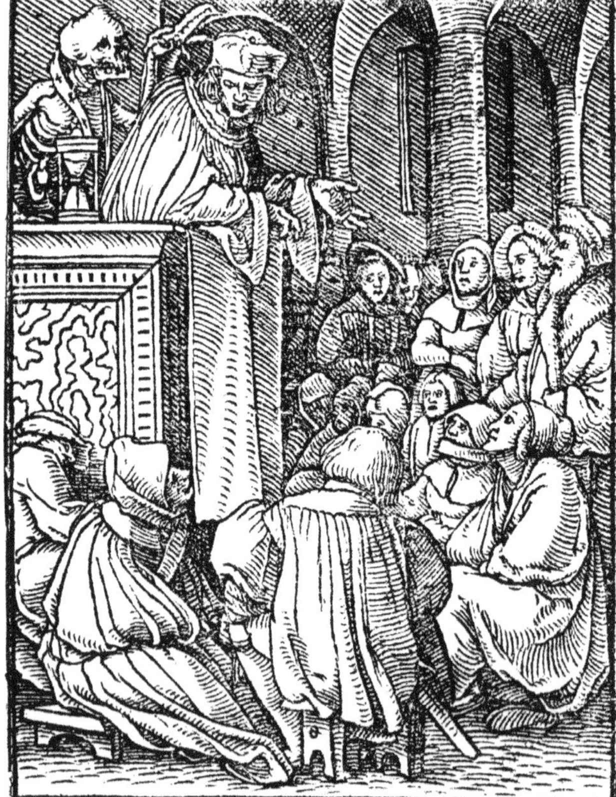

161. Death and the Judge, Hans Holbein the Younger.

162. Death and the Advocate, Hans Holbein the Younger.

163. Death and the Councillor, Hans Holbein the Younger.

164. Death and the Preacher, Hans Holbein the Younger.

165

166

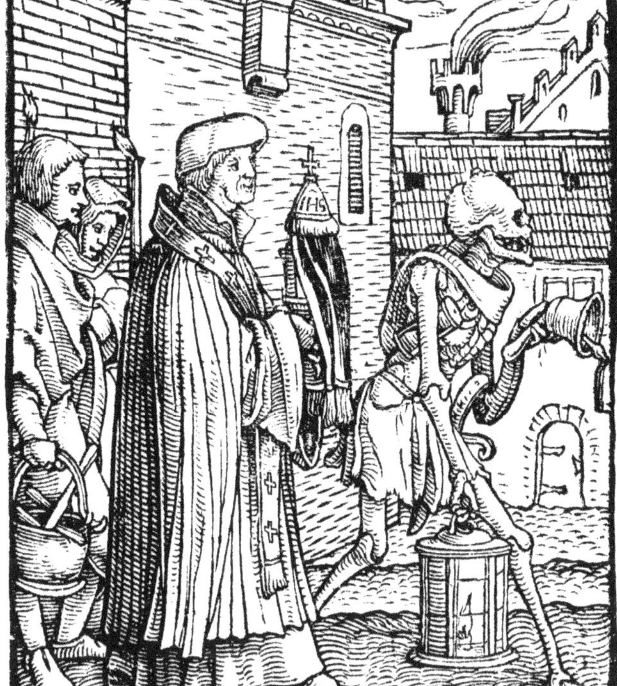

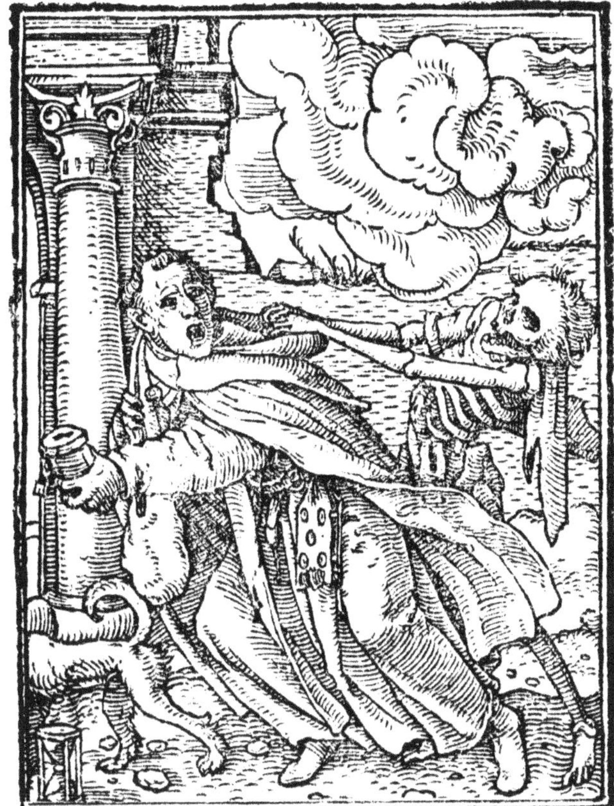

167

168

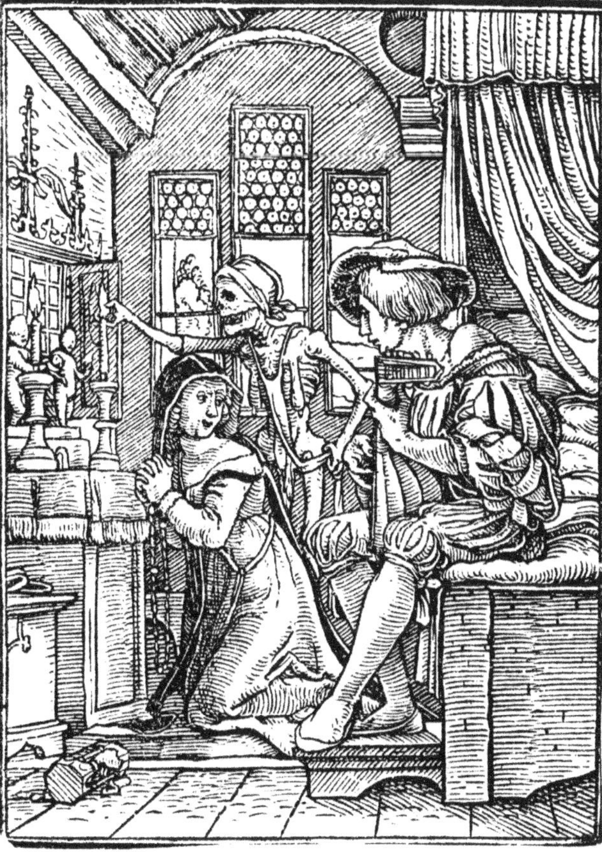

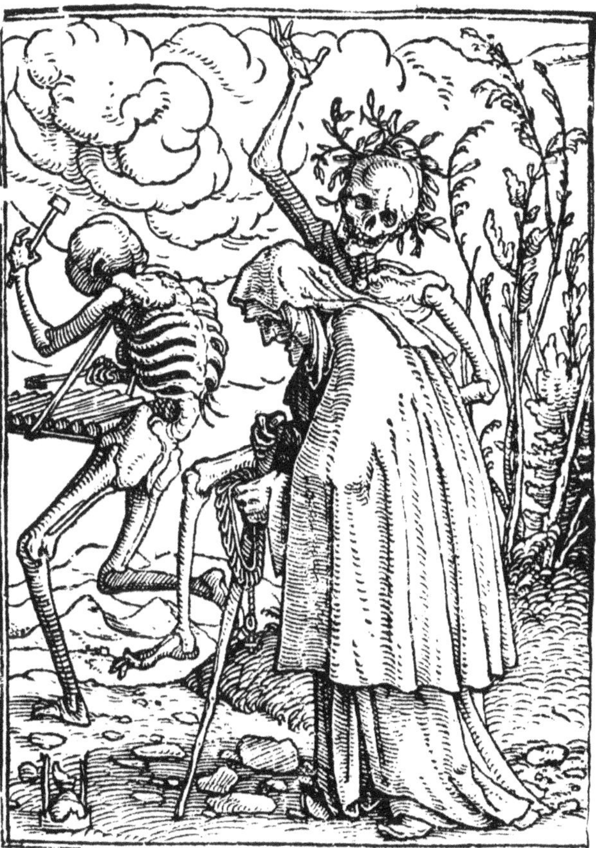

165. Death and the Priest, Hans Holbein the Younger.

166. Death and the Mendicant Friar, Hans Holbein the Younger.

167. Death and the Nun, Hans Holbein the Younger.

168. Death and the Old Woman, Hans Holbein the Younger.

169

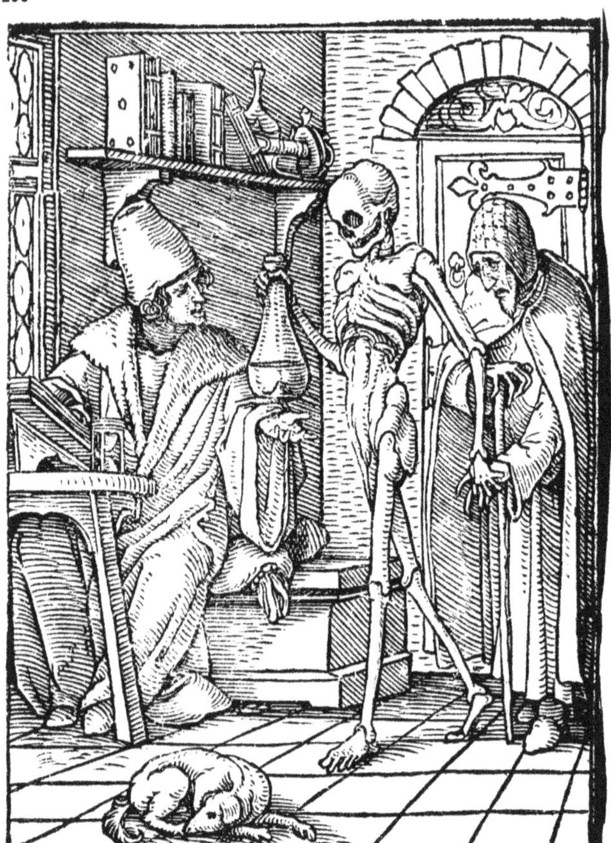

170

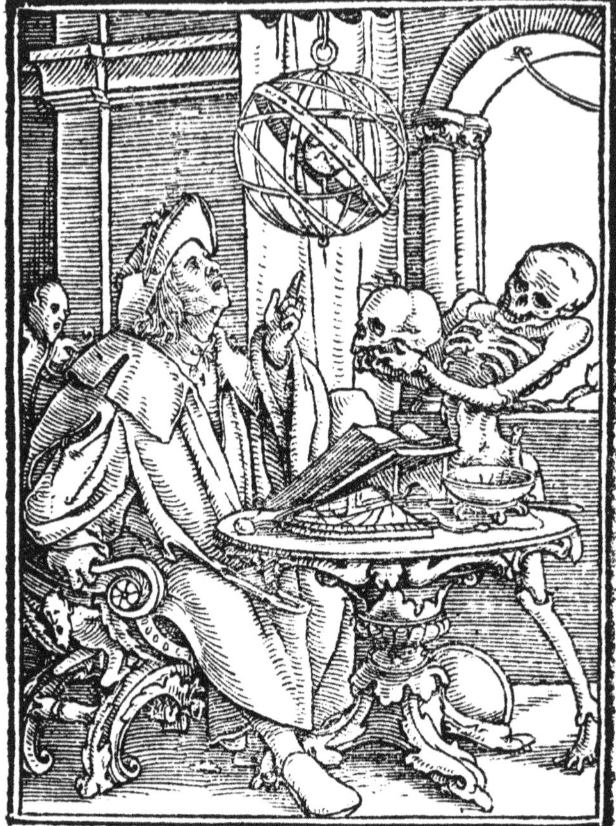

171

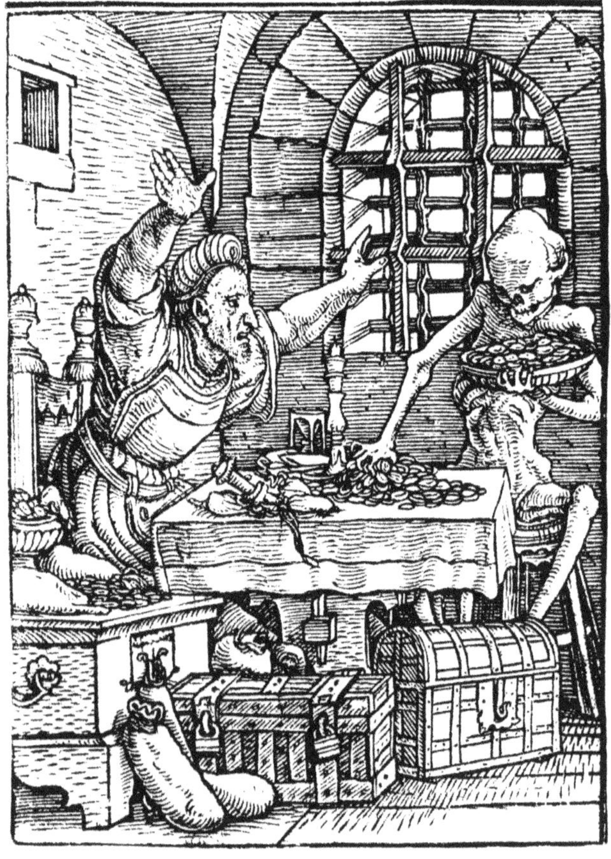

172

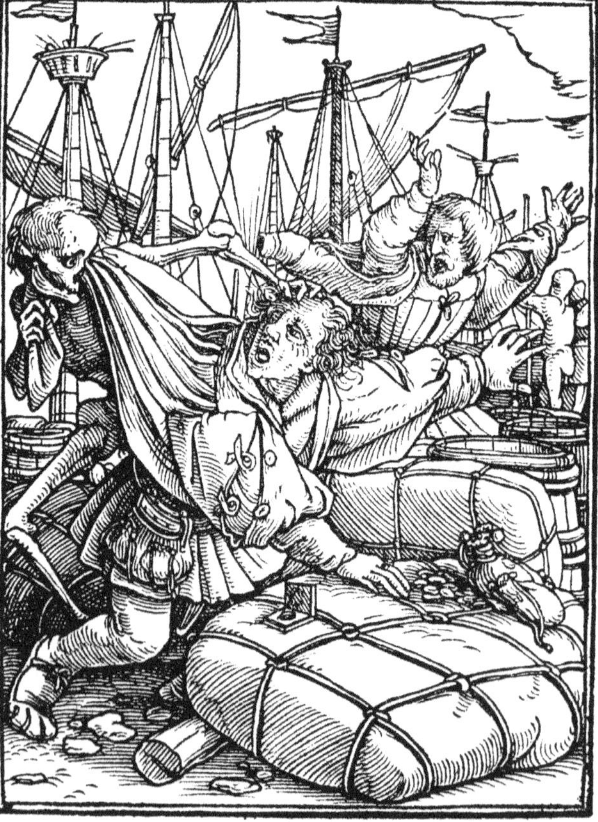

169. Death and the Doctor, Hans Holbein the Younger.

170. Death and the Astrologer, Hans Holbein the Younger.

171. Death and the Rich Man or Miser, Hans Holbein the Younger.

172. Death and the Merchant, Hans Holbein the Younger.

173

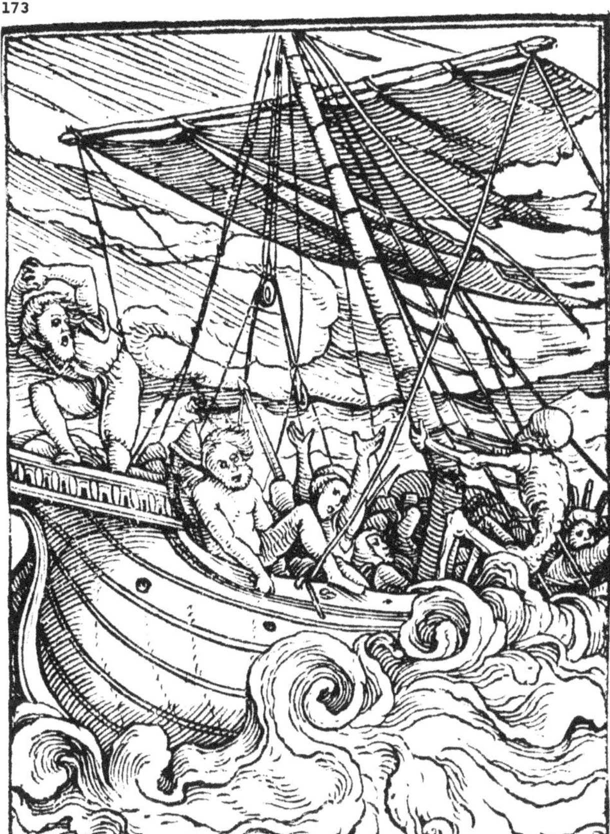

174

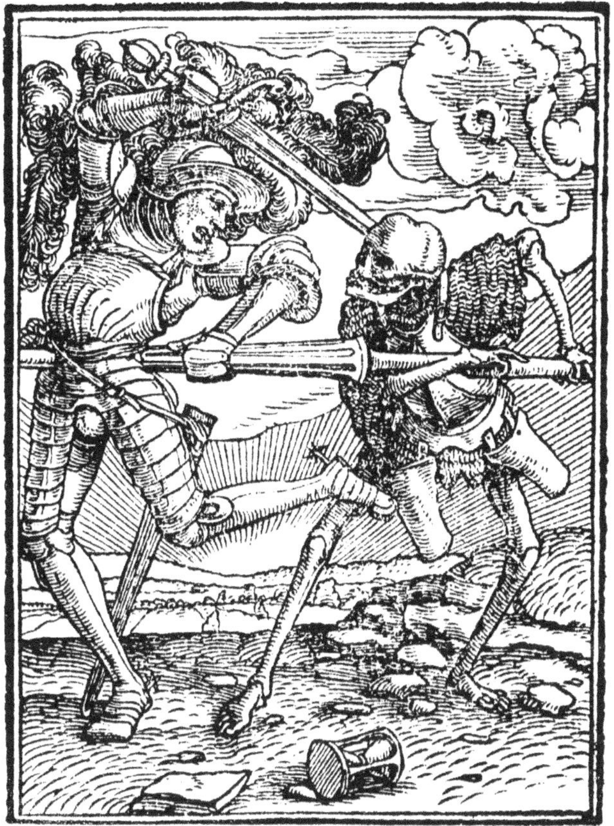

175

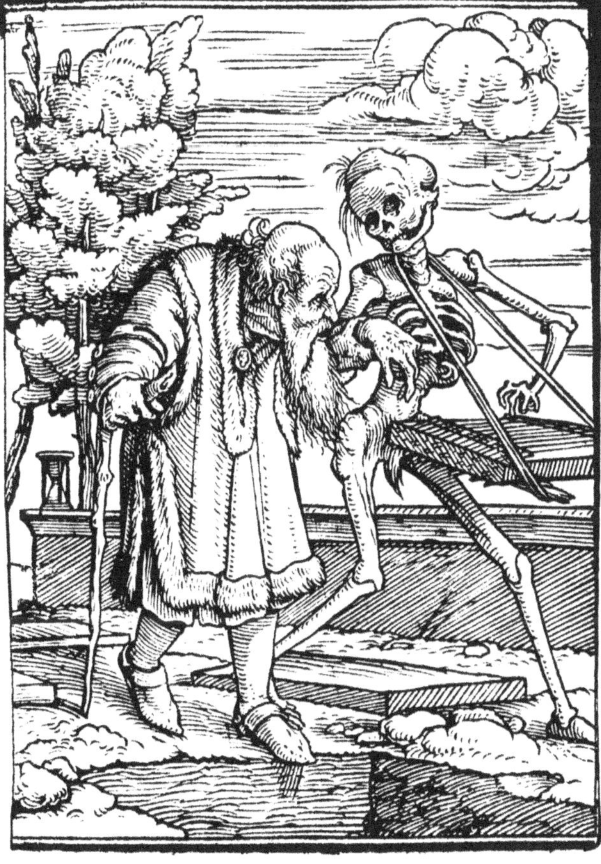

176

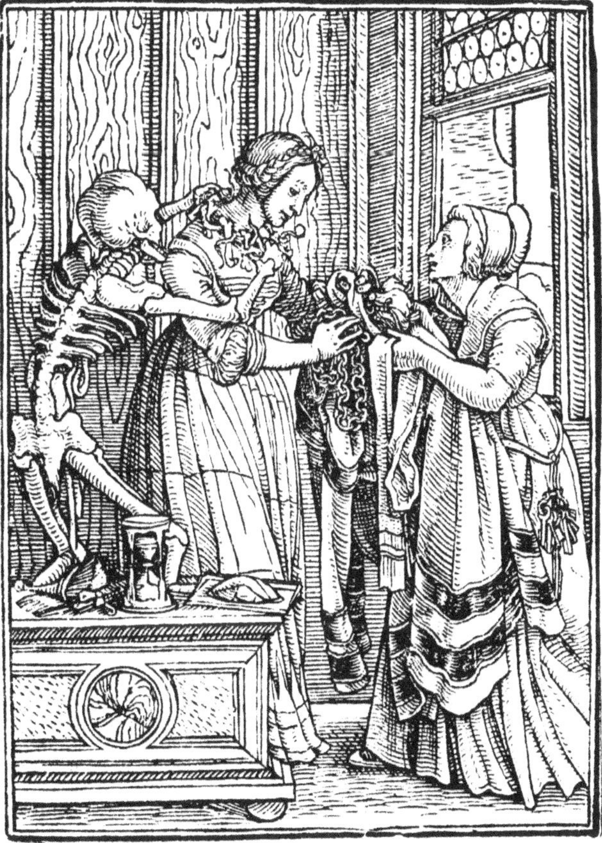

173. Death and the Sailor 2, Hans Holbein the Younger.

174. Knight and Death, Hans Holbein (II), 1538.

175. Death and the Old Man, Hans Holbein the Younger.

176. Death and the Countess, Hans Holbein the Younger.

177

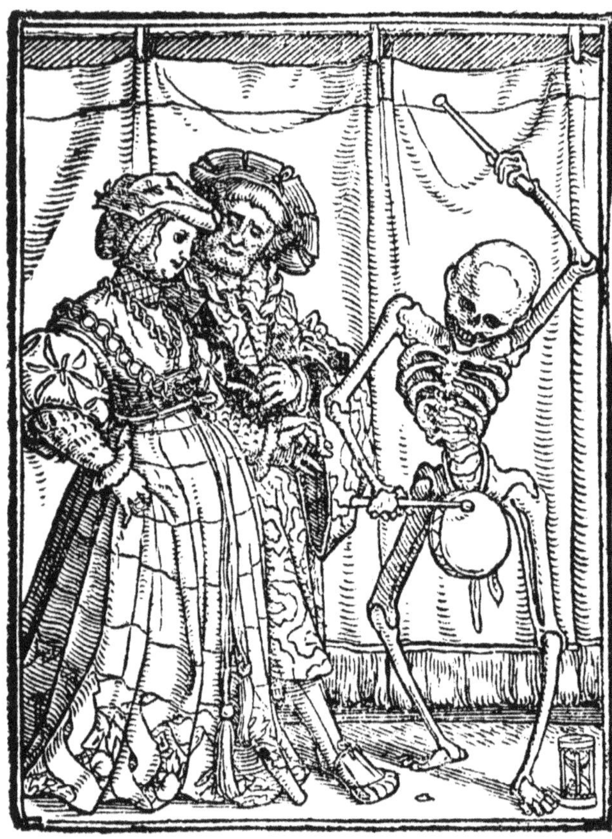

178

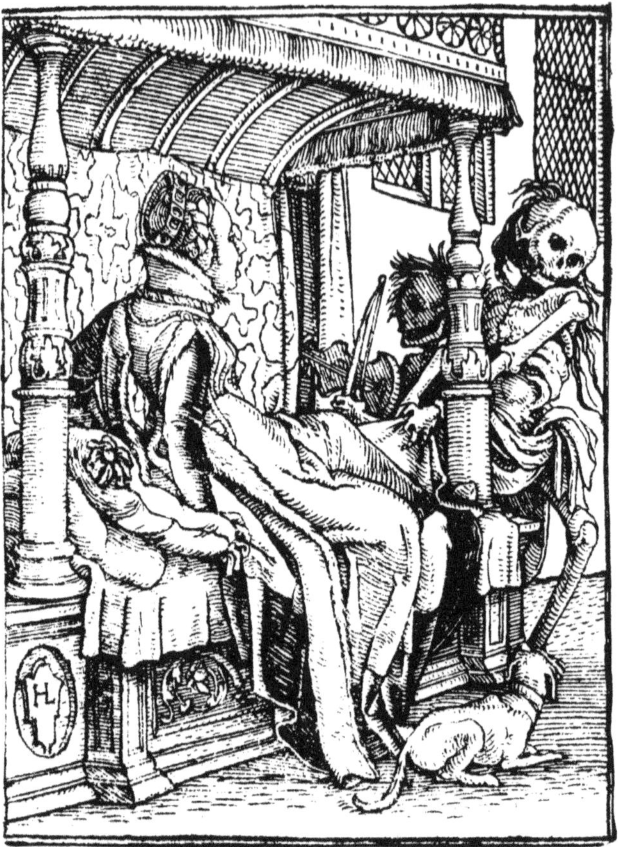

179

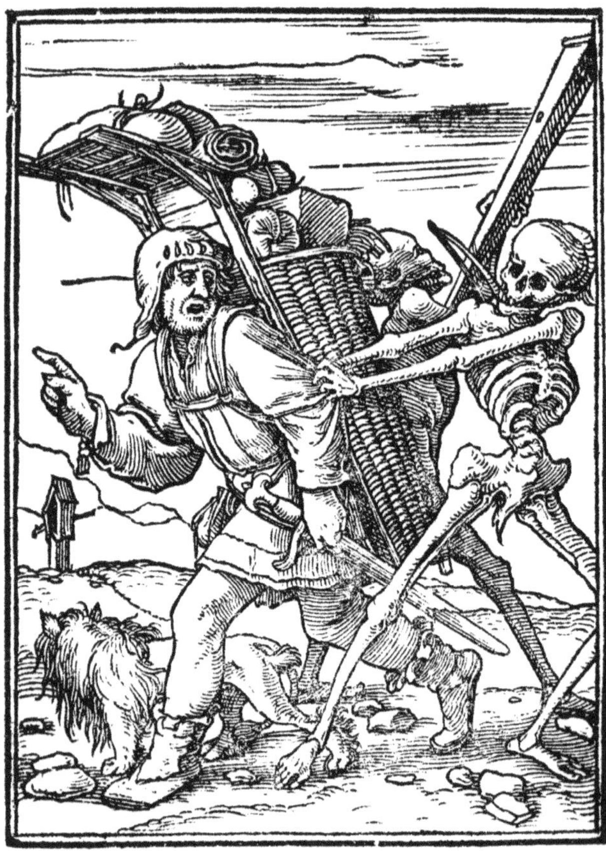

180

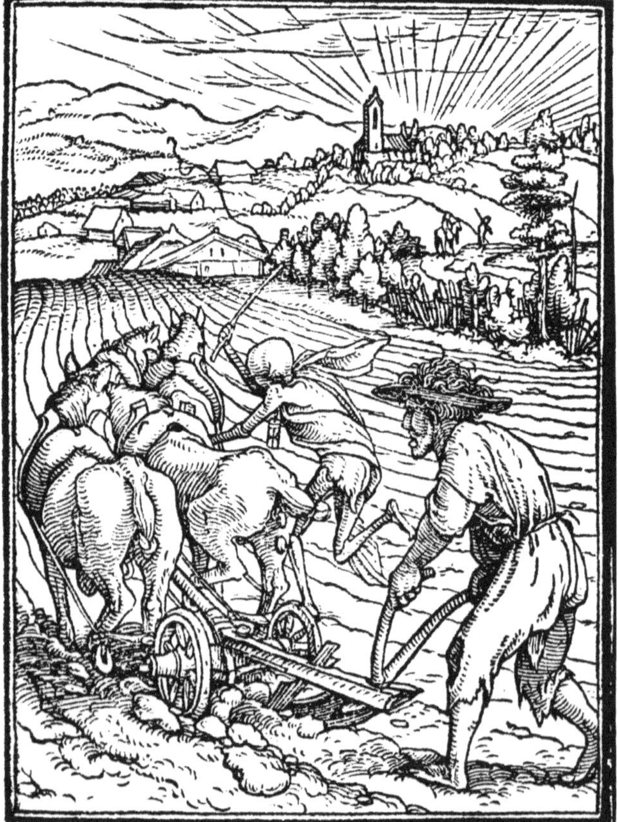

177. Noblewoman and Death, Hans Holbein (II), 1538.

178. Death and the Duchess, Hans Holbein the Younger.

179. Pedlar and Death, Hans Holbein (II), 1538.

180. Death and Ploughman, Hans Holbein the Younger.

181

182

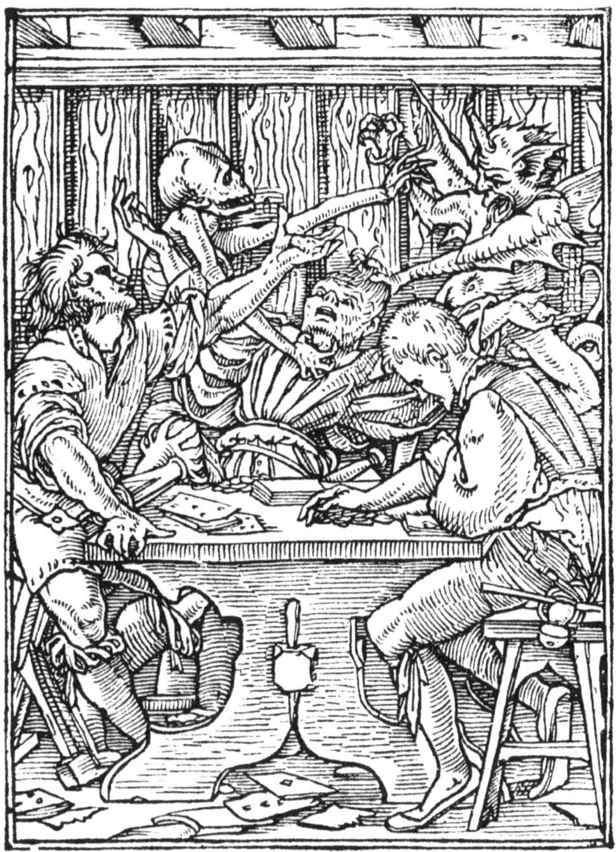

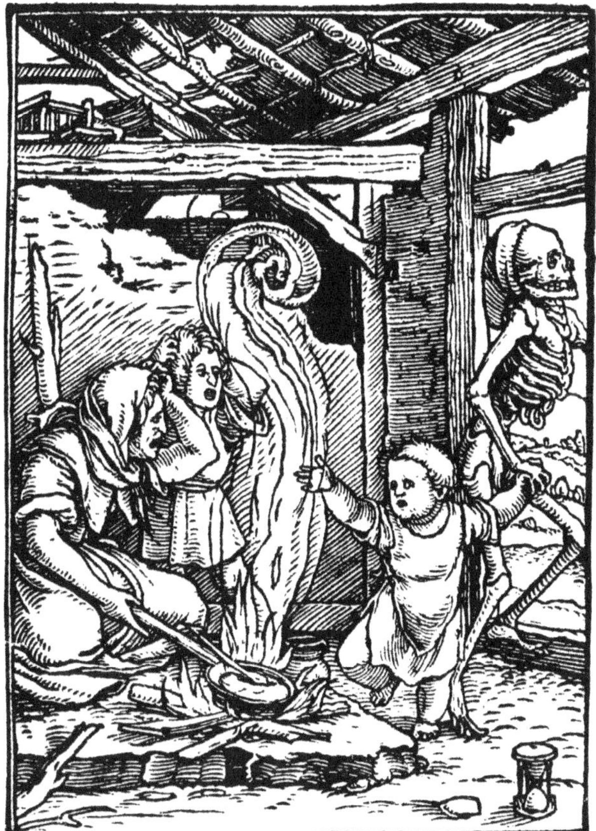

183

184

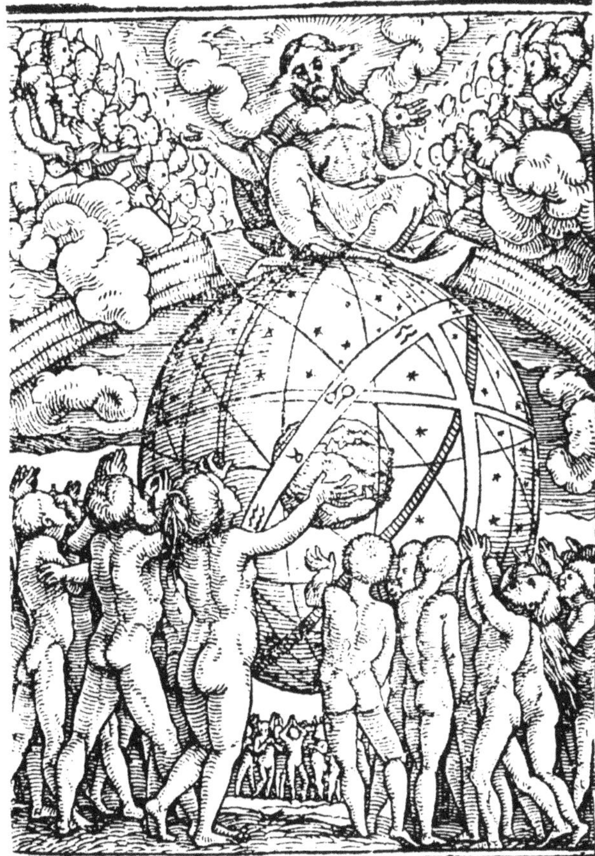

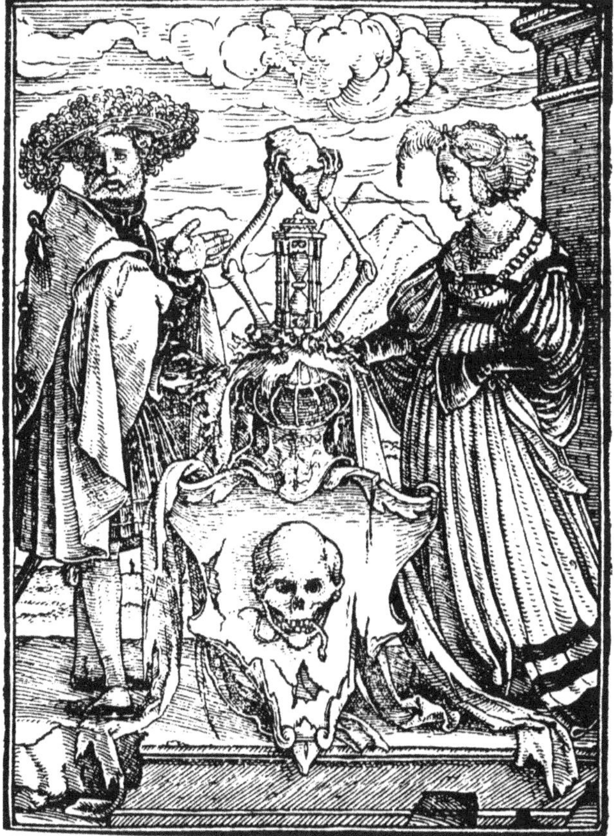

181. Card Players and Death, Hans Holbein (II), 1538.

182. Death and the Child, Hans Holbein the Younger.

183. The Last Judgement, Hans Holbein the Younger.

184. The Coat of Arms of Death, Hans Holbein the Younger.

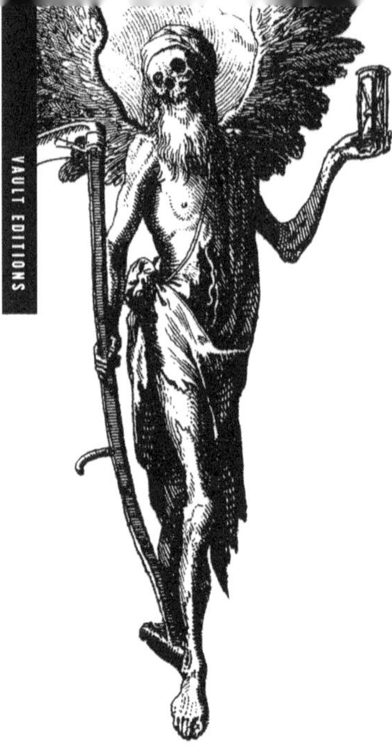

LEARN MORE

At Vault Editions, our mission is to create the world's most comprehensive collection of image archives for the practical use of artists and designers. If you have enjoyed this book, you can discover more of our titles at vaulteditions.com

REVIEW THIS BOOK

As a family-owned and operated independent publisher, reviews are essential to the success of our business. Please leave an honest review of this book wherever you purchased it.

JOIN OUR COMMUNITY

Are you the creative and curious type? If so, you will love our community on Instagram. Every day, we share bizarre and beautiful artwork ranging from 17th and 18th-century natural history and scientific illustrations to mythical beasts, ornamental designs, anatomical drawings and more; join our community of 280K+ people today by searching @vault_editions on Instagram.

DOWNLOAD YOUR FILES

STEP ONE

Enter the following web address in your web browser on a desktop computer.

www.vaulteditions.com/pages/dod

STEP TWO

Enter the following unique password to access the download page.

doda23363828sxda

STEP THREE

Follow the prompts to access your high-resolution files.

TECHNICAL ASSISTANCE

For all technical assistance, please email: info@vaulteditions.com

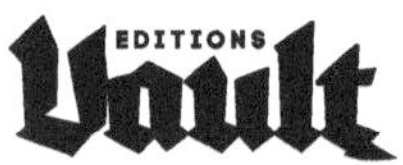

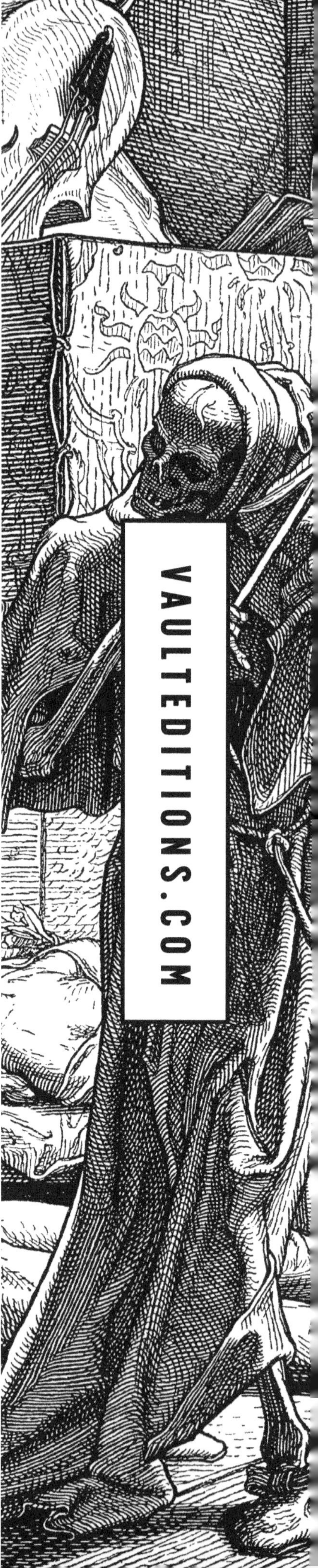